The Canadian Red Cross Society

Swimming and Water Safety

The Canadian Red Cross Society

Swimming
and Water Safety

St. Louis Baltimore Boston Carlsbad Chicago Naples New York Philadelphia Portland
London Madrid Mexico City Singapore Sydney Tokyo Toronto Wiesbaden

Mosby
Lifeline
Dedicated to Publishing Excellence

A Times Mirror
Company

Copyright © 1995 The Canadian Red Cross Society

Adaptation of: Swimming and Diving
Copyright © 1992 The American National Red Cross

A Mosby Lifeline imprint of Mosby–Year Book, Inc.

Printed in the United States of America

Composition by Mosby Electronic Production
Color Separation by Accu•color
Printing/binding by William C. Brown

Mosby–Year Book, Inc.
11830 Westline Industrial Drive
St. Louis, Missouri 63146

International Standard Book Number 0-8151-1498-2

95 96 97 98 99 / 9 8 7 6 5 4 3 2 1

NOTES TO READERS

SOCIAL JUSTICE AND DIVERSITY POLICY

In keeping with the Fundamental Principles of the Red Cross, The Society is committed to social justice in the elimination of Society structures and actions that oppress, exclude, limit or discriminate on the basis of race, gender, ethnicity, financial ability, sexual orientation, religion, disability, or age.

It is imperative that all programs and services provided by The Society reflect its commitment to social justice.

The Society will make every effort to make its volunteer and employee workforce representative and reflective of the communities in which its services are provided.

THE CANADIAN RED CROSS SOCIETY, WATER SAFETY SERVICE

Aim To prevent water-related injuries and fatalities.
Goal To reduce drowning and water-related injuries and fatalities by providing Canadians with:

- the awareness and knowledge to recognize and avoid dangerous situations;
- the knowledge and skills required to save their own lives;
- the basic rescue skills to enable them to save others; and
- the knowledge and awareness to recognize hazardous aquatic environments and equipment in their communities and to provide solutions.

This book is a reference for the Red Cross Water Safety Service and Program and should not be considered a substitute for Red Cross water safety lessons offered by authorized providers: municipal recreation programs, fitness clubs, educational institutions, camps, and private swim schools.

ACKNOWLEDGMENTS

The original version of this manual was developed and produced through a joint effort of the American Red Cross Society and Mosby. Our sister Society kindly authorized us to use their materials and shared with us the success they had with Mosby. The Canadian Red Cross Society wishes to express our appreciation to the volunteers and staff of the American Red Cross Health and Safety Services Department who made this project possible. The Society also wishes to acknowledge the efforts of the many volunteers and staff involved in the Canadian development of this manual. Their commitment to excellence made this resource possible.

A very special thank you to the volunteer members of the Society's Text Development Team: Tim Bradshaw, Edward Madill, Larry Maloney, Gary Otte, Brent Page, Brenda Pichette, Judy Quillin, and Cathy White. Thank you also to our text reviewers: Steve Box, Sandy Davis, and Jane Woodley. The Mosby editorial, production, and manufacturing team members included: David T. Culverwell, Publisher; Claire Merrick, Executive Editor; Ross Goldberg, Editor; Deborah Vogel, Project Manager; Mary Drone, Senior Production Editor; Ginny Douglas, Senior Production Assistant; Jodi Willard, Associate Production Editor; Lin Dempsey, Electronic Production Director; Joan Herron, Senior Electronic Production Editor; Kay Michael Kramer, Art and Design Director; Susan Lane, Senior Designer; Jerry Wood, Manufacturing Director; and Theresa Fuchs, Manufacturing Manager. Thanks go to Steve O'Hearn and Allan Orr of Times Mirror Professional Publishing.

Special thanks go to Tom Lochhaas, Ed.D., Developmental Editor; Elizabeth Rohne Rudder, Freelance Designer; and Studio Montage, Design and Electronic Imaging.

Portions of the photography in this text were taken from the American Red Cross text *Swimming and Diving*. Thanks go to their contributing photographers. Additional Canadian photography is by Gary Otte; other photography sources are listed on page 293. Appreciation goes to the following locations for their assistance in the photography:
- Canadian Aquatic Hall of Fame, Winnipeg, Manitoba
- Port Hood Beach, Cape Breton, Nova Scotia
- Bridgewater Pool, Bridgewater, Nova Scotia
- Lido Pool, Chester, Nova Scotia
- Piscine de St. Léonard, St. Léonard, Québec
- Piscine de Repentigny, Repentigny, Québec
- Piscine Olympique Pool, Montreal, Québec
- City Centre Aquatic Complex, Spani Pool, Coquitlam, British Columbia
- Maple Ridge Leisure Centre, Maple Ridge, British Columbia
- Ladner Leisure Centre, Delta, British Columbia
- Calgary Canoe Club, Calgary, Alberta
- Canada Games Sportsplex, Brandon, Manitoba
- U.B.C. Aquatic Centre, Vancouver, British Columbia
- Stan Stronge Pool, Percy Norman Pool, Vancouver, British Columbia
- Eileen Dailly Pool, Burnaby, British Columbia
- Terrace S.A.R. Water Rescue Team, Terrace, British Columbia
- Granville Island Marine, Vancouver, British Columbia

CONTENTS

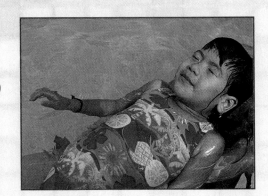

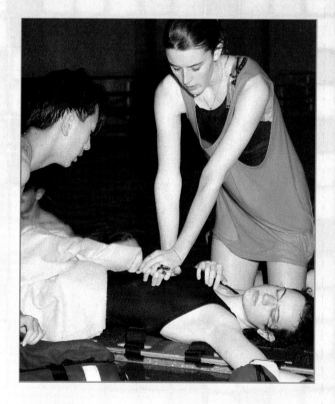

Introduction

Being prepared for a safe aquatic experience involves having the knowledge and skills needed to prevent water-related injury or death.

Staying safe during an aquatic experience involves putting your knowledge and skills into action in ways that help prevent injury and death.

Surviving or helping others survive an emergency that may occur during an aquatic experience involves knowing how to use rescue techniques and how to render first aid.

Some people live to swim. You'll find some at pools and beaches all summer or in competition year 'round. Others quietly swim their laps and keep track of their distance. Still others join teams for water polo, diving, or synchronized swimming.

Other people swim to live. The lives, not just the livelihoods, of sailors and commercial fishermen depend on their ability to function in, on, and near the water.

Most of us fall between these two extremes. Some of us want to know how to swim well enough to be safe around the pool. Others might be curious about the new ways of doing the strokes we learned long ago. Still others have incorporated aerobic exercise in the water into our fitness programs.

Safety in and around the water is a major concern for organizations such as The Canadian Red Cross Society because the loss of life due to drownings can be prevented. Safety education is an integral part of learn-to-swim programs offered by The Canadian Red Cross Society. Even though the number of people participating in swimming and other water activities has increased dramatically, the Canadian drowning rate has been on a downhill trend over the last 40 years.

This chapter reviews the development of water safety and swimming within The Canadian Red Cross Society, examines the history of swimming, highlights some notable Canadian swimming achievements, and briefly looks to the future.

THE CANADIAN RED CROSS SOCIETY
Fundamental Principles

The Canadian Red Cross Society is part of The International Red Cross and Red Crescent Movement, which was established in 1863 to alleviate pain and suffering. Its founder was Henri Dunant. Countries around the world soon were attracted to the humanitarian purpose of the first Red Cross organization, and at present over 150 countries and their citizens benefit from the work of The Red Cross and Red Crescent Movement. The Society is the largest humanitarian volunteer organization in the world.

The Red Cross and Red Crescent Movement was established on the basis of principles that have guided its development over the years. As its work expanded, the principles guiding the Red Cross and Red Crescent Movement evolved. In the mid-1960s, The International Red Cross and Red Crescent Movement officially adopted a set of seven fundamental principles. These principles work together and are mutually supportive. They are arranged in a hierarchy as shown in Figure 1-1.

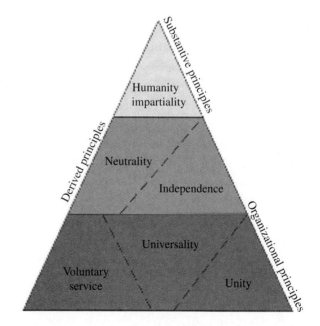

The seven fundamental principles that Red Cross follows

Figure 1-1. The seven fundamental principles of the Red Cross.

The two principles that have been at the core of Red Cross since the beginning in 1863 are *humanity* and *impartiality.* They are the **substantive principles.** This means that they are the core values, the essence of the Red Cross and Red Crescent Movement.

Neutrality and *independence* are the **derived principles** that are necessary to put the substantive principles into action.

Voluntary service, unity, and *universality* are the **organizational principles** describing the practical and operational nature of the Red Cross and Red Crescent Movement.

On the basis of these seven principles, and with the goal of reducing the loss of life and suffering from drownings, The Canadian Red Cross Society began developing a swimming and water safety program in 1944.

Swimming and Water Safety
Early development

In 1944, Dr. R.W.I. Urquart, Chairman of the National Committee on First Aid of The Canadian Red Cross Society, spoke about the growing concern over the number of injuries that were occurring and lives that were being lost in water environments. The Canadian Red Cross Society then started a swimming and water safety program *"in an effort to reduce unnecessary fatalities that occurred at bathing beaches and summer resorts."*

Proponents of the swimming and water safety program strongly believed that The Canadian Red Cross Society was the appropriate organization to deliver this service. Although other organizations were involved in swimming instruction in a small way, The Canadian Red Cross Society could reach all of the Canadian population.

The Canadian Red Cross Society recognized that, along with developing swimming skills, it is *equally important to focus on injury and fatality prevention through water safety education.*

Services of The Canadian Red Cross Society

1. *International*: Assistance to other countries in times of war or natural disasters.
2. *Blood Transfusion*: Provision of blood and blood products to the Canadian public.
3. *Emergency Services*: Assistance to the public in times of domestic disaster in conjunction with municipal government.
4. *Water Safety*: Provision of knowledge and skills to the public to prevent water-related injuries and fatalities.
5. *First Aid*: Training and information for the Canadian public to prevent injury and save lives.

Also important for reducing drownings and water-related injuries and fatalities is the *training and education of instructors* (Figure 1-2). In 1945 the first instructor course at the Charlottetown Yacht Club certified 13 new instructors.

Pupil achievement awards were also established at the Junior, Intermediate, and Senior levels. In 1950 a fourth level, Beginner, was added to bridge a gap in the transition from non-swimmer to swimmer.

The proponents of the national safety education program proved correct in their analysis of the need. In the first year (1945), 16,414 individuals enrolled in classes in the formal Swimming and Water Safety program. In 1952, enrollment had grown to 82,220. This steady growth continued, reaching 654,000 in 1968 and 1.3 million in 1993!

Figure 1-2. Early Canadian Red Cross swimming instructors.

The Big Numbers

S ince the establishment of the Red Cross Water Safety program in 1945,
Over 25 million pupils have been enrolled in the Learn-to-Swim program.
Over 440,000 people have been trained as instructors and leaders.

Similar participation trends occurred with instructor training: in 1946, 980 instructors were qualified; 26,000 were qualified in 1993.

Cooperation: a key principle

From the beginning the Red Cross "pioneers" who developed the swimming and water safety program recognized that a two-pronged approach was needed to address the problem of

Staff and Volunteers—a Critical Partnership

T he swimming and Water Safety program of the Canadian Red Cross Society has depended on a very dedicated and talented group of staff members and thousands of committed volunteers. Together these people have combined to research and develop programs, instructional techniques, and materials to support programs for the elimination of drownings and water-related injuries.

drownings and water-related injuries. On the one hand, a program was needed for personal *swimming and safety skills* for Canadians. On the other hand, *lifesaving* skills and knowledge were necessary for proper supervision of swim-

Unique Delivery of Services

The Canadian Red Cross Society has worked to ensure access to water safety and swimming instruction. The use of portable pools and river barges on the MacKenzie River are but two successful innovations.

ming areas and proper management of emergency situations.

In 1945 The Canadian Red Cross Society began to develop a cooperative relationship with the Royal Life Saving Society of Canada (RLSSC) to prevent duplication of services. Both organizations saw a need for public education in aquatic safety. The Canadian Red Cross Society focused on teaching swimming and safety education, and the Royal Life Saving Society of Canada focused on lifesaving and life guarding.

Concern for diversity

Consistent with the seven principles of The Canadian Red Cross Society, the Water Safety program has sought to address the needs of all sectors of the Canadian public, including those with special needs. Programs and instruction were designed for people with disabilities. In 1950, for example, a program for people with visual impairment was begun in Regina, Saskatchewan. Another program for persons with a physical disability was offered in Manitoba.

Starting in 1954, special attention was given to training instructors who would be serving Canadians with disabilities. Since that time research and development have continued. Special instructor trainer modules have been offered all across Canada to prepare individuals to face these special challenges (Figure 1-3). In 1996, Canadians with disabilities will be fully integrated within the Water Safety program.

A new program

Until the late 1970s, volunteers and staff of the Water Safety program focused on expanding services in teaching and leadership development to meet the ever-expanding demand for programs in Canadian communities.

In the late 1970s The Canadian Red Cross Society began to reassess the Learn-to-Swim program, examining it in light of developments in technology, teaching methodology, psychology of learning, motor development, and other advances in knowledge. The goal was to develop the best possible programs to meet the needs of Canadians.

In this extensive research program, parents, community organizations, pupils, instructors, and recreation agencies shared their thoughts

Figure 1-3. Canadians with disabilities have individualized training.

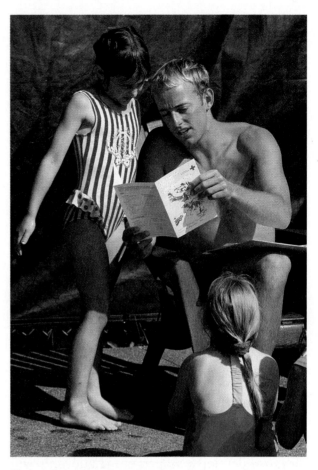

Figure 1-4. A swimming instructor evaluates student learning using progress cards.

on the Swimming and Water Safety program of The Canadian Red Cross Society.

On the basis of this research, the program was revised, and in 1981 a new eight-level Learn-to-Swim program was launched. This revised program made progress from one level to the next much easier. It also emphasized continuous progressive evaluation, progress cards, and instructor-based evaluation and testing (Figure 1-4).

In 1954 the Canadian Red Cross recognized the needs of members of the Royal Canadian Air Force and their families who were posted overseas. Since then, The Canadian Red Cross Society has provided instructor training courses to overseas military bases. Swimming and Water Safety programs are offered at military bases in Canada to support programs for the elimination of drownings and water-related injuries.

Injury prevention: an evolving focus

In the last 20 years, The Canadian Red Cross Society has concentrated more resources on research into drownings and water-related injuries and their causes. Cooperative work with provincial coroners and the Royal Life Saving Society of Canada led to recent National Drowning Reports, which analyze all drownings in Canada to understand causes of and factors involved in water-related deaths.

This research has revealed important facts about drownings:

- Many drownings are alcohol related.
- Drowning is most common among males between 14 and 25 years of age.
- Many drowning deaths are related to boating.
- The greatest percentage of drownings occur in ocean, lakes, and rivers.
- Many toddlers drown when left unsupervised.

Drowning is ranked as the fourth major cause of accidental death in Canada, accounting for almost 6% of deaths, according to Statistics Canada. For males, drowning ranked as the third leading cause of accidental death, whereas for females, drowning was the sixth leading cause. Later chapters in this book address how to prevent such drownings.

The Canadian Red Cross Society recognizes the need for an approach that focuses on **prevention.** With this information, The Canadian Red Cross Society Water Safety Service adopted an aim (see sidebar) and the following objectives to fulfill the aim in 1993:

1. Preparation of an annual report on unintentional water-related fatalities in Canada.
2. Distribution of safety promotion information.
3. Institution of a Water Safety Training program based on national safety standards.
4. Institution of a Leadership Development program.

In 1996 a new Water Safety program is being launched, which emphasizes prevention of injuries in all three stages of participation in aquatic activities:

1. Preparation: Get ready before beginning the activity.
2. Staying Safe: Engage in the activity in a safe manner.
3. Survival: If something does go wrong, know what to do to survive.

At each of these stages, three factors influence safe participation:

• Personal factors
• Equipment-related factors
• Environmental factors

Chapter 3, Water Safety, explains this injury prevention model and its implications in more detail. This new approach will help all Canadians understand what actions and attitudes can help prevent injuries and deaths.

The Red Cross and public education

One of the goals of The Canadian Red Cross Water Safety program is to develop "water-safe communities." Teaching people swimming skills is one way to promote safe participation in aquatic sports and activities.

However, it is also important to develop a safety-conscious attitude throughout the community. The Canadian Red Cross Society has

Water Safety Service Aim

Aim
To prevent water-related injuries and fatalities.

Goal
To reduce drowning and water-related injuries and fatalities by providing Canadians with—
• The awareness and knowledge to recognize and avoid dangerous situations.
• The knowledge and skills required to save their own lives.
• The basic rescue skills to enable them to save others.
• The knowledge and awareness to recognize hazardous aquatic environments and equipment in their communities and provide solutions.

developed a wide range of public education programs to meet this goal of injury prevention. Films, videos, books, pamphlets, educational week themes, demonstrations, public service announcements on radio and television, posters, school programs, and many other techniques have been used to bring to the public the message that, although there are dangers in the aquatic environment, it can be enjoyed without injury if one prepares and acts in a reasonable and responsible manner.

The Water Safety programs of The Canadian Red Cross Society continue to involve thousands of pupils, instructors, and volunteers every year. The Canadian Red Cross Society will continue to analyze the needs of the Canadian public and develop new programs in an ongoing drive to reduce injuries and fatalities in all aquatic environments.

THE PAST: SWIMMING IN HISTORY
Beginnings

Ancient civilizations left ample evidence of their swimming abilities. Bas-relief artwork in an Egyptian tomb from around 2,000 BC shows an overarm stroke like the front crawl. The Assyrians showed an early breaststroke in their stone carvings. The Hittites, the Minoans, and other early civilizations left drawings of swimming and diving skills. Even the Bible refers to movement through the water. Competitive swimming is at least as old as 36 BC, when the Japanese held the first known swimming races.

The earliest published work on swimming was written in 1538 AD by Nicolas Wynman, a German professor of languages. In 1696, *The Art of Swimming* by the French author Thevenot, first described a type of breaststroke done with the face out of the water and an underwater arm position. This stroke gives the swimmer good stability, even in rough water.

Swimming research pioneer Benjamin Franklin.

AN EARLY RESEARCHER

In the 1700s, Benjamin Franklin researched buoyancy, back floating, and gliding, using his kite for propulsion and devising an early form of hand paddles and fins.

As he wrote, "When I was a boy I made two oval palettes, each about ten inches long and broad, with a hole for the thumb, in order to retain it fast in the palm of my hand. They much resembled a painter's palettes. In swimming I pushed the edges of these forward, and I struck the water with their flat surfaces as I drew them back. I remember I swam faster by means of these palettes, but they fatigued my wrists. I also fitted to the soles of my feet a kind of sandals; but I was not satisfied with them...."

After the English translation of Thevenot's work became the standard swimming reference, the breaststroke was the most common stroke for centuries.

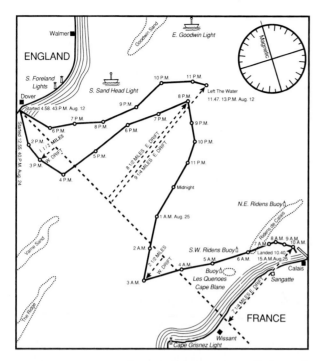

Figure 1-5. Map showing the routes of Captain Matthew Webb's English Channel swims in August 1875. His first attempt was abandoned after 6 hours because he drifted far off course. His second attempt was completed in 21:44:35.

The Rise of Competitive Swimming

The English are considered the first modern society to develop swimming as a sport. By 1837, when modern competitive swimming began in London, several indoor pools already existed. The National Swimming Society regulated competition. The breaststroke and the recently developed sidestroke were used. In 1844, Native Americans swam in a London meet. Flying Gull swam 130 feet in 30 seconds to defeat Tobacco and win a medal. Their stroke was described as thrashing the water with their arms in a motion "like a windmill" and kicking in an up-and-down motion. This early form of the front crawl was successful in that race, but the English continued to prefer the breaststroke for competition.

The English also liked to compete against nature. In 1875, Captain Matthew Webb first swam the English Channel (Figure 1-5). With the breaststroke, he swam the 21.26 miles in 21 hours and 45 minutes. The first woman to swim the channel was Gertrude Ederle in 1926. In 1955, the Canadian Marilyn Bell, at the age of 17 years, became the youngest person ever to cross the channel—in a time of 14 hours and 30 minutes. Marcus Hooper in 1979 at age 12 then became the youngest person to complete the swim. In 1983, Ashby Harper swam the channel just a few days before his 66th birthday, making him the oldest. Penny Dean has held the world record for the channel swim since 1978. Another Canadian of note, Cindy Nichols, recorded a record time for a two-way crossing of the channel in 1977. She also completed her sixth crossing, the most by any woman at the time. This challenge continues to attract distance swimmers as the ultimate feat in this sport.

Early Interest in Stroke Development

Throughout the 1800s, a series of swimming strokes evolved. The sidestroke, in which the swimmer lies on one side, was soon modified to become the overarm sidestroke. One arm was recovered above the water for increased arm speed. The legs were squeezed together in an uncoordinated action. In 1895, J. H. Thayers of England, using the overarm sidestroke, swam a record 1:02.50 for 100 yards.

John Trudgen developed the hand-over-hand stroke, which was then called the trudgen. He copied the stroke from South American Indians and introduced it in England in 1873. Each arm recovered out of the water as the body rolled from side to side. The swimmer did a scissors kick with every two arm strokes. This stroke was the forerunner of the front crawl. Kick variations included different multiples of scissors kicks or alternating scissors and flutter kicks. F. V. C. Lane showed the speed of the trudgen in 1901 by swimming 100 yards in 1:00.0.

MODERN TIMES: SWIMMING IN THE TWENTIETH CENTURY
The Development of Modern Strokes

Although people have swum since ancient times, swimming strokes have been greatly refined in the past 100 years. Competitive swimming—notably the modern Olympic Games, begun in Athens, Greece, in 1896—increased interest in strokes. Scientific stroke analysis has helped produce more varied strokes, greater speeds, and a better understanding of propulsion through the water.

Front crawl

The inefficiency of the trudgen kick led Australian Richard Cavill to try new methods. He used a stroke he observed natives of the Solomon Islands using, which combined an up-and-down kick with an alternating overarm stroke. He used the new stroke in 1902 at the International Championships and set a new world record (100 yards in 58.4 seconds). This stroke became known as the Australian crawl.

The Australian men's swimming team introduced a front crawl stroke with more body roll at the 1956 Olympic Games in Melbourne. This roll decreased the water resistance and thus increased speed.

Backstroke

In the early 1900s, swimming on the back was not done in competition. Since the breaststroke was still the stroke of choice, the backstroke was done like an upside-down breaststroke. However, as the front crawl became popular, swimmers tried the alternating overarm style on the back. Combined with a flutter kick, this stroke was faster than the breaststroke. In 1912, the backstroke became a competitive event. The continued effort to gain greater speed, along with studying and experimenting with the stroke, led to the back crawl as we know it today.

Breaststroke and butterfly

Swimming research has helped the breaststroke evolve. Other strokes are faster, but the breaststroke is still a competitive event. Until the 1950s, the breaststroke was the only stroke with a required style. The underwater recovery of both arms and legs in the breaststroke is a natural barrier to speed.

In 1934, however, David Armbruster, coach at the University of Iowa, devised a double overarm recovery out of the water. This "butterfly" arm action gave more speed but required greater training and conditioning. Then in 1935, Jack Sieg, a University of Iowa swimmer, developed the skill of swimming on his side and beating his legs in unison like a fish's tail. He then developed the leg action face down. Armbruster and Sieg combined the butterfly arm action with this leg action and learned to coordinate the two efficiently. With two kicks to each butterfly arm action, Sieg swam 100 yards in 1:00.2. This kick was named the dolphin fishtail kick (Figure 1-6).

Even though the butterfly breaststroke, as it was called, was faster than the breaststroke,

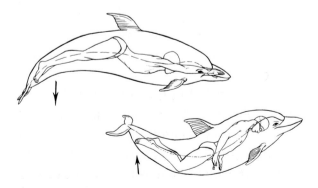

Figure 1-6. The dolphin butterfly kick.

Early Champions

In the first half of the 20th century, American swimmers were very successful in Olympic competition and often brought innovations to stroke mechanics. Three names seem most prominent: Duke Kanhanamoku, Johnny Weissmuller, and Buster Crabbe.

Stroke mechanics is the analysis of the hydrodynamic principles that affect how swimmers move in the water and can improve propulsion.

"Duke" Kahanamoku, a Hawaiian who learned the front crawl by watching native Hawaiian swimmers, further changed how this stroke was done. His stroke was characterized by a truly vertical six-beat flutter kick. The Duke was an Olympic record holder and an Olympic gold medal winner for the 100-yard front crawl in both the 1912 and the 1920 games.

Johnny Weissmuller (who also played Tarzan in the movies) influenced the stroke as well. He dominated sprint swimming in the period, including the 1924 and 1928 Olympic Games. In 1927, Weissmuller swam 100 yards in 51 seconds flat in a 25-yard course, setting the record for almost two decades. His style featured a deep kick, which allowed the chest and shoulders to ride higher; a rotating of the head for inhalation that was inde-

Johnny Weissmuller and teammate Buster Crabbe at the 1932 Olympics.

pendent of the action of the arms; and an underwater arm action in which the elbow was bent slightly for greater positive action.

The popularity of Duke Kahanamoku, Johnny Weissmuller, and Buster Crabbe, an Olympic swimming champion in 1932 who succeeded Weissmuller as Tarzan in the movies, contributed greatly to the development of the front crawl. Their popularity also led to this becoming the stroke used to teach beginners.

the dolphin fishtail kick was declared a violation of competitive rules. For the next 20 years, champion breaststrokers used an out-of-water arm recovery (butterfly) with a shortened breaststroke kick. In the late 1950s, the butterfly stroke with the dolphin kick was legalized as a separate stroke for competition. Many swimmers say the "wiggle" is the key to

the stroke and that a swimmer who can undulate through the water naturally can more easily learn the butterfly.

Competitive Swimming

As swimmers refine strokes or make changes, the best way to test the new stroke is to use it in competition. This is why so much attention is paid to speed and endurance records.

Variety of swimming events

The first modern Olympic Games had only four swimming events, three of them freestyle. The second Olympics in Paris in 1900 included three unusual swimming events. One included an obstacle course; another was a test of underwater swimming endurance; the third was a 4,000-metre event, the longest competitive swimming event ever. None of the three was ever used in the Olympics again.

> *Freestyle is a competitive event in which any stroke is allowed. The term is frequently used for the front crawl, since it is the stroke most often used in this event.*

> *Individual medley is an event in which the competitor swims one quarter of the total distance using a different competitive stroke in a prescribed order (butterfly, backstroke, breaststroke, freestyle).*

Women were excluded from swimming in the first several Olympic Games. In 1896 and again in 1906, women could not participate because the developer of the modern games, Pierre de Coubertin, held firmly to the assumption, common in the Victorian era, that women were too frail to engage in competitive sports. In 1900, the committee organizing the Paris games allowed women to participate in golf and tennis, since these were popular sports in Europe. (Until the International Olympic Committee was formed, events at Olympic Games were chosen by the host committee.)

The 1904 games in St. Louis were dominated by the President of the Amateur Athletic Union (AAU), James E. Sullivan, who allowed women to participate only in archery, a demonstration sport. Women's swimming made its debut in the 1912 games at the prompting of the group that later became the International Olympic Committee.

From the humble beginning with four swimming events, the Olympics Games have developed to 32 swimming races, 16 for men and 16 for women.

Competition for people with disabilities

Swimming competition for people with disabilities also has a long history. In 1924, the Comité International des sports des sourds (CISS—the International Committee for Sports for the Deaf) held the first Summer World Games for men and women who were deaf. Athletes with cognitive disabilities first joined in international swimming competition in 1968, with the International Summer Special Olympics. The most recent Special Olympics had 22 events for men and 22 for women. In the summer of 1994 swimming events for persons with a disability were included in the Commonwealth Games held in Victoria, B.C. (Figure 1-7).

Swimmers setting records

Alfred Hajos of Hungary won the first Olympic men's swimming gold medal in the Olympic

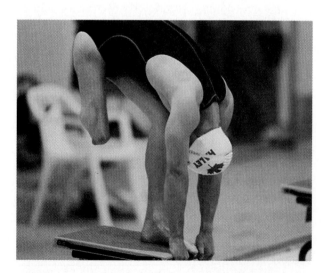

Figure 1-7. Swimming competitions are now integrated.

Games in Athens in 1896. He had a time of 1:22.20 for the 100-metre freestyle, a competitive event in which any stroke is allowed. Since then, new swimming records have been set regularly. At this writing, the world record for that event is 48.21, set by Alexander Popov in the summer of 1994.

Although names have come and gone from the record books, several U.S. swimmers have left their mark on the swimming world. Johnny Weissmuller won 5 Olympic medals and 36 national championships and never lost a race in his 10-year career. His record of 51 seconds for the 100-yard freestyle stood for over 17 years. Mark Spitz won seven gold medals in the 1972 Olympics in Munich, more than any other swimmer in the history of Olympic competition.

Research and Training Techniques

Unlike walking and other motions, swimming is not a natural activity for the human body. A standing position on land does not translate easily to a horizontal swimming position. Therefore throughout history people have experimented with different ways to swim better. We can use a variety of swimming techniques because of the ball-and-socket joints of our shoulders and hips.

Early swimmers experimented by trial and error and watched others. In 1928 David Armbruster first filmed swimmers under water to study strokes. The Japanese photographed and studied world-class athletes, using their research to produce a swim team that dominated the 1932 Olympic Games. This marked the beginning of research into stroke mechanics.

At the same time, others advanced the role of conditioning. The 1956 Olympic Games in Melbourne, Australia, showed the value of conditioning. The fantastic success of the host team was due to their training program, not their

stroke technique. American swimming coaches began adopting training methods like those used by track coaches to help runners break the 4-minute mile.

Current research focuses on the forces that act on a body moving through the water. The main points of this science, hydrodynamics, are presented in Chapter 6.

Hydrodynamics is the science that studies the motion of fluids and forces on solid bodies in fluids.

Other Water Sports
Competitive diving

Although it is a water sport, competitive diving is closer to gymnastics and tumbling than it is to swimming. In fact, competitive diving grew out of the gymnastic movement in Germany and Sweden. People may have been diving throughout history, but written reports date from 1871, when divers plunged from London Bridge and other high places.

Springboard diving began as an Olympic event in the 1904 games in St. Louis. American Jim Sheldon won gold medals in the 1- and 3-metre events. An event called distance plunging also was held. Each diver performed a racing dive into the pool, followed by a prone glide for distance. W. E. Dickey won the gold with a plunge of 62 feet, 6 inches in the only Olympics that included this event.

Men's platform diving (10 metres) began in the 1908 games in London, and women's diving events started in the next two Olympic Games—platform diving in 1912 and springboard diving in 1920.

Important in diving history is the evolution of the diving board. Changes improved safety and allowed for greater variety in dives. Before the mid-1940s, diving boards were wood planks covered with cocoa matting to prevent slipping. Many subsequent changes enabled divers to add

Text continues on page 18.

Great Moments in Canadian Aquatic Sports

Swimming

George Hodgson

In 1912 at the Stockholm Olympics, George Hodgson captured a gold medal in the 1500-metre freestyle. On his way to completing the 1500 metres, he set a world record at 1000 metres. After completing the 1500 metres, he continued without stopping to finish the mile. These three events in one race were all new world records! Four days later, he won a gold medal in the 400-metre freestyle event!

Marathon swimming

Marilyn Bell

On the evening of September 9, 1954, Marilyn Bell exited the waters of Lake Ontario at Toronto's Canadian National Exhibition grounds—she had just become the first person to swim across the lake, having left Youngstown, New York 22 hours and 58 minutes earlier!

A year later at the age of 17, she swam the English Channel in 14 hours and 30 minutes to become the youngest person to complete this crossing.

George Hodgson

Marilyn Bell

Swimming

Elaine "Mighty Mouse" Tanner

At the 1968 Olympic Games in Mexico City, Elaine Tanner won the silver medal in the 100 and 200 metre backstroke events and was a member of Canada's 4 × 100 metre freestyle relay team. Through this accomplishment she became the first Canadian woman to win three Olympic medals at a single game.

Swimming

Alex Bauman

In 1984 at the Los Angeles Olympics, Alex Bauman captured gold medals in the 200-metre and 400-metre individual medley events. Both of these were in world record times and were the first Olympic gold medals for Canada since the 1912 games.

Elaine Tanner

Alex Bauman

Great Moments in Canadian Aquatic Sports—cont'd

Swimming

Nancy Garapick

At the age of thirteen, Nancy set a world record in the 200 metre backstroke at the Canadian swimming championships in 1975.

Later that summer at the World Championships, she won silver and bronze medals in the 200- and 100-metre backstroke events.

Swimming

Mark Tewksbury

In 1992 at the Barcelona Olympics, Mark Tewksbury captured a gold medal in the 100-metre backcrawl and a bronze medal in the 4 × 100 medley relay.

Synchronized swimming

Helen Vanderburg

Between 1978 and 1979 Helen competed in four major international events and won a total of seven gold medals. In three other major competitions before 1978, she won another gold and five silver medals. Her accomplishments came in solo and duet events.

Synchronized swimming

Carolyn Waldo-Baltzer

Carolyn Waldo earned her first national title at the age of 14. In 1984 at the summer Olympic games, she won a silver medal in her first international experience as a soloist.

When she retired, Carolyn had won gold medals in all solo and duet international competitions that she entered, except for one!

Mark Tewksbury

Carolyn Waldo-Baltzer

Synchronized swimming

Sylvie Frechette

Between 1988 and 1992, Sylvie Frechette won gold in solo competition in 19 of 25 major national and international competitions. In 1991, she won the World Aquatic Championships with seven perfect scores of 10!

In 1992 she was awarded the silver medal at the summer Olympic Games. One of the judges admitted to recording an inaccurate score in the computer that prevented Sylvie from reaching the gold. However, this injustice was corrected a year later when the International Olympic Committee and the International Swimming Federation presented her with a gold medal.

This accomplishment capped a truly exceptional career as an aquatic athlete.

Synchronized swimming

Penny and Vicky Vilagos

After 6 years on the Canadian National Team, these two sisters retired from a successful synchronized swimming career. They returned again to competition, and in 1992 they won a silver medal in duet competition at the summer Olympic games.

Penny and Vicky Vilagos

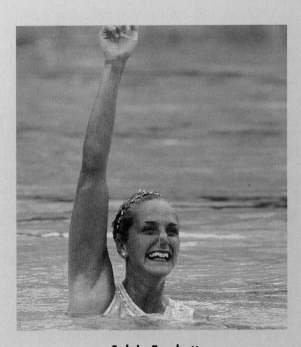

Sylvie Frechette

more somersaults and twists to dives. Originally there were only 14 platform and 20 springboard dives. Competitors and coaches have now assembled 87 different dives from the basic "ingredients": forward, backward, or inward takeoff; handstands and twists; and somersaults and reverse dives—performed in a straight, pike, or tuck position from boards or platforms at various heights.

Water polo

Water polo combines soccer and rugby skills and is played in deep water. It requires tremendous stamina and skill. It was made a sport in 1885 by the Swimming Association of Great Britain and became an official Olympic sport in 1908. Today it is a popular high school, college, and Olympic sport.

Synchronized swimming

Synchronized swimming is a creative sport for swimmers at any level. It may be purely leisure swimming or competitive. Beulah and Henry Gundling, founders of the International Academy of Aquatic Art, deserve much credit for its development. Esther Williams, who was inspired by Eleanor Holmes, popularized synchronized swimming in the movies and teamed with Johnny Weissmuller in the 1940 San Francisco World's Fair Aquacade. In competition, swimmers are judged on intricate skills and synchronization of routines set to music.

THE FUTURE

Participation in aquatic activities continues to grow each year, as does the diversity of activities. Aquatic environments provide an opportunity for enjoyable leisure participation for millions of Canadians each year.

Part of the reason for this tremendous increase in participation is the work done by a multitude of organizations that promote aquatic sports and activities. Although competitive swimming has a high profile in Canadian

Participation in Aquatic Activities

According to Campbell's *Survey of Well-Being in Canada* in 1981 and the Canada Fitness Survey in 1988, swimming is the third most popular physical recreation activity among Canadians. Among Canadians 10 years old or older, the participation rate in swimming as a physical recreation activity increased from 36% in 1980 to 42% in 1988.

society, organizations that promote water polo, synchronized swimming, diving, rowing, canoeing, yachting, and sailing can claim similar achievements.

Although their specific interests differ, these organizations have in common the goal of safe and enjoyable aquatic activities. All of them provide wonderful opportunities for Canadians to learn new skills. Chapter 2 provides information on many of these organizations and gives directions for contacting them.

Young people continue to engage in competitive aquatic activities as they have in the past; and similar opportunities now exist also for older competitors. For example, the Master's Swimming movement has expanded dramatically over the last 20 years, and participants engage in competitions at the local, national, and international levels.

All Canadians continue to be increasingly interested in personal fitness and well-being. Both individuals and governments see the need for people to maintain a minimal level of fitness to remain healthy, productive members of society. Swimming and aquatic activities do much to meet this need. Chapter 11 describes aquatic activities for leisure and lifetime fitness.

A wide variety of traditional and innovative facilities have been built to provide swimming instruction and leisure aquatic activities

Figure 1-8. West Edmonton Mall is an example of Canada's innovative aquatic facilities.

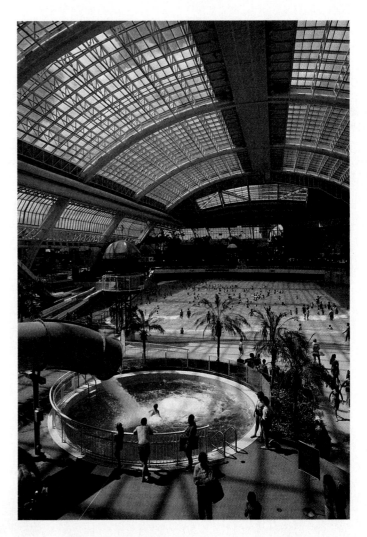

(Figure 1-8). More pools are being built with the latest technology to meet the needs of high level competitors.

In addition, municipalities and companies have built new facilities for leisure and fun aquatic activities: wave pools, water slides, bumper cars. Chapter 4, Aquatic Environments, describes many types of locations and settings in which these aquatic activities occur.

Although these new and expanding programs and facilities provide wonderful opportunities for Canadian citizens of all ages, they also present potential dangers if safety is not the primary concern of participants and organizers. *Water safety knowledge and attitudes, combined with swimming skills, are the basis for safe participation in aquatic activities.* This book is intended to help achieve the goal of safe and enjoyable participation in aquatic activities.

REFERENCES

1. Wallechinsky D (1988). *The complete book of the Olympics.* New York: Penguin Books.
2. Tihany J, Bauman A (1989). *Swimming with Alex Bauman: a program for competitive and recreational swimmers.* Toronto: Key Porter Books Limited.
3. McAllister R (1954). *Swim to glory: The story of Marilyn Bell and the Lakeshore Swimming Club.* Toronto: McClelland & Stewart Ltd.
4. MacDonald D, Drewery L (1981). *For the record: Canada's greatest women athletes.* Rexdale, Ontario: John Wiley & Sons Ltd.
5. The Canadian Encyclopedia (1985). Edmonton: Hurtig Publishers.
6. Firby H (1975). *Howard Firby on Swimming.* London: Pelham Books.

Aquatic Opportunities

In any recreational or sports activity in or on the water, the more you know about it and the more you improve your skills, the safer you will be. Organizations for those participating in aquatic activities are an excellent source of information and instruction that help you prepare for the activity and stay safe while experiencing it.

Many aquatic opportunities are available in Canada. For most of these activities, there is an organization or association that provides information or instructions. These groups have much to offer both for beginners and for the experienced. Not only can you have more fun if you participate with others in the activity, but you can learn from them at the same time.

Most aquatic organizations have programs and activities that can help you learn the activity or perfect your skills. Many offer programs or classes for different ages and skill levels. Most also publish and disseminate information. As you join with others to enjoy the activity, you learn more about it and become better at it—which makes the experience safer and more enjoyable.

The following sections describe organizations related to these aquatic activities:

- Canoeing
- Competitive swimming
- Diving
- Kayaking
- Personal watercraft
- Power boating
- Rowing
- Sailing and boardsailing
- SCUBA
- Synchronized swimming
- Water exercise
- Water polo
- Water rescue and lifesaving
- Water skiing

The information in the following sections comes from the organizations themselves. For additional information, contact the organizations directly at the addresses provided.

CANADIAN AMATEUR DIVING ASSOCIATION
Aim and Purpose

The purpose of the Canadian Amateur Diving Association is to provide all divers, from beginners to Olympic competitors, with an opportunity to achieve personal excellence in diving through programs that focus on safety and fun.

Activities Offered

The Association offers diving programs in two tiers:

- The Learn to Dive recreational program teaches safe, fun diving in municipal pools and clubs all across Canada. The program is organized in four levels to help divers progress in their skills, and participants are recognized for their success at multiple stages in each level. Participants learn safety skills they can apply in various aquatic environments to prevent injuries.

- The Tier II Competitive program continues the Learn to Dive program by offering opportunities for advanced and competitive divers to continue to progress in their skills.

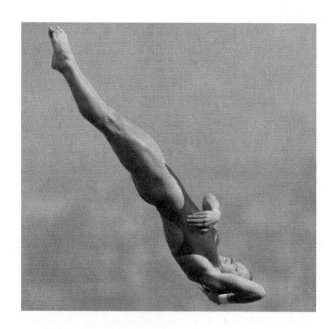

Programs and Materials

The Learn to Dive and Tier II Competitive classes are taught in local diving clubs and municipal facilities. There is also a 2-day instructor course for those wishing to teach in the Learn to Dive program.

Contact

For more information, contact your provincial diving office or the Canadian Amateur Diving Association, 1600 James Naismith Drive, Gloucester, Ontario K1B 5N4. Tel: (613) 748-5631. FAX: (613) 748-5766.

CANADIAN CANOE ASSOCIATION
Aim and Purpose

The purpose of the Canadian Canoe Association (CCA) is to increase Canadian participation in canoeing. To promote canoeing, CCA provides athletic development programs and membership support.

Activities Offered

CCA clubs across Canada offer activities in many kinds of canoeing:

- Olympic sprint racing
- White water, marathon, dragonboat, and outrigger canoeing
- Canoe polo

The volunteer-based clubs offer courses such as canoe and water safety and technical training sessions. There are competitive programs for various age groups, a "Canoe Kids" day camp, social activities, and tours. CCA provides training for competition or for enjoying the sport as a leisure activity.

Programs and Materials

CCA offers a certificate program for children to learn individual and team boat skills. Many clubs also offer recreational paddling programs for both children and adults. The Masters Racing Class for females age 25 and older and males age 30 and older offers competitive opportunities.

Contact

For more information, contact Canadian Canoe Association, 709-1600 James Naismith Drive, Gloucester, Ontario K1B 3K9. Tel: (613) 748-5623. FAX: (613) 748-5700.

CANADIAN POWER AND SAIL SQUADRON
Aim and Purpose

The mission of the Canadian Power and Sail Squadron (CPSS) is to maintain high standards of navigation and seamanship among boaters in Canada. To achieve this, CPSS provides facilities and instruction in boating, seamanship, piloting, navigation, and the safe handling of boats of all kinds.

Activities Offered

CPSS provides boating instruction as a public service. Most of the 177 squadrons across Canada offer a boating course in the spring and fall. Times, dates, and locations of course sites are published locally or may be obtained by calling 1-800-268-3579. Public seminars are offered year-round to promote boating safety awareness.

Programs and Materials

Successful completion of the boating course qualifies candidates for CPSS membership. Courses open to the public include the following:

- Boatwise (8- to 12-year-olds)
- Boat Pro (basic knowledge for the first-time boater)
- Ride Smart (a rider's guide to personal watercraft)
- Ad Hoc Skipper (prepares crew members to take charge if boat operator is incapacitated)
- VHF (preparation for the Department of Communications' Restricted Radiotelephone Operator's Certificate Exam)

Advanced and elective courses for members include:

- Seamanship
- Advanced Piloting
- Junior Navigator
- Navigator
- Seamanship Power
- Seamanship Sail
- Weather
- Marine Maintenance
- Maritime Electronics

Contact

For more information, contact Canadian Power and Sail Squadron, 26 Golden Gate Court, Scarborough, Ontario. Tel: (416) 293-2438. FAX: (416) 293-2445.

CANADIAN RECREATIONAL CANOEING ASSOCIATION
Aim and Purpose

The Canadian Recreational Canoeing Association (CRCA) serves canoeists, kayakers, and sea kayakers. Its four aims are:

- To provide safety and certification
- To protect the environment
- To preserve the heritage of the canoe in Canadian culture
- To provide information to the public about Canada's waterways.

Activities Offered

CRCA runs the annual Canadian Canoe Route Environmental Cleanup Project, in which more than 15,000 participants remove garbage and debris from Canada's waterways. National "Let's

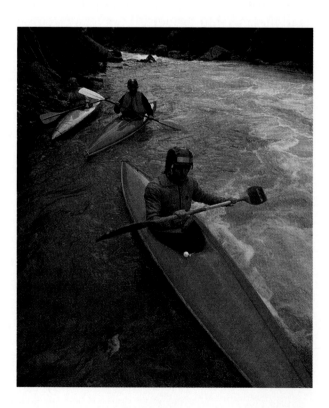

Go Paddling" Week is also operated by CRCA to involve new paddlers. Canoe, kayak, and sea kayak trips are available through Canada's Canoe Adventures (contact CRCA for catalogue).

Programs and Materials

CRCA provides instructor training and basic canoe courses. It also has the world's largest collection of information on canoeing, kayaking, and sea kayaking in Canada, including books, maps, videos, instructional manuals, and route guides. Other programs include the following:

- Liability insurance for members attending sanctioned canoeing and kayaking events operated by instructors, volunteers, or canoe clubs
- *Kanawana Magazine*, a 72-page, full-colour quarterly publication
- The Bill Mason Memorial Scholarship Fund
- Annual photography contest co-sponsored by Nikon Canada

Contact

For more information, contact Canadian Recreational Canoeing Association, 1029 Hyde Park Road, Suite 5, London, Ontario. Tel: (519) 473-2109. FAX: (519) 473-6560.

CANADIAN YACHTING ASSOCIATION
Aim and Purpose

The Canadian Yachting Association (CYA) is Canada's national sailing organization. It promotes sailing through its membership of individuals, sailing clubs and schools, summer camps, class associations, and provincial sailing associations.

Activities Offered

CYA has programs in the following areas:
- Sailing
- Windsurfing
- Cruising
- Instructor certification in all disciplines of sailing

CYA also sponsors annual nationwide sailing championships for young people, women, and open categories; and it operates the Canadian Sailing Team.

Programs and Materials

- Sailing, cruising, and windsurfing lessons are offered through CYA member clubs and schools.
- Instructor-training programs are provided through Canada's Provincial Sailing Associations.
- Learn to Sail student texts are available through the Provincial Sailing Associations.
- The CYA Recommended Cruising Checklist.

Contact

For more information, contact Canadian Yachting Association, 504-1600 James Naismith Drive, Gloucester, Ontario. Tel: (613) 748-5687. FAX: (613) 748-5688.

ROWING CANADA AVIRON
Aim and Purpose

Rowing Canada Aviron (RCA) is the trade name of the Canadian Amateur Rowing Association. This is the governing body of rowing in Canada, whose purpose is to promote, encourage, and develop the sport of rowing.

Activities Offered

RCA promotes both sliding seat and fixed seat rowing. The RCA Rowing Club offers a variety of programs, including learn-to-row programs, recreational programs, and national and international racing programs. In addition, provincial rowing associations offer Coaching and Officials Development Programs in cooperation with RCA.

Programs and Materials

To become a member of RCA, you must first join a rowing club. There are recreational and competitive memberships. Services members receive include the following:

- *Aviron Canadian Rowing* (bimonthly rowing magazine)
- Videotape library
- Access to RCA archives
- Athlete and other awards
- Coaching Certification Program and related materials
- Qualified RCA licensed officials for regattas
- Rules of Racing Handbook
- Talent Identification Program
- Access to competitive RCA regattas such as the Rowing Canada Cup, Royal Canadian Henley, and the Canadian Masters Championships
- The Regatta Schedule/Regatta Watchers Guide

Contact

For more information, contact Rowing Canada Aviron, 1600 James Naismith Drive, Suite 716, Gloucester, Ontario K1B 5N4. Tel: (613) 748-5656. FAX: (613) 748-5712.

THE ROYAL LIFE SAVING SOCIETY CANADA

Aim and Purpose

The purpose of the Royal Life Saving Society Canada (RLSSC) is to prevent drowning and water-related injuries by providing education and training.

Activities Offered

RLSSC works to increase awareness of the responsibility of everyone involved in water sports and recreation. RLSSC provides education in water rescue, resuscitation, lifeguarding, and aquatic risk management. The society also offers leadership training and development for lifesaving and lifeguarding programs and activities.

Programs and Materials

RLSSC offers the following programs:

- Twelve lifesaving programs and resources that focus on self-rescue and the voluntary rescue of others
- Lifeguarding programs and resources that focus on professional responsibility for preventing injuries and intervening in aquatic emergencies
- Leadership programs and resources that train instructors and examiners in lifesaving and lifeguarding education
- Water Smart Campaign and resources, delivering personal water safety information and lifesaving education

Contact

For more information, contact The Royal Life Saving Society Canada, 287 McArthur Avenue, Ottawa, Ontario K1L 6P3. Tel: (613) 746-5694. FAX: (613) 746-9929.

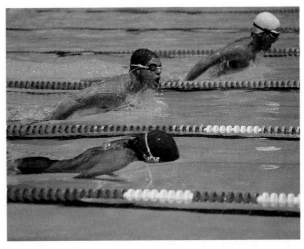

SCUBA

SCUBA stands for self-contained underwater breathing apparatus, referring to the equipment one uses in SCUBA diving. SCUBA is an increasingly popular aquatic activity. When you swim underwater, you can observe fish and other marine plants and animals in their natural habitat. Many people find the undersea world exciting and beautiful.

To safely use the equipment and know what to do in any underwater situation, you must take a certified SCUBA training course. A medical examination and swim test are recommended before beginning this training. To learn about SCUBA classes in your area, contact your local dive shop or other aquatic recreational facilities.

SWIMMING/NATATION CANADA
Aim and Purpose

Swimming/Natation Canada (S/NC) assists with the design, coordination, and operation of educational and recreational swim programs in Canada. Its mission is to help swimmers reach their maximum potential. Each of S/NC's 10 provincial sections conducts competitions and recreational programs to meet the needs of swimmers in each region.

Activities Offered

In addition to coordinating the National Swim Team, S/NC does the following:

- Provides progressive educational materials
- Promotes the development of swimmers competing in meets from local to international levels

Programs and Materials

- ESSO Swim Canada
- National Coaching Certification Program for all swimming coaches
- Educational programs for swimmers, parents, officials, and coaches
- Development of swimming skills for all age groups

Contact

For more information, contact Swimming/Natation Canada, 1600 James Naismith Drive, Gloucester, Ontario K1B SN4. Tel: (613) 748-5673. FAX: (613) 748-5715.

Synchro Canada
Aim and Purpose

Synchro Canada is an independent research, education, and service organization dedicated to encouraging and improving synchronized swimming in Canada.

Activities Offered

Synchro Canada provides support services to swimmers, coaches, officials, volunteers, and provincial member associations. Working to improve the quality of synchro programs and aquatic facilities, it operates through a national volunteer board of directors and action committees comprised of interested members across Canada.

Programs and Materials

Synchro Canada teaches synchronized swimming to young people ages 8 to 17. Adults can also participate in synchronized swimming, singly or in groups, through the society's programs. These include:

- See It—Try It, a beginner's-level program
- Star Awards Program, a five-level program that teaches basic synchro figures set to music

- Superstar Awards Program, a five-level advanced program
- Synchro Fit Circuit, a complete fitness program

Qualified members can judge and coach at the national level and contribute to the management of Canadian synchronized swimming. Services members receive include the following:

- National membership directory
- Communique, Synchro Canada's national newsletter
- Synchro Resource Centre catalogue
- Discounts on publications, videos, and Synchro Canada products

Contact

For more information, contact Synchro Canada, 1600 James Naismith Drive, Gloucester, Ontario K1B 5N4. Tel: (613) 748-5674. FAX: (613) 748-5724.

Water Polo Canada
Aim and Purpose

The purpose of Water Polo Canada (WPC) is to promote water polo to the Canadian public as a sport and a leisure activity.

Activities Offered

To increase the participation of youngsters between 8 and 14 years of age in water polo activities, Water Polo Canada developed the Skills Award Program. One of the objectives of the Skills Award Program is to disprove the idea that water polo is difficult to teach. Other WPC activities are:

- Mini-polo, which has modified rules and a smaller field of play
- Inner-tube water polo
- Competitive water polo

Programs and Materials

Services provided to members include:

- Skills Award Program manual including certificates and decals
- Posters and achievement certificates for students
- Educational material and videos

Contact

For more information, contact Water Polo Canada, 1600 James Naismith Drive, Gloucester, Ontario K1B 5N4. Tel: (613) 748-5682. FAX: (613) 748-5777.

WATER SKI CANADA RECREATION AWARDS PROGRAM
Aim and Purpose

Water Ski Canada provides new and developing water skiers, kneeboarders, and wakeboarders with the opportunity to learn these sports and develop their skills.

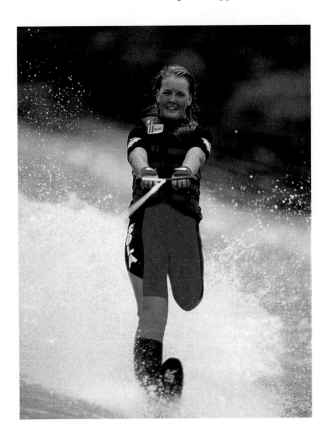

Activities Offered

The Recreation Awards Program leads beginners through a progression of skills to increase their knowledge and abilities. The program is divided into three award levels for water skiing and one for kneeboarding and wakeboarding. Knowledge, safety, and skill acquisition are emphasized at every level.

Programs and Materials

In addition to the programs described above, available materials include the following:

- Packs for organizers that include certificates for participants at each level
- Recreation Awards Program Handbook
- General information on water skiing and water skiing safety
- Organizer progress chart
- List of provincial water ski contacts

Contact

For more information, contact Water Ski Canada Recreation Awards Program, 1600 James Naismith Drive, Gloucester, Ontario K1B 5N4. Tel: (613) 748-5683. FAX: (613) 748-5867.

YOUNG MEN'S CHRISTIAN ASSOCIATION CANADA
Aim and Purpose

The Young Men's Christian Association (YMCA) is a worldwide fellowship dedicated to individual personal growth in spirit, mind, and body. YMCA seeks to create a sense of individual responsibility to others and the human community. Health and aquatic programs are one element of this personal growth.

Activities Offered

YMCA Canada owns and operates swimming pools throughout Canada, with many local YMCAs and YMCA-YWCAs located in all 10 provinces. Programs offered include health, fitness and recreation, and camping.

Programs and Materials

YMCA aquatic and swimming programs include the following:

- Preschool swimming
- Children and Adult Learn-to-Swim
- Advanced Swimming
- Lifesaving
- Canoeing
- Recreational Swimming
- Aquatic Clubs
- Instructor Training
- Aquatic Fitness
- Special Aquatic Sports
- Competitive Swimming

Contact

For more information, contact YMCA Canada, 2160 Yonge Street, Toronto, Ontario M4S 2A9. Tel: (416) 485-9447. FAX: (416) 485-8228.

YOUNG WOMEN'S CHRISTIAN ASSOCIATION (YWCA) OF CANADA

Aim and Purpose

YWCA of Canada is a voluntary organization of member associations that provides programs and services in response to community needs. YWCA works to develop and improve the status of women and improve social and economic conditions.

Activities Offered

YWCA provides leisure and recreational activities, including the following:

- Swimming lessons
- Lifesaving
- Aquafitness
- Family activities

Programs and Materials

YWCA of Canada offers these related publications:

- *A Fitness Leader's Guide to Osteoporosis (L'Osteoporose Guide de L'Animateur en Condition Physique)*
- *The Leader's Guide to Aquafitness (Guide du Moniteur de Conditionnement Aquatique)*

Contact

For more information, contact YWCA of Canada, 80 Gerrard St. East, Toronto, Ontario M5B 1G6. Tel: (416) 593-9886. FAX: (416) 971-8084.

SUMMARY

Joining an aquatic organization can introduce you to new ways to enjoy your favourite activities while you also become safer in the water. These organizations will help you learn to work within your own abilities to develop your personal potential to its fullest.

Water Safety

Be prepared before you head for water.

Know what to do to stay safe in, on, and around the water.

Know how to save yourself or another in a water emergency
and how to give first aid when needed.

- Safely enjoying the water involves common sense and basic skills. By reviewing these principles and skills, you may be able to avoid an emergency.

- Know your swimming ability and that of your companions. Be aware of the factors that may cause fatigue during water activities.

- Understand the aquatic environment: in the water and on the shore, dock, or deck. Be able to respond if a hazardous condition arises, such as wind, waves, poor weather, or too much sun.

- Know how to use equipment you take into the water. Understand how to choose a flotation device, how to put it on, its proper use in the water, and how to care for it.

- By becoming properly trained in basic first aid and basic water rescue techniques, you will enhance your ability to effectively help yourself or someone else in distress.

If you watch television, listen to the radio, or read the newspaper, you know that some people die while engaging in water activities. The tragic reality is that many of these deaths could have been prevented by using the right equipment and common sense. Do not let yourself or someone you know become a casualty. Learn how to prevent injuries and stay safe in, on, and around the water. Not only will you minimize the risk of injury, but you will more fully enjoy your aquatic activities.

NATIONAL SAFETY STANDARDS

Canadian National Safety Standards, as developed by The Canadian Red Cross Society Water Safety Service, are defined as the knowledge, skills, and attitudes that individuals need to prevent water-related incidents and death and save themselves or others in an emergency. These standards are noted at the beginning of every appropriate chapter.

INJURY PREVENTION

Learning, exploring, and developing new skills always involve some challenges—and often some risk! It is everyone's responsibility to make sure injuries don't happen as a result of this risk. Planning for "safety" is the most effective tool for preventing injuries.

Whether you are at a lake, river, or backyard pool—whether you are swimming, boating, or just splashing in the surf, the principles and practices of injury prevention are the foundation for ensuring your safety.

Injury prevention is an organized way to—

- Prevent, minimize, or control exposure to the risk of injury.
- Reduce the severity of an injury that does occur by providing prompt treatment.
- Reduce the severity of the consequences of an injury.

The Problem

Injury is damage to the body caused by a destructive force in the environment. The damage can be minor, serious, life threatening, or fatal. It can range from a cut finger to a drowning. In, on, or around aquatic environments, people, especially young children and recreational boaters, are dying. Others are left with a lifelong disability such as paralysis. Many more must live with the loss of a loved one. These people are members of our community. It can overtake and change the familiar shapes and patterns of life, family, finances, and the future.

In Canada more than 9,000 people per year lose their lives to injury. Injuries are the leading cause of death among toddlers of both sexes, with approximately 1 fatal injury per 5,000 boys and 1 per 10,000 girls each year.

Drowning is the second most common cause of injury-related deaths among toddlers.

The Solution

Injury prevention depends on both individual and community action. As individuals, we all practice injury prevention to varying degrees. As a community activity, it is a new, evolving movement. Community action focused on injury prevention can—

- Help people become aware that injuries can be prevented.

- Mobilize action that results in fewer injuries and better protection of people in the community.

An approach to injury prevention

Injury prevention for aquatic activities is a simple approach involving three stages:

Stage 1—Prepare: Includes everything you do before you head to the water (Figure 3-1).

Stage 2—Stay Safe: Includes the things you do during water activities to stay safe (Figure 3-2).

Stage 3—Survive: Includes the actions you take to ensure the safety and survival of yourself and others if something does go wrong (Figure 3-3).

Figure 3-1. Prepare for your water experience in advance.

Figure 3-2. Staying safe in the water includes adult supervision and following safety guidelines.

Figure 3-3. Know how to give first aid for injuries that may occur in aquatic activities.

In each stage, the following factors play a major role in safety in, on, and around the water:

- **Personal factors:** Your knowledge, skills, and behaviour

- **Equipment:** Knowing, supplying, wearing, carrying, and using the right equipment for the activity

- **Environment:** The conditions of the site, your surroundings, the weather, and the water

If you understand and think about the stages of injury prevention, you are more likely to anticipate problems and learn the skills needed either to avoid them or to properly respond to them. You can also initiate community action and promote safer environments to prevent and eventually eliminate injuries and water-related fatalities.

PREPARE BEFORE YOU HEAD TO THE WATER

Preparation includes being personally prepared, checking your equipment, and checking the environment.

Personal Preparedness

Being personally prepared involves having the correct knowledge, skills, and attitude. Follow these guidelines:

- Through the Red Cross or other agencies, learn about swimming, boating, and first aid; and be sure that others in your group are well informed.
- Know the rules of the recreational site.

- Teach your children about water safety. Even very young children can learn basic safety rules.
- Plan water activity with your children ahead of time to ensure that you will not be distracted or interrupted while you supervise them.
- Know your swimming limits, based on your own level of capability.
- Learn the safe and proper way to dive and know when and where it is safe to do so.
- Have an emergency plan in case of a water emergency, regardless of how well you swim.

Check Your Equipment

- Keep boating equipment in repair and ready for use.

- Ensure that your pool has access to a telephone. The gate into the pool area should be self-latching and self-closing and at least 1.2 metres high. (See later section on becoming Pool Perfect.)
- Have a first aid kit at the site and know how to give first aid.
- Apply sun protection and dress appropriately for the weather conditions.
- Have the appropriate safety equipment readily available and in working order and know how to properly use it. (See Chapter 13, Water Rescue.)
- Wear your flotation device.

Check the Environment

- Swim in supervised areas.
- Avoid swimming in open water with strong currents, heavy boat traffic, or excessive debris in the water.

- Always check the depth before entering the water.
- Check for inclement weather.

WHO DROWNS?

Research shows that deaths related to water involve people of all ages, ranging from very young children to the elderly. However, certain groups of people are at greater risk. Most casualties are males. The majority of water-related fatalities are concentrated in the following age groups:

- Young males 15 to 24 years of age

- Older males 45 to 54 years of age

- Elderly people over 75 years of age

- Toddlers 1 to 4 years of age

Often the casualties had not intended to be in the water at all. The vast majority of deaths from drowning and other water-related injuries are associated with boating and other recreational activities. Drowning most commonly occurs during the following:

- Boating

- Aquatic activities

- Walking near the water (and falling into the water)

Research shows other patterns of risk in water-related deaths.

- Use of alcohol is the most common contributing factor in all water-related deaths.

- Children 1 to 4 years old have a high drowning rate. A key factor in many of these deaths is lack of supervision and access to water hazards in and around the home.

- Poor swimming ability is a contributing factor for some water-related deaths, despite the availability of learn-to-swim programs. More people need to learn swimming and water safety skills.

- In boating incidents most drowning casualties were not wearing a personal flotation device (PFD).

Data from The Canadian Red Cross Society, National Drowning Report, 1993. The source of this information is the Canadian National Surveillance System for Water-Related Fatalities, developed by the Canadian Red Cross Society in collaboration with several other organizations.

Water-related Death

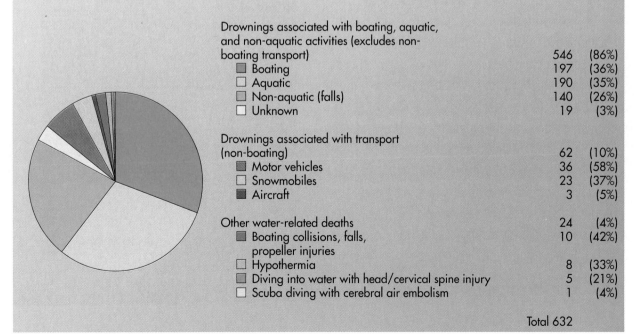

Drownings associated with boating, aquatic, and non-aquatic activities (excludes non-boating transport)	546	(86%)
■ Boating	197	(36%)
☐ Aquatic	190	(35%)
☐ Non-aquatic (falls)	140	(26%)
☐ Unknown	19	(3%)
Drownings associated with transport (non-boating)	62	(10%)
■ Motor vehicles	36	(58%)
☐ Snowmobiles	23	(37%)
■ Aircraft	3	(5%)
Other water-related deaths	24	(4%)
■ Boating collisions, falls, propeller injuries	10	(42%)
☐ Hypothermia	8	(33%)
■ Diving into water with head/cervical spine injury	5	(21%)
☐ Scuba diving with cerebral air embolism	1	(4%)

Total 632

- Know the local water hazards. In some urban or industrial settings, for example, swimming is not recommended if the daily pollution count is high. Check with local authorities.
- In winter, telephone your local community authority for ice safety reports.

Stay Safe During Water Activities

Staying safe in the water involves doing the right things personally, with your equipment, and with the environment.

Personal Safety

- If you feel cold and are shivering, stop and warm up. Have something hot to drink.
- Swim with a buddy.
- Refrain from the use of alcohol and other drugs when you are swimming.
- Always enter feet first if you do not know the water depth.
- Stay within your swimming capabilities.
- Watch out for the "dangerous too's": too tired, too cold, too far from safety, too much sun, too much rough play.
- Do not chew gum or eat while you swim; you could easily choke.
- Give children your undivided attention. Let the phone ring, leave the laundry out in the rain, put off lunch and chores. It only takes a moment for a child to drown.

Learning to Swim

The best thing you can do to stay safe in and around the water is to learn to swim. Learning to swim is fun for everyone! Swimming can open up a whole new world of enjoyment and recreational activity. The Canadian Red Cross Society offers water safety and learn-to-swim classes through municipalities, camps, fitness facilities, and private organizations.

Knowing how to swim is important even if you don't intend to swim regularly. It may even save your life at some time when you hadn't planned to swim. Many drownings in Canada occur each year when the person never intended to be in the water.

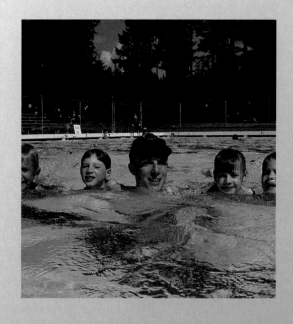

TODDLER DROWNINGS

Drowning is the second most common cause of death from injury among toddlers in Canada.

For every toddler who drowns, another 6 to 10 are hospitalized because of near drowning, and 20% of these suffer permanent brain damage.

Only 5% of toddlers who drowned are in the company of an adult when the incident occurs.

Most commonly, the drowning casualty was either playing or walking near the water.

Drowning hazards in and around the home account for 53% of all toddler drownings. The remaining incidents occur in large bodies of water such as lakes and rivers.

The rate of swimming pool drownings among toddlers is many times higher than in other age groups. Home swimming pools are the most common location of toddler drownings. In or near the home, the bathtub is the second most frequent site.

Ninety-seven percent of swimming pool drownings in Canada occurred in a pool **not** equipped with a self-latching, self-closing gate and standard fence.

Highlights of the Special Research Report on Drownings Among Children Aged 1 to 4 in Canada, 1994. Information from The Canadian Red Cross Society,

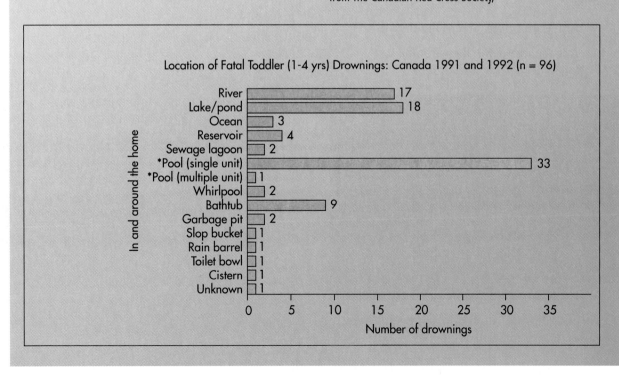

Location of Fatal Toddler (1-4 yrs) Drownings: Canada 1991 and 1992 (n = 96)

Location	Number of drownings
River	17
Lake/pond	18
Ocean	3
Reservoir	4
Sewage lagoon	2
*Pool (single unit)	33
*Pool (multiple unit)	1
Whirlpool	2
Bathtub	9
Garbage pit	2
Slop bucket	1
Rain barrel	1
Toilet bowl	1
Cistern	1
Unknown	1

In and around the home

Equipment Safety

- Monitor the use of buoyant toys. They are fun but must not be relied on for safety. They may deflate suddenly or be carried by wind or waves into deep water (Figure 3-4).

Environmental Safety

- Swim only in a pool where you can see the bottom at the deep end.

- Swim in supervised areas (Figure 3-5).

- Monitor the weather and environment continually.

Figure 3-4. Be sure children playing with buoyant toys are supervised by an adult.

THE BUDDY SYSTEM

A buddy system should be used to be sure participants in an aquatic activity, particularly children, can be accounted for at all times. You can use this system whenever you are supervising a group in the water. Every person is paired with another person of about equal ability, and they are asked to stay near each other and watch out for each other. Periodically you call for a "buddy check," and each pair holds their hands up together. Count the number of pairs to be sure everyone is accounted for.

Camps, municipal pools, and other programs often use an organized buddy system for the same purpose. Participants check in at the "buddy board" before entering the water and check out when they leave the water, allowing supervisors and lifeguards to know who is in the water and to have an accurate count to compare with the count during a buddy check.

SURVIVE

 Know what actions to take to ensure the safety and survival of yourself and others if something does go wrong. Like preparing and staying safe, surviving depends on personal preparedness, the effective use of equipment, and paying attention to the environment.

Personal Factors

• Stay in a safe position when performing a reaching assist. (See Chapter 13, Water Rescue.)

• If you fall into the water, use survival positions such as the huddle or help position, described in Chapter 4, Aquatic Environments. If a boat capsizes, stay with the boat.

• Stay calm, do not panic.

• Follow the lifeguard's instructions if there is an emergency.

• Know how to perform first aid.

Equipment Factors

• Use a reaching or throwing assist.

• Put on a flotation device.

• Use your sound signal device attached to your flotation device.

• Use your first aid kit.

Environmental Factors

• Find shelter from the cold or overexposure to the sun.

• Remove yourself from the hazard (such as rough waves) or remove the hazard (such as broken glass on pool deck).

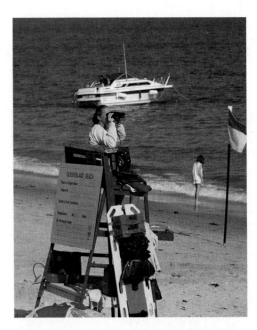

Figure 3-5. Swim only in supervised areas.

GET POOL PERFECT

Injury prevention activities are crucial for those who own or use backyard pools. The following pool perfect checklist is to help prevent drownings, spinal injuries, and other incidents in your backyard pool. Safe enjoyable swimming for your family and friends is up to you. Carefully think about each of the following questions, and be honest with yourself in your answers.

Pool Perfect Checklist

Who's the boss?

Are swimmers constantly supervised by an adult pool supervisor who knows and is trained in—

• The safety equipment and emergency procedures?

• Water rescue and first aid?

• How to use approved PFDs rather than toys to support weak swimmers?

• POOL PERFECT TIP: BE WISE—SUPERVISE!

REAL DROWNING STORIES

A 32-year-old male who had been drinking decided to swim the 50 metres across the Fraser River to Crescent Island. No one was with him; no one saw him drown.

A 5-year-old boy wandered out onto the tidal flats near the ocean while his grandparents set up a picnic lunch. When they looked up, he was gone. His body was found the next day floating face down in the sea.

A mother left a 1-year-old boy in the tub alone with his 3-year-old sister in 15 cm of water for just 10 minutes. He was dead when she returned to the bathroom.

A 22-year-old man was fishing with two friends in a small boat on a lake on a windy day when a large wave rocked the boat and threw them overboard. The boat was still running and moved away from them. The two friends were wearing life jackets and survived to be picked up by a passing boat, but the 22-year-old was not wearing his life jacket and drowned.

Good fences make good pools

Does the fence around your pool—

- Prevent direct access from the house?
- Meet municipal height regulations?
- Have a self-closing, self-latching gate with inside latch?
- Not have any gaps larger than 10 cm?
- Prevent climbing?
- POOL PERFECT TIP: PREVENT ACCESS TO YOUR POOL.

Safe diving, jumping, and getting wet

Few backyard pools are safe for diving. Have you—

- Clearly marked pool depths and unsafe diving areas?
- A floating safety line between deep and shallow water?

- Informed guests of safe entry techniques?
- Ensured sufficient depth for entire path of entry on slide or dives?
- Told guests about sliding feet first only?
- Restricted activities to one at a time on a slide or in a diving area?
- POOL PERFECT TIP: BEFORE THEY PLUNGE, EXPLAIN AND EDUCATE.

You're the bottom line in poolside entertainment

Do you communicate pool guidelines to family and friends by posting them?

- Swim only with pool supervisor present.
- Play with care!
- Walk, don't run.
- Keep your head! Feet first entries only.

Do you inform your guests of pool safety procedures? Let them know that alcohol and pools don't mix—alcohol is involved in about 50% of drowning incidents.

POOL PERFECT TIP: SEAL THEIR FATE—COMMUNICATE!

Be aware—always prepare

Do you always have the following safety equipment poolside?

- Non-metal reaching pole.
- Throwing line with buoyant aid.
- First aid kit.
- Telephone with posted emergency numbers, your address, and phone number.
- Properly fitted flotation devices for toddlers around the pool.

Are you familiar with emergency procedures for water safety and first aid?

Do you keep pool chemicals stored under lock and key?

POOL PERFECT TIP: BE PREPARED WITH EQUIPMENT AND TRAINING.

Self-Assessment

If you answered Yes to all these questions, congratulations!

If you answered No to any of them, make changes and become "Pool Perfect!"

Take Action

Organize an annual spring community safety check to verify that all swimming pools in or near residential areas with children are appropriately fenced and fitted with self-latching and self-closing gates (Figure 3-6).

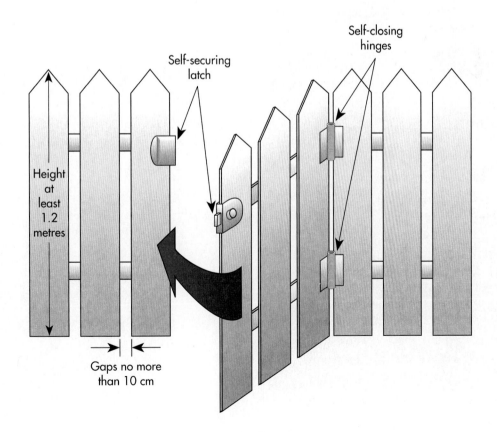

Figure 3-6. A safe home pool is fenced and has a self-latching, self-closing gate.

Be Sun Smart

Summer is a great time to be outdoors, but the sun's rays can be harmful to skin. When you or your child is swimming or playing outdoors, you should take precautions against the damaging effects of the sun's rays. Exposed skin during winter activities is equally as susceptible.

It doesn't matter how old you are or what colour your skin is. You are still susceptible to skin damage from the sun.

Why should you be concerned? When skin is exposed to the sun, it can be damaged by two different ultraviolet rays in sunlight:

- Ultraviolet B (UVB) rays affect the outer layer of skin, causing sunburn.

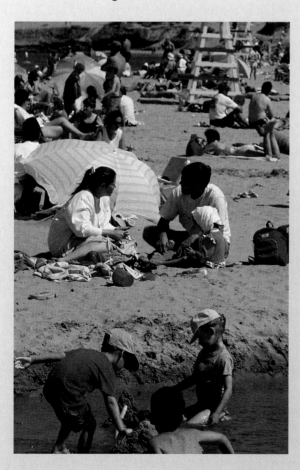

- Ultraviolet A (UVA) rays go deeper into the skin, possibly causing damage that may result in the development of cancer at a later time.

UVA and UVB rays are both known to damage the skin and cause cancer. The most dangerous part of the day is from 11 am to 4 pm.

What can you do?

Reduce your exposure to the sun. To be protected from the sun's rays, be sure that you and your family—

- Wear a hat with a wide brim or peak.

- Wear sunglasses. Sunglasses are sunscreen for your eyes and provide important protection from UV rays. Ophthalmologists recommend sunglasses that have a UV absorption of at least 90%.

- Wear light clothing to cover as much skin as possible.

- Use sunscreen with a minimum sun protection factor (SPF) of 15, and reapply it frequently (every 3 to 4 hours). Sun-screen should be applied 15 to 30 minutes before exposure to the sun.

- Use sunscreen also on cloudy and hazy days. Clouds do not block UV rays.

- Remain in shaded areas, especially if you don't have sunscreen.
- Take extra care around the water. Water reflects the sun's rays and can cause sunburn.
- Keep infants under 1 year old out of the sun altogether.
- Drink lots of water or juice to prevent dehydration.

How do you choose a sunscreen?

When choosing a sunscreen, read the label carefully and look for:

- SPF of 15 or higher, as recommended by the Canadian Dermatology Association and the Canadian Cancer Society.
- The word "waterproof" or "water resistant."
- Protection against both UVA and UVB.
- The Canadian Dermatology Association seal of approval.

NOTE: If a rash appears after using the sunscreen, contact your physician.

SKIN CANCER

Cancer of the skin is the most common of all cancers.

About 44,000 new cases of skin cancer are detected each year in Canada.

Skin cancer can usually be cured, if detected early.

Information provided by the Canadian Cancer Society.

PFDs AND LIFE JACKETS

Statistics on water-related fatalities in Canada show that most drowning casualties never intended to be in the water. Many were either enjoying boating activities or playing near the water. Because they did not intend to enter the water, they were not wearing the most important piece of safety equipment: a life jacket or personal flotation device (PFD).

The Department of Transportation (DOT) requires that there must be one approved PFD or approved life jacket for each person in a craft (under 5.5 metres). Flotation devices should be WORN by everyone in the boat.

Choosing a Life Jacket

Following are some guidelines for selecting a DOT-approved flotation device.

Approved label

When a flotation device passes a test for design performance, quality control, and flotation materials, an approval label is sewn, silk-screened, or etched in. Make sure it is DOT-approved, *since flotation devices approved by the U.S. Coast Guard are not recognized on Canadian boats as required safety equipment* (Figure 3-7).

Colour

Only red, yellow, gold, and orange flotation devices meet Canadian government requirements.

Size

Life jackets and personal flotation devices must fit properly to work efficiently. They should be easy to put on and take off. Choose a device that permits you to bend freely when wearing it and to walk easily and sit comfortably. First, check the label, which provides size information based on chest size or body weight. Then try on the device, and tie or zipper all the fasteners (Figure 3-8). To test a PFD, pull the device at the collar to ensure that it does not ride up and interfere with movement or breathing.

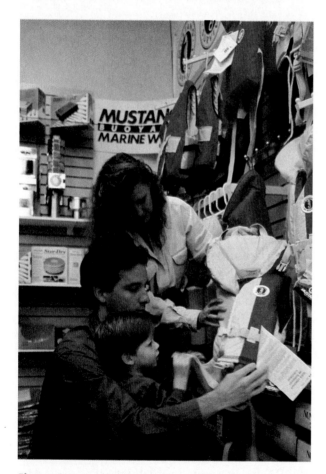

Figure 3-7. Different kinds of flotation devices are appropriate for different activities in or on the water. Being prepared for a safe water experience includes choosing the right type of device. Check the label to make sure that it is DOT approved.

Figure 3-8. Try on a PFD to ensure correct fit before buying it.

Condition

To ensure the most efficient performance in an emergency situation and to ensure DOT approval, snaps, belts, tapes, or zippers must work; and the device must not be ripped.

Types of Flotation Devices

Standard life jackets

The approved standard life jacket is available in one keyhole style and in two sizes: for body weights over or under 40 kg, also called adult and child sizes. The main feature of the standard life jacket is its ability to turn an unconscious person in the water from a face-down to a face-up position so that the person can breathe. This is also known as a self-righting capability.

Put on a standard life jacket in the following manner:

1. Place your head through the keyhole.
2. Tie the neck ties.
3. Encircle your waist with the straps and tie them at the front, against your stomach, *never on top of the life jacket.*
4. Ensure you can cross your arms under the tied life jacket to allow proper flotation to occur.

The standard life jacket is available with either kapok or foam flotation. They are reversible.

Small-vessel life jackets

Small-vessel life jackets are less buoyant than standard life jackets, but they will also turn an unconscious person in the water from a face-down to a face-up position. They may be carried on any pleasure craft.

Personal flotation devices

PFDs are designed to keep a conscious person afloat but have less buoyancy and turning ability than DOT-approved life jackets. PFDs are designed for constant wear and provide varying degrees of protection against cold water. They are available in a variety of styles (vest and over-the-head, or keyhole) and sizes, giving the wearer greater comfort and versatility. PFDs are acceptable only on pleasure crafts or for use around the water.

Flotation devices for children

There are PFDs and small-vessel life jackets designed specially for children. When purchasing a child's flotation device, look for the following features:

- Label stating DOT approval
- Red, yellow, gold, or orange colour
- Large collar for head support
- Sturdy rust-proof zipper
- Neck ties
- Waist ties with snug-fitting drawstring or elastic in front and back
- Safety strap between the legs to prevent flotation device from slipping over the child's head
- Buckle on safety straps
- Reflective tape
- A signal device such as a plastic whistle can easily be attached to a PFD at the zipper or shoulder

Make sure that the flotation device is comfortable yet snug (Figure 3-9). Do not buy a PFD that is too large in the hope that the child will grow into it. Loose, ill-fitting PFDs are dangerous.

Warning: A life jacket or PFD is not a substitute for adult supervision.

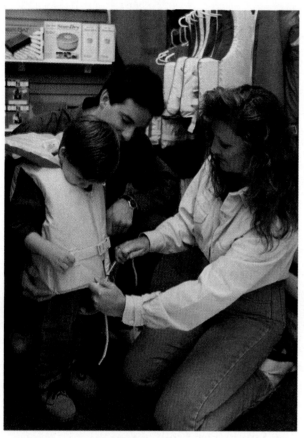

Figure 3-9. Make sure that the child's PFD fits correctly.

Snowmobilers

If you must snowmobile over ice-covered lakes or rivers, wear a buoyant snowmobile survival suit.

Test Your Flotation Device

While wearing your life jacket or PFD, wade out into chest-deep water in a supervised pool or beach. Bend your knees, then float on your back. Make sure that your flotation device keeps your chin above water and that you can breathe easily. Practice swimming a short distance on your stomach, and then on your back. Finally, try a position in which you can easily propel yourself forward (Figure 3-10).

Remember to test your flotation device at the start of each season.

If you are responsible for children, allow them to experiment with their flotation devices under your supervision so that they can become familiar with them.

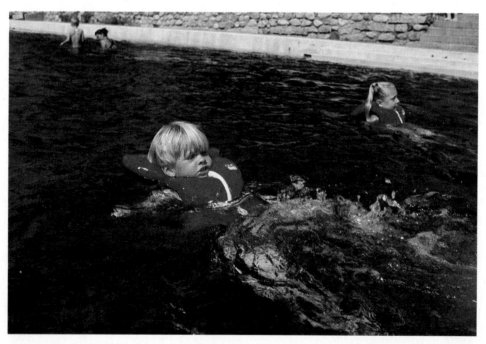

Figure 3-10. Practice floating in a position in which you can easily propel yourself forward.

ALCOHOL AND WATER DON'T MIX

LIFE ON THE WATER—FREEDOM!?

There's nothing like getting out on or near the water and relaxing with family and friends. Those are times worth looking forward to. For many, this is life at its best.

HERE'S SOME VALUABLE INFORMATION.

The most common contributing factor in deaths in and around the water is alcohol.

Many people are not aware how dangerous drinking alcohol is during aquatic activities and that operating a boat while intoxicated is a crimi-nal offence. The laws for drinking and driving apply just the same to drinking and boating.

More important than the possible jail sentence, fine, loss of your driver's license, and criminal record are the injuries or death that can result.

DON'T LIMIT YOUR FREEDOM!!

Information from The Canadian Red Cross Society, National Drowning Report, 1993.

Care and Maintenance of Flotation Devices

Flotation devices are designed to be worn. Do not use them as cushions or boat fenders. Rinse salt water off flotation devices immediately after use, and hang them to dry away from direct heat. Once dry, store them in a cool, ventilated area. Use mild soaps to remove dirt; do not dry clean. Repaired accessories such as replaced ties, snaps, and buckles no longer have DOT approval.

SUMMARY

If you're not used to thinking about water safety and preventing injury, this chapter may at first overwhelm you with seemingly burdensome details. However, once you're in the habit of preparing for your water activities in advance and following safety guidelines when you arrive at the water, you'll find that you can apply these safety precautions in a few minutes. You can lessen or even completely eliminate the risk of injury or drowning; and, because you have peace of mind, you'll also have a lot more fun.

4

Aquatic Environments

Know what environmental conditions might occur in your location and their effects on swimmers or boaters.

Have the skills necessary to deal effectively with various water conditions.

Understand the potential dangers of aquatic life in open water.

Understand and recognize the body's response to cold and heat, and know how to prevent hypothermia and heat illnesses.

Know how to establish and maintain a safe environment at pools and hot tubs.

Obey posted rules and other regulations at open water sites and pools.

Continually monitor environmental conditions to detect any changes that may affect swimming or boating.

Monitor the body's response to hot and cold conditions and respond appropriately to prevent problems.

Know how to cope with dangerous environmental conditions.

Know how to treat stings and wounds from aquatic life.

Know the appropriate first aid to give for hypothermia and heat illness.

- Know what environmental conditions might occur in your location and their effects on swimmers and boaters.

- Understand and recognize the body's response to cold and heat, and know how to prevent hypothermia and heat illnesses.

- Know how to give appropriate first aid.

- Know how to perform self-rescue techniques:

  Heat escape–lessening position

  Huddle position

  Staying with or entering an overturned craft

  Emerging after falling through ice

PREPARE FOR THE AQUATIC ENVIRONMENT

 As you learned in earlier chapters, safety in and around the water begins with being prepared. Part of that preparation is knowing what hazards may exist in the particular aquatic environment. This chapter describes common hazards at pools, other facilities, and open water environments. Knowing the hazards and how to avoid problems in the particular aquatic setting will help you stay safe and prevent injury while you enjoy yourself.

STAY SAFE IN POOLS AND OTHER FACILITIES

 Safety in pools and other facilities depends on knowing the potential hazards.

Private Pools
In-ground pools

In-ground residential pools at homes, apartments, condominiums and hotel/motel pools have many sizes and shapes. They generally range from 1 metre to 2.5 metres in depth. Since most head and neck injuries in residential pools result from dives into shallow water, pool owners are urged to take these precautions:

- Do not allow any diving unless there is ample clearance from the point of entry to the upslope in front of the diving board (Figure 4-1).

- Clearly mark depths on the deck near the edge of the pool and on the side.

- Clearly mark the location of the breakpoint between shallow and deep water with a float line.

- Place "No Diving" signs on the deck near shallow water and on the fence or wall around the swimming pool.

- Follow the "Pool Perfect" rules listed on page 41.

Even deep water in home pools may be dangerous because of the shape of the bottom and sides of the pool or the placement of the diving board. The average backyard pool is not long enough or deep enough for safe springboard diving. Chapter 3 gives more information about safety guidelines for home pools, and Chapter 7 describes safe diving in deep pools.

Above-ground pools

No one should ever dive into an above-ground pool. People have been injured by diving from the deck, the rim, or a structure above the edge. Swimmers should enter on the ladder or ease into the pool. Above-ground pools linked to the home by a deck at the level of the pool surface, require a barrier and gate between the deck and pool (see Chapter 3).

Public Pools

Hotel/motel, apartment, and condominium pools may not be required to employ lifeguards, and therefore during your activity there may not be someone trained to assist you immediately if a problem occurs.

Many public facilities provide lifeguards who are employed to supervise patrons while the pool is open. These individuals are trained according to provincial requirements and must prevent injuries and render assistance if required. When entering a public facility, approach the lifeguards and inquire about the facility's rules.

Spas and Hot Tubs

Spas and hot tubs in the home or at a facility are often not formally supervised, so you must take responsibility for your activity (Figure 4-2). Follow these guidelines:

- The maximum safe water temperature is 40° C.
- Soaking too long at too high a temperature can raise your body temperature. Limit soaking to 15 minutes.
- When not in use, a tub should be securely covered to prevent anyone from falling in.
- Pregnant women or people with heart conditions and other medical conditions such as diabetes, epilepsy, and high blood pressure should not use a spa or hot tub without their physician's approval.
- Never use a spa or hot tub when drinking or using drugs.
- Children under 5 years of age should not go in water above 39° C.
- After being in a spa, it is a good practice to wait at least 5 minutes before swimming because of the effects of a sudden change in water temperature.

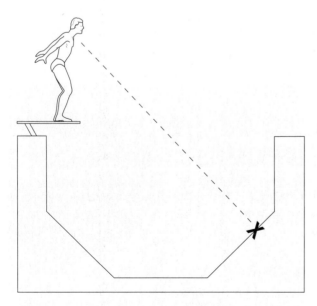

Figure 4-1. For safe diving, there must be ample clearance from the point of entry to the upslope in front of the diving board.

Figure 4-2. Follow safety guidelines for hot tubs and spas.

Water Parks and Water Slides

Water parks and water slides have become very popular. Water park pools and slides have many different sizes and shapes (Figure 4-3). Slides also vary in length, height, and angle and direction of descent. With the proper precautions, they can be very safe and enjoyable.

To prevent injury on a water slide, follow these guidelines:

- Follow slide attendants directions or posted instructions.
- Slide feet-first and after landing, move quickly away from the area in front of the slide (Figure 4-4).
- Be sure the slide is anchored securely to the deck.
- If the slide has a lip higher than the surface of the water, be sure there is sufficient water depth to keep you from striking the bottom.
- On speed slides, cross your legs and keep your arms close to your body to help prevent injuries (Figure 4-5).

Splash pads or water play areas are a popular attraction at water parks and are becoming more common in community-operated parks (Figure 4-6). These areas vary from standing

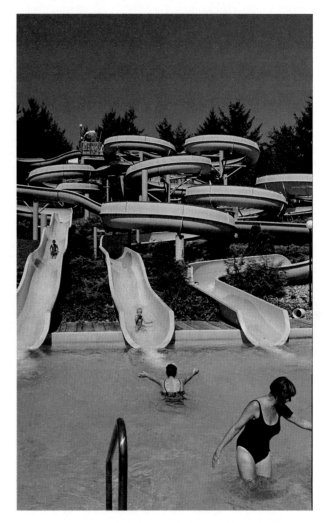

Figure 4-4. Always slide feet-first down a water slide.

Figure 4-3. Water park pools and slides are enjoyable and safe when you take the proper precautions.

Figure 4-5. Cross your legs to help prevent injuries on speed slides.

Figure 4-6. Adult supervision is needed in water play areas.

shallow water (wading pools) to fountains, waterfalls, and hand-activated "water cannons." Primarily designed for children, these areas require no swimming skills. Adult supervision is required in water play areas as in any play area in a park.

STAY SAFE IN OPEN WATER

 In open-water areas, the water usually has limited visibility and for many reasons may be more hazardous than that in pools. Even when a lifeguard is present, you must be more careful when swimming in open water. In an ocean, river, lake, or other open water, you may encounter potentially dangerous conditions different from those with which you are familiar. Conditions may also change from hour to hour in some waters. Before swimming in a new area, check it out carefully and watch for the hazards described in the next sections.

Waves

Any open-water area may have waves (Figure 4-7). Waves can change quickly with the weather. A sudden wave may carry or push a non-swimmer into deep water. Any swimmer can be knocked over by a wave breaking close to shore. The wave may roll you under the surface or slam you into the sand. Children playing at the water's edge can be knocked down by even a small sudden breaking wave. Parents should be with their children to supervise them at a shore-line.

Currents

Currents in oceans and rivers can be hazardous to swimmers.

Ocean currents

On guarded ocean beaches, flags or other signals are often used to alert swimmers to water conditions. A green flag means that the water is safe, a yellow flag means that caution should be

Figure 4-7. Always pay attention to surf conditions.

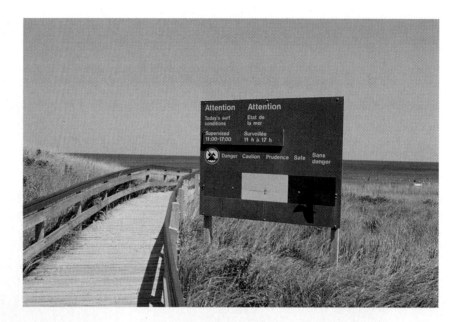

exercised when swimming because of currents or other conditions, and a red flag means that the area is closed because conditions are unsafe. Check with lifeguards on duty to become familiar with the system in use at the beach you visit. Swimming at unguarded beaches increases your risk. Should you find yourself in distress, assistance may not be close at hand.

If you swim in the ocean, watch for the three types of currents that can become dangerous. Drift or side currents move parallel to the shore (Figure 4-8, *A*). Undertows move down the slope of the beach, straight out, and under incoming waves (Figure 4-8, *B*). Undertows are common. Drift currents and undertows can be dangerous if you are not careful. An unexpectedly strong undertow can pull your feet out from under you, causing you to fall. They are especially hazardous to small children, who can easily fall into the water. Drift currents can move you rapidly away from the spot where you entered the water.

Rip currents move straight out to sea beyond the breaking waves. They often occur if a sandbar has formed offshore. A band of water a few feet wide may rush back from the beach through a gap in the sandbar made by breaking waves. You can sometimes spot a rip current because of the narrow strip of choppy, turbulent water that moves differently from the water

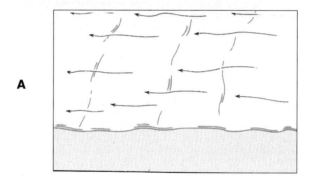

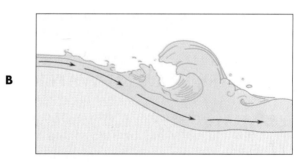

Figure 4-8. A, Drift or side current. B, Undertow.

on either side of it. A rip current can take you in over your head or move you a frightening distance from the beach.

Do not stand in breaking waves if the undertow is strong enough to knock you down. If a drift current carries you parallel to shore, try to swim toward shore while moving along with the current. If you are being carried away from shore by a rip current, swim out of the current, not against it, by moving parallel to the shore. Once you are free, turn and swim toward shore (Figure 4-9).

River currents

River currents are often unpredictable and fast moving. They may change direction abruptly because of bottom changes. You might not see the current on the water surface, even though it may be strong below the surface. A current can slam you into a rock or other unseen object. If you are being carried by a river current, roll over onto your back and go downstream feet-first to avoid crashing head-first into a rock or other obstacle (Figure 4-10). When you are out of the strongest part of the current, swim straight toward shore. Because of the current,

you will actually move downstream at an angle toward the shore (Figure 4-11). If your boat has overturned, hang on to the upstream end of the boat (see Chapter 12).

Hydraulics

Hydraulics are whirlpools that happen as water flows over an object, causing a strong downward force that may trap a swimmer or small boat (Figure 4-12). The water surface may look calm and fool you because the hydraulic does not show from the surface. To avoid this hazard, do not swim or boat near areas where the water drops off, such as below a dam. If you are caught in a hydraulic, instead of fighting it, you should swim to the bottom and swim out with the current and then reach the surface.

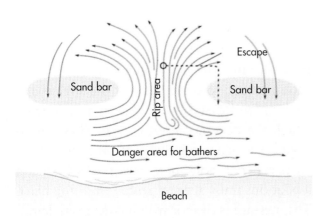

Figure 4-9. How to escape from a rip current area.

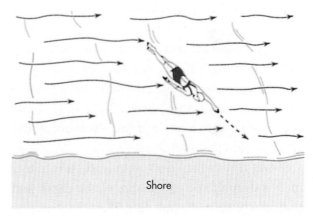

Figure 4-11. Angle toward shore to get out of a river current.

Figure 4-10. Travel downstream feet-first in a river current.

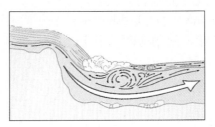

Figure 4-12. Hydraulic current.

Underwater Obstacles

There may be underwater obstacles such as rocks, stumps, and remains of old structures in any open water. Even in some ocean waters there may be large unseen obstacles. With wind, currents, and heavy rains, some obstacles on the bottom may move or change shape. You can be seriously injured if you jump, slide, or dive into water and hit any object. Always enter open water slowly, carefully, and feet-first.

Small Lakes and Quarries

Although in small lakes and quarries the hazards of waves and currents may be less, the bottom may present hazards. Wind and waves can move submerged debris close to shore. Submerged tree stumps or logs may be close to shore. In lakes and especially in quarries, boulders may be hidden underwater (Figure 4-13).

Unless you know that precautions have been taken to make an area safe for swimming, diving, or boating, do not assume that it is. Never run and dive or jump in the water in an unsupervised or unmarked area. Wade into chest-deep water before swimming. Any head-first entry could cause injury.

Never dive from a dock into water less than 2 metres deep. If you are unsure of the depth and bottom contour, do not dive. The water may be shallower than you expect. Each time you swim in open water, lower yourself into the water feet-first or wade in from shore the first time you go in. Never dive into a quarry. Carefully check the bottom and depth before entering from any height. Ease in feet-first to check the bottom and depth.

Dams

Dams are common on rivers, lakes, and ponds. When the floodgates open, the water level can rise quickly below the dam, making a wall of water. If the dam is part of a hydroelectric power plant, the current made when the gates are open can pull swimmers and even boaters above the dam into danger. Therefore always avoid both swimming and boating above or below a dam.

Lowhead dams are particularly dangerous. These are small dams without floodgates, usually only 1 to 3 metres high, over which water constantly flows quickly (Figure 4-14). They are dangerous in part simply because they do not look dangerous, particularly from a canoe or small boat upstream. The flow of water below the dam can cause powerful hydraulics that can suck a person to the bottom of the stream and back up and then down again in a cycle from which the person cannot escape. These situations are so dangerous that even professional rescuers generally will not approach a hydraulic in a boat but must attempt rescue from the bank. The message is clear: stay well away from dams.

Self-rescue techniques for all open-water settings are described in more detail in Chapter 13, Water Rescue.

Figure 4-13. Boulders or tree trunks may be hidden underwater in a lake or quarry.

Figure 4-14. Lowhead dams are dangerous because of the hydraulic currents they produce.

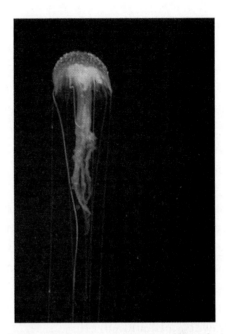

Figure 4-15. Jellyfish have stingers along their trailing tentacles.

Rafts: a Risk for Young People

A well-constructed and solidly anchored raft used as a summer diving platform in deep water can be fun. In many Canadian lakes and popular swimming areas, however, home-made rafts are often put together from old wood, fenceposts, oil drums, and similar materials. These can be floating menaces that every year are responsible for deaths of young people playing, diving, or fishing from them. If your swimming area has a floating raft, check to ensure it is in good repair.

Aquatic Life

There may be potentially dangerous plants and animals in some open-water locations. Weeds, grass, and kelp often grow thickly in open water and can entangle a swimmer. If you find yourself becoming caught, avoid frantic movements that may only entangle you more. Try to swim slowly and gently out of the plants, preferably along with the current. If you see a patch of plants on the surface or feel plants underwater, avoid the area.

Aquatic animals seldom pose a danger to swimmers. However, in the ocean you may be stung by a jellyfish (Figure 4-15) or other aquatic life with less severe stings. A sting can be very painful and may cause illness or even death if the affected area is large. The tentacles of stinging jellyfish may extend far below the body of the jellyfish you see on the surface. Even stepping on a dead jellyfish can cause a sting. The stinging cells may be active hours after the creature dies.

You can treat a sting with a simple method:

1. Rinse the skin with sea water—not fresh water. Do not use ice and do not rub the skin.

2. Soothe the skin by soaking it in vinegar or isopropyl alcohol. If these are not available, use diluted ($1/4$ strength) ammonia, a baking soda paste, or a paste of unseasoned meat tenderizer for relief.

3. Call for emergency medical help if the person—

   Does not know what caused the sting.

   Has ever had an allergic reaction to a sting from marine life.

   Is stung on the face or the neck.

   Develops any problem that seems serious, such as difficulty breathing.

Some ocean areas contain sea urchins with spines that can break off in the foot and cause a painful wound. Some types of coral also sting. Stingrays and other marine animals have stings that may be dangerous. Before going into any ocean, find out what local marine life may be dangerous, how to avoid it, and how to care for any injuries.

If you swim in fresh water, you might encounter snakes or leeches. Snakes rarely pose a threat. Leave them alone and swim away slowly. You will usually not see a leech, but you may come out of the water and find one on your skin. Do not panic if you find one. You can sprinkle salt or hot sand on the leech, and it will withdraw its head and fall off.

Inclement Weather Conditions

Always try to stay aware of inclement weather that may be coming. Television and radio stations broadcast weather reports all day. CB radios and scanners also can keep you informed. Many areas have 24-hour telephone service for weather reports. Watch the sky. Rolling, dark clouds or large clouds with cauliflower-like tops announce a storm.

Whether in a pool or open water, use common sense and do not swim in storms, fog, or high winds. Leave the water when rain starts or at the first sound of thunder or sight of lightning. Since water conducts electricity, being in the water during an electrical storm is dangerous. If you are boating, go to the nearest shore.

Do not swim after a storm if the water seems to be rising or if there is flooding because currents may become very strong. The clarity and depth of the water may change, and new unseen obstacles may become hazards. If a body of water or beach area is prone to pollution, pollution counts may be higher after a storm as a result of storm water run-off. Consult with local authorities before swimming.

SURVIVE AN EMERGENCY

 Two kinds of emergencies can develop in outdoor environments: hypothermia caused by exposure to cold water or air, and heat illness caused by exposure to sun and hot air. Both can become life-threatening conditions. Know how to care for yourself and others to prevent a cold or heat situation from becoming an emergency.

Exposure to Cold Water

Falling off a dock, breaking through ice on a lake, being thrown into the water as your boat swerves—these incidents can put you in water suddenly and thus put you at risk for hypothermia.

Hypothermia is a life-threatening condition in which the body's warming mechanisms cannot maintain normal body temperature and the body cools. Contributing factors for body cooling include air temperature, humidity, wind, and the condition of your skin (wet or dry).

Cold water is generally considered 21° C or colder. However, if exposure is lengthy, hypothermia can occur even in water as warm as 27° C. As a general rule, if the water feels cold, it is cold.

Here's what happens after you fall into cold water:

- The temperature of your skin and of the blood in your arms and legs drops quickly.

- At first you may have trouble breathing, and you may slowly become unable to use your hands.

- The temperature of your heart, brain, and other vital organs gradually drops.

- You start shivering.
- You may become unconscious. If you are in the water, you can drown.
- If your temperature drops more, you can die of heart failure.

Preventing hypothermia

Protect yourself from hypothermia in the following ways:

- Don't start an activity in, on, or around cold water unless you know you can get help quickly in an emergency.

- Wear a Department of Transportation (DOT)-approved personal flotation device (PFD) while boating. Have PFDs at hand whenever you are near cold water. A PFD will help you float in a rescue position if you fall in cold water, and some styles provide insulation against cold water.

- If you're near water in cooler weather, wear rain gear and/or wool clothes. Wool insulates you even when it is wet. Wear layers of clothing, and wear a hat. As much as 60% of body heat loss occurs through the head.

- Carry matches in a waterproof container. You may need to build a fire to warm up after a fall into cold water.

- Carry a chocolate bar or high-energy food containing sugar. Glucose stimulates shivering, the body's internal mechanism for rewarming itself.

- If you must snowmobile over ice-covered lakes and rivers, wear a buoyant snowmobile survival suit.

Benefits of winter clothes People who fall into the water wearing winter clothes, especially heavy boots or waders, usually panic because they think they'll sink immediately. But winter clothes can actually help you float. Heavy clothes also help delay hypothermia. Tight-fitting foam vests and PFDs with foam insulation can double your survival time.

If you fall into the water wearing a snowmobile suit or other heavy winter clothes, air will be trapped in the clothes and help you float. If you are very close to shore, lie back, spread your arms and legs, and perform a "winging" motion with your arms to move toward safety (Figure 4-16).

Hip boots, waders, and rubber boots often trap air if you fall into water. Relax and bend your knees and let the trapped air in your boots bring you to the surface quickly (Figure 4-17). While on your back, you can float in a tuck position. Bring your knees up to your chest, let your hips drop, and keep your head up and back. Then paddle backward with your hands to safety.

You can also float on your front. Keep your head raised and bend your knees. Paddle forward with your arms in the water (Figure 4-18).

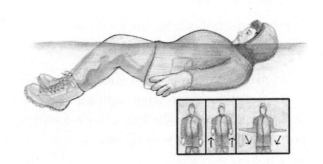

Figure 4-16. If you fall into water wearing heavy winter clothes, float on your back and "wing" with your arms to move to safety.

Figure 4-17. Trapped air in your boots can help bring you back to the surface.

Figure 4-18. You can float on your front and paddle forward with your arms.

Falling into cold water with a PFD

If the air is warm and even if you are a good swimmer, wear a PFD when you are near cold water. If you fall into cold water wearing a PFD, keep your face and head above the surface. Keep all your clothes on, even your hat. Wet clothes help you retain body heat.

In cold water you must decide whether to try to reach safety or float and wait for help. Remember that you can't swim as far in cold water as in warm water. Trying to swim beyond 100 metres is dangerous. Consider these factors:

- The likelihood of rescue
- The flotation and insulation you're wearing
- Your age
- Your body size
- Any medical conditions you have
- Water and wind conditions

Swim in a way that keeps your arms underwater. If you can get to safety with a few strokes, do so. If not, float in the heat escape–lessening position (HELP) and wait for rescue.

Waiting to be rescued

There are two floating rescue positions you can use in cold water in a PFD. Because both of these positions are hard to maintain, you may want to practice them in warm shallow water. Practice only when supervised by someone with the water safety skills so that they can assist you. **Heat escape–lessening position** In the HELP position, draw your knees up to your chest, keep your face forward and out of the water, hold your upper arms at your sides, and fold your lower arms across your chest (Figure 4-19). **Huddle position** This position is for two or more persons. Put your arms over one another's shoulders so the sides of your chests are together. Sandwich a child between adults (Figure 4-20).

Special situations

If your boat capsizes, do not assume the HELP position; instead, try to climb up onto the boat to get more of your body out of the water. If you cannot get onto the capsized boat, position yourself on the lee (downwind) side of the craft. This procedure is described in Chapter 12, Boating Safety.

If you fall into cold water and a swift current is carrying you toward some danger, swim to safety. If you are not in immediate danger but are far from shore, float on your back and go downstream feet-first. Let your PFD support you as you flow with the current. Swim to shore when appropriate.

Figure 4-19. HELP position.

Falling into cold water without a PFD

If you fall into cold water without a PFD, you must get out of the water as quickly as possible before hypothermia sets in. Chapter 13, Water Rescue, describes self-rescue techniques to use.

Helping yourself once you're ashore

You or someone with you may still be at risk for hypothermia after getting out of cold water. Follow these guidelines:

- Your clothes will be heavy with water. Stand still to let some of the water drain away before you try to move.

- Change into dry clothes or a blanket immediately if you can. If not, take off the wet clothes and wring them out. Put them back on, unless the air is unusually warm. Even damp clothes will help keep you warm, especially if they're wool.

- Get inside a building. If there is no building nearby, start a fire to keep warm.

- When you've warmed up, wait 30 minutes to be sure your body is completely warmed before starting to walk to safety. Leave the fire only if you know where you are and where you can get help. If you don't know which way to go, stay by the fire and wait for rescue. The smoke from the fire will help rescuers find you.

Figure 4-20. Huddle position.

- If you cannot build a fire and you don't know which way to go, stay out of the wind and cold as much as possible while you wait for help.

- Even if you are in a building, if you feel at all weak or dizzy, call for emergency assistance immediately. If you have not removed all wet clothing, do so and put on warm dry clothing. A warm fire, hot water bottles, and a warm non-alcoholic beverage will help you feel more comfortable and warm up.

- As soon as you can, drink warm fluids.

Caring for someone with hypothermia

Anyone in cold water or in wet clothes for a long time may develop hypothermia. Children under 12 and the elderly are particularly vulnerable. You need to recognize the signals of hypothermia in order to act quickly and get emergency help. Bluish lips and shivering may be the first things you see. Other signals include a feeling of weakness, confusion, a slow or irregular pulse, numbness, slurred speech, and semi-consciousness or unconsciousness. Exposure to cold water is a severe physical shock.

Follow these guidelines to help another person who has hypothermia from being in cold water:

1. Treat the person very gently and monitor breathing carefully.

2. Remove wet clothes, dry the person, and move him or her to a warm environment.

3. Wrap the person in blankets or put on dry clothes. Do not warm the person too quickly by immersing him or her in warm water. Rapid warming may affect heart rhythms. Remember that hypothermia can be life-threatening.

4. If available, put hot water bottles, heating pads (if the person is dry), or other heat sources on the body, keeping a blanket or towel between the heat source and skin to avoid burns.

5. If the person is alert, give warm liquids to drink.

Heat Illness
Heat exhaustion

Heat exhaustion is a form of shock that often results from strenuous work or exercise in a hot environment. Heat exhaustion is the most common heat illness and may be an early stage of more serious illness. Those who are active for too long or stay too long in the sun may experience it (Figure 4-21). Being near the water magnifies the effects of exposure to the sun. You can help prevent problems by wearing sunblock, light clothing, a hat, and sunglasses; staying in a shaded area; not drinking alcoholic beverages; and drinking plenty of water. A person may be experiencing heat exhaustion if the skin is cool, moist, pale, or red and if the person has a headache, nausea, faintness, dizziness, or

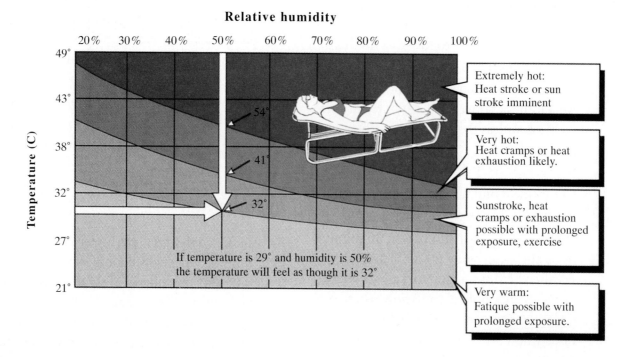

Figure 4-21. High humidity can intensify the effects of temperature.

exhaustion. Follow these guidelines to care for heat exhaustion:

1. The person should be moved to a cool environment and allowed to rest.

2. Give $^1/_2$ glass of cold water every 15 minutes.

3. Loosen tight clothes and remove any clothes soaked with sweat.

4. Put cool, wet cloths next to the skin.

If the person's condition does not improve within 30 minutes or if the person vomits, refuses water, or becomes less alert or unconscious, call for medical help immediately. These may be signals that the person's condition is progressing to heat stroke.

Heat stroke

Heat stroke is a life-threatening condition that develops when the body's cooling mechanisms are overwhelmed and body systems start to fail. It usually occurs when people ignore the signals of heat exhaustion. Sweating stops as the body's cooling mechanisms shut down; and the person has hot, red, dry skin and a very high body temperature (often as high as 41° C). Breathing may be rapid and shallow. The person may vomit and may lose consciousness. Heat stroke is a life-threatening emergency. Give the following care:

1. Call for emergency help immediately.

2. Remove the person from the sun or hot environment.

3. Cool the person. Apply cool, wet cloths, such as towels or sheets, to the person's body if you have not already done so. If you have ice packs or cold packs, apply them to the wrists, ankles, neck, and armpits to cool the large blood vessels.

SUMMARY

In other chapters in this book you will learn more about different kinds of activities you can enjoy in, on, or around the water. When you enjoy such activities, always remember to think also about the environment itself. The same activity (for example, swimming) in different waters (a backyard pool or a river) can become a very different experience. Whatever the environment, consider its possible hazards and adjust your activity accordingly. This way, the experience will be as safe for you and those with you as it is fun.

Ice Safety

Understand ice and the environment. Prepare yourself by wearing appropriate clothing, using the right equipment, and being physically prepared for the ice activity. Know the emergency procedures and first aid.

Monitor ice conditions as well as your own physical abilities and your level of fatigue. Constantly supervise children around the ice.

Know how to rescue yourself and others if you break through the ice. Know the appropriate first aid for hypothermia and frostbite.

- **Understand the qualities and hazards of ice.**

- **Know how to ensure your own safety and the safety of others on ice.**

- **Should you or someone else fall through the ice, know how to use the appropriate survival and rescue techniques.**

Many non-residents perceive Canada to be the land of the frozen north, home of the north pole and of long, cold winters. In reality, Canada has wide seasonal variations and different climatic regions, but winter snow and ice still play a significant role in the lives of most Canadians.

A deep freeze in Ottawa or a dip below the zero mark in Vancouver provides Canadians with snow and ice and a variety of exciting recreational activities. As a group, Canadians look forward to winters for skating, curling, ice fishing, skiing, snowmobiling, snowshoeing, and, of course, our favorite sport—hockey!

Ice does more than provide recreational opportunities. Particularly in northern Canada, ice affects the daily activities of many Canadians.

Just as you must take certain precautions when you are outside in cold weather, if you are on a frozen body of water, you must have special knowledge and skills to stay safe and prevent injury. This chapter is about safety on or near the ice. You will learn how to prepare for an ice experience, how to stay safe when on the ice, and how to rescue yourself or another in an ice emergency.

In Canada every year there are many deaths related to ice activities. Typically about two thirds of these occur while snowmobiling, and others die while walking, fishing, or playing on ice. If all Canadians fully prepared for ice activities, knew how to stay safe on the ice, and had effective rescue skills, most of these deaths could be prevented.

PREPARE FOR ICE ACTIVITIES

 Being prepared for your ice experience—whether for a recreational activity, sport, or work—not only will help you stay safe, but it will help you enjoy the experience more fully. Take a few minutes to think ahead and plan. Consider both personal preparedness and the equipment and clothing you need to prevent problems.

Personal Preparedness

Personal preparedness means that you know what to do to stay safe on the ice and that you take the appropriate steps before you begin. Follow these guidelines:

- Before starting any activity outside, be physically prepared for it. For example, if you've never been on skates before, don't try to plunge right into the middle of a hockey game on a frozen lake! If you're getting on a snowmobile for the first time, learn from an experienced rider. Being physically fit for the activity and learning the skills needed will make the activity safer and more enjoyable.

- In winter just as in summer, outdoor activities expose parts of your skin to ultraviolet (UV) rays. Use sunscreen with a high sun protection factor (SPF) on all exposed skin before you start. The winter sun can be just as harmful as the summer sun.

- Learn basic first aid skills in a Red Cross first aid course, including care to give for frostbite and hypothermia (see later section in this chapter).
- Before starting, be sure everyone in the group knows what to do if someone breaks through the ice. Time spent discussing rescue procedures could save a life.
- Pay attention to weather forecasts before going into isolated areas. Don't let a sudden blizzard catch you unprepared and unable to get back to safety.
- If you are traveling over the ice, plan your route in advance and leave a route map with a responsible individual.

Equipment for Ice Activities

All activities on ice require specialized equipment. Whether it be warm clothing, skates, or fishing gear, proper equipment is important for your fun and safety.

Clothing

Snow and ice activities expose you to the winter elements. The right clothing limits your exposure to wind and low temperatures (Figure 5-1). Follow these guidelines for choosing the appropriate clothing:

- Clothing should be layered. You can easily remove top layers if your body temperature goes up as the day gets warmer or if your activity warms you too much. You can also add or replace layers if your body temperature starts to cool.
- The layer of clothing next to the skin should absorb moisture and perspiration to keep you dry and comfortable. Many of today's brands of long underwear have this quality.
- On top of the first layer, wear warm insulating layers. Wool, for example, holds warm air next to your body even if it gets wet. Choose clothing made of tightly woven fibres that trap warm air.

- Wear a windproof outer garment. It should also be water resistant or repellent in case you get wet.
- Your head loses heat much faster than the rest of the body. Always wear a hat in cold weather. Protect your ears and nose as well. Carry a neck warmer and face protector to use if the temperature drops or the wind picks up.
- Sunglasses are a must in the winter to avoid snow blindness and to cut glare.
- Make sure your hands and feet have proper covering. The layering concept works here also!

When planning for the particular activity, consider the following questions to help determine what kind and how much clothing to wear.

1. Will I be moving or stationary?
2. Will I be near shelter or exposed to the elements during the activity?
3. Does this activity require specific protective gear, such as hockey pads?
4. Will I be on the ice for a long time and thus encounter changes in wind and temperature changes?

Figure 5-1. Choose appropriate clothing to protect yourself from low temperatures, wind, sun, and snow glare.

Recreational and transportation equipment

In many ice activities you can go much farther than you can when walking. This is true when snowmobiling, skiing, and snowshoeing (Figure 5-2). But this also means that you become more dependent on your equipment because you may face a long walk back if it breaks down. A few minutes on a snowmobile could mean hours of walking if your engine stops! Therefore being prepared includes paying attention to your equipment as well:

- Know your equipment and check it before each use. Keep it in good working order. Know what problems are most likely to occur and the best quick-fixes.

- Your equipment is only as good as your ability to use it. Learn how to use it properly and use it responsibly. If you are new at an activity, take lessons or learn from someone who is experienced.

- Even with the best equipment, don't go out alone. No equipment is guaranteed *forever*, and being stranded miles from safety with possible bad weather coming can become a life-threatening situation.

Figure 5-2. A snowmobile can carry you farther afield than you can walk back. Be sure it won't break down—check your equipment carefully!

Safety equipment

Take safety equipment with you when you are on the ice. It need not be cumbersome, and it could save a life!

- For activities in a defined area, such as skating, curling, or hockey, have a long pole or weighted line for a rescue in case someone breaks through the ice. Keep this equipment nearby.

- When traveling by foot over ice, it is not practical to carry heavy rescue equipment. However, a strong lightweight rope is an excellent rescue aid easily taken along.

- Carry matches in a waterproof container. You may need to build a fire if someone falls through the ice.

- When traveling by vehicle for long distances or in isolated areas, carry extra safety or survival equipment, including the following:

    First aid kit

    Blanket

    Dry clothing

    High energy food

STAY SAFE ON THE ICE

 Your knowledge of the winter environment, including ice, will help ensure your activities stay enjoyable and safe.

Understand the Environment

Ice forms on fresh water when the surface water temperature falls to 0° celsius. Salt water and water containing dissolved impurities freeze at a lower temperature. Freezing also depends on various factors, including the following:

- Air temperature
- Solar radiation
- Wind speed

- Snow cover

- Waves, currents, and tides

- The size and depth of the body of water

- Underwater vegetation

For example, a small lake freezes earlier in the winter than larger lakes. A fast-moving river freezes later in the season or perhaps not at all.

Characteristics of Ice

The better you understand ice, the safer you will be on it. Your understanding should be based on the colour of ice and on other aspects that determine its strength.

Colour

The colour of ice is an indication of its quality and strength.

- **Clear blue**—strongest

- **White opaque or snow ice**—formed when water-saturated snow freezes on top of ice, making an opaque white ice that is usually only half as strong as clear ice

- **Grey ice**—the greyness indicates that water is present, usually from thawing

Strength and thickness

Clear blue ice is the strongest type of ice. Its strength increases as the temperature drops further below 0° celsius. However, if the temperature drops very quickly, such as overnight, internal stress within the ice itself can weaken it. Likewise, removing snow from an ice surface may result in a temperature drop within the ice that weakens the ice. Thus, if you clear snow from lake or pond ice for hockey or skating, consider this ice to be only half as strong as it appears.

Large vehicles such as pick-up trucks or cars compress the ice when they drive over it. The ice returns to its original qualities after the load is removed. The movement of the vehicle across the ice also creates a wave in the water under the ice that weakens it. After vehicles have been on the ice, recheck its thickness.

Before an activity on the ice, measure the ice to determine whether it is thick enough to support the people and equipment for the activity, and check that the ice is uniformly thick.

Some recreation departments and community groups measure ice thickness in areas for public use during the winter months. Find out if this service is available in your community or in areas to which you are traveling.

If you must determine ice thickness yourself, drill test holes 15 metres apart in a river or 30 metres apart in a lake (Figure 5-3). When going onto the ice to drill these holes proceed with caution in case of ice breakthrough.

For recreational use, make sure the ice is thick enough for the particular activity. Use the following guidelines for blue ice thickness. Be sure the thickness is uniform throughout the area.

- **Individual or partner activities**—15 cm thick.

- **Group activities**—20 cm thick.

- **Operation of snow machines**—25 cm thick.

- **Operation of heavy vehicles**—40 cm thick.

Figure 5-3. Drill holes in the ice to test its thickness.

General Safety Principles

In addition to understanding the environment of cold and ice, staying safe during your ice activities includes following certain safety guidelines while engaged in the activity:

- As with any physical activity, always drink plenty of water or other fluids to avoid dehydration. Warm fluids help maintain body temperature. But avoid alcohol, which hinders the body's ability to produce heat and may hasten the onset of hypothermia.

- Know and respect the changing qualities of ice and changing weather. A sunny day may be perfect for pleasure skating, but the ice could be melting right under your feet!

- Keep children safe. Constantly supervise children on ice. They may wander onto unsafe surfaces (Figure 5-4).

- To really enjoy winter activities, you need to be in control. Never mix alcohol with activities on the ice. Alcohol reduces your reaction time, dulls your judgment, and makes you more susceptible to the cold.

- Use the buddy system when snowshoeing, skiing, or walking across the ice. It's safer and more fun!

- If you start to shiver, get out of the cold as soon as possible and let your body warm up before returning to your activity.

- Watch for the signs of hypothermia: shivering, numbness, lack of coordination, or confused behaviour. If these occur to you or someone with you, get out of the cold immediately (see Chapter 4, Aquatic Environments).

SURVIVING AN ICE EMERGENCY

 If you follow the guidelines for preparing for and staying safe during ice activities, the chances of breaking through the ice or having an emergency due to cold are greatly reduced. Yet even the most careful person can end up in an ice emergency where a rescue or first aid is needed. Knowing the right techniques to use can help you survive such emergencies.

Self-Rescue

When you are on ice, it is safest to stay with a partner. But if you are alone and break through the ice, follow these self-rescue steps:

1. Resist the urge to try to climb out onto the ice. It is likely to be weak in the area where you fell in.

2. Quickly get into a floating position on your stomach. Your winter clothing can actually help you float and can increase your survival time. When you enter the water, air will be trapped in your clothes and provide flotation.

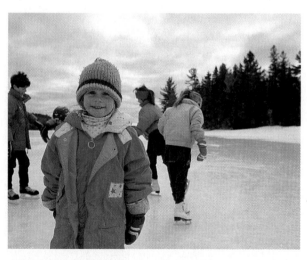

Figure 5-4. Constantly supervise children playing on or near the ice.

3. Reach forward onto the broken ice, but do not push down on it (Figure 5-5, *A*). Use a breaststroke or other kick to push your torso onto the ice.

4. Once most of your body is on the ice, don't stand up. Crawl or roll away from the break area, with your arms and legs spread out as far as possible to distribute your weight on the ice surface (Figure 5-5, *B*).

A   **B**

Figure 5-5. A, If you fall through the ice, reach forward onto the ice and kick yourself up onto the ice. **B,** Once on the ice crawl or roll away from the break area.

A Snowmobile Fatality (the Typical Case)

The guys had been drinking heavily all evening when they decided to go snowmobiling on the lake. Joe was drunk and not paying attention to the ice. He hit an area of thin ice and, snowmobile and all, crashed through into the freezing water. His buddies didn't even notice he's gone for several minutes, and when they did notice, they didn't know what to do to try to rescue him.

If Joe had been sober, he might have been able to use his heavy winter clothes as a flotation aid to help stay afloat. In his impaired condition, however, the wet heavy clothes hindered his attempts to climb back out on the ice. Once in the cold water, hypothermia set in quickly and soon made it difficult for him to move. He drowned within minutes.

This is a typical snowmobiling fatality. Most casualties are male teenagers or young adults, and most have been drinking. Most incidents occur on weekend evenings.

5. Rewarm yourself by changing into dry warm clothes, getting to a warm place, and drinking warm fluids. (Chapter 4 describes hypothermia and its treatment in more detail.) If necessary, call emergency medical assistance.

Ice Rescues

If someone has fallen through the ice, it is crucial to act quickly and correctly. The longer the person is in the water, the slimmer are the chances of survival.

Rescuing a person on or in ice may be very dangerous. Follow these guidelines to stay safe yourself while effectively helping the person:

1. If at all possible, do not go onto the ice yourself. The ice may give way, and there will be two people in the water instead of one. It is always safest to perform the rescue from a secure place on shore.

2. If the person has fallen through in the middle of a large body of water, consider whether you quickly can get help for the rescue. Trained professionals such as police, fire, or ambulance are better prepared to deal with rescue from the ice surface.

3. If you must go out onto the ice, carry a long pole or branch to test the ice in front of you by hitting the ice or putting pressure on it with the extended end of the pole. Wear a personal flotation device (PFD) if available. Take along something to reach or throw to the person, such as a pole, weighted rope, or line with a aid on the end (Figure 5-6). If these are unavailable, even a tree branch can work.

4. When approaching the break in the ice through which the person fell, lie down and slowly crawl toward the hole. This distributes your weight over a greater surface area and should prevent you from falling through. Stay as far away from the breakthrough as possible while attempting the rescue (Figure 5-7).

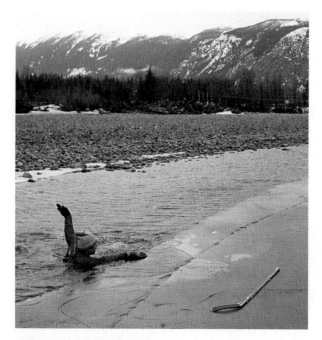

Figure 5-6. A hockey stick could be used as a reaching aid.

Figure 5-7. Stay low and as far away from the breakthrough as possible while extending the aid.

5. From a secure position on land or lying on the ice, extend or throw the emergency rescue device to the person. While extending the aid, stay low to avoid slipping on the ice or toward the hole.

6. Tell the person to keep kicking while you pull him or her out. This will help propel the person out of the hole while you're pulling.

7. Move the person to a secure position, on shore or where you are sure the ice is thick. Re-warm the person in dry warm clothes in a warm place, and give him or her warm fluids (see hypothermia). If necessary, call emergency medical assistance.

Cold Injuries

Low temperatures can lead to cold injuries, particularly when there are high winds or when the body becomes wet. Try to prevent cold injuries by dressing appropriately and not staying in the cold too long. Hypothermia and frostbite can occur together or separately in such cases. If someone in your group does suffer hypothermia or frostbite, you should know what to do.

Hypothermia

Hypothermia is a cooling of the body to the point at which the body's natural rewarming mechanisms cannot be maintained. This condition may occur if a person is dressed inappropriately for the cold, stays in the cold too long, or becomes wet from perspiration or falling into water. The care for hypothermia is described in Chapter 4.

Frostbite

Frostbite is a type of cold injury occurring in specific body parts exposed to the cold. In frostbite, body tissues freeze. In superficial frostbite the skin is frozen but not the tissues below. In deep frostbite both the skin and underlying tissues are frozen. Both types of frostbite are serious (Figure 5-8).

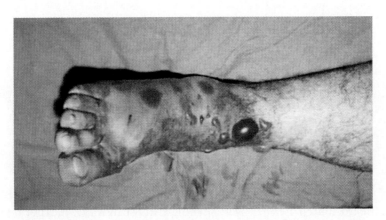

Figure 5-8. Blisters and swelling caused by frostbite under a tight boot.

Frostbite can usually be prevented with common sense. Follow these guidelines:

- Avoid exposing any part of the body to the cold.
- Wear a hat and layers of clothing.
- Drink plenty of warm fluids or water.
- Avoid alcohol.
- Take frequent breaks from the cold.

Depending on the circumstances and how long the person is exposed to the cold, frostbite may occur by itself or along with hypothermia. Signs and symptoms of frostbite are—

- Lack of feeling in the affected area.
- Skin that appears waxy.
- Skin that is cold to the touch.
- Skin that is discoloured (flushed, white, yellow blue).

The specific care for frostbite includes the following:

1. Cover the affected area to keep it warm until you can immerse it in water.
2. Handle the area gently and never rub it because rubbing causes further damage.
3. Warm the area gently by immersing the affected part in water warmed to 40.5° C. If possible, use a thermometer to check the water (Figure 5-9).
4. Keep the frostbitten part in the water until it looks red and feels warm.
5. Bandage the area with a dry, sterile dressing. If fingers or toes are frostbitten, place cotton or gauze between them. Avoid breaking any blisters.
6. Get the person to medical care.

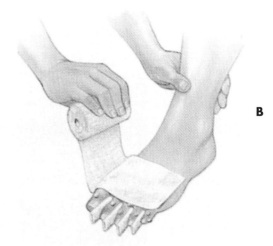

Figure 5-9. A, Warm the frostbitten area gently by soaking it in warm water. **B,** After rewarming, bandage the area with a dry, sterile dressing. If fingers or toes are frostbitten, place gauze between them.

SUMMARY

Any ice activity for recreation, work, or daily living can be just as safe as outdoor activities in the summer. There is no reason for deaths and injuries to occur. By taking a little time to make sure you and those with you are prepared, have proper equipment, follow safety precautions, and know what to do in an emergency, you help ensure that everyone has the best possible time.

The Science of Swimming

Everyone's body reacts differently to water and moves differently in it. We all need to experience and understand how our body moves in the water so that we are aware of our limitations and can prepare well for participating in any water activity.

This chapter discusses many scientific principles involved in hydro-dynamics and kinetics, the principles of how we float and move in water. The more we understand them, the better we can control our movement in the water. Experiment with these principles in the water by trying the activities this chapter suggests. This experience will help you be better prepared for water activities.

Physics Is Phun! Students used to write this on the chalkboard before class to irritate the teacher. Both students and teacher faced the same problem—how to keep the students awake for the whole period. Many people find science boring. The concepts seem too hard, too confusing, or simply irrelevant to what matters to them.

You might even be asking yourself, "Why do I have to know anything about physics to be a good swimmer?" You don't. You can simply use trial and error and practice, practice, practice. But good swimmers do not rely on practice alone. They mix their practice with an understanding of physics.

For a long time people have tried to understand how the human body moves through the water so that they can swim faster or easily. Researchers have spent years trying to discover how to help people swim even a little faster. The science of swimming builds on the science of hydrodynamics. In this chapter you will learn how the science of swimming can help you swim better.

Hydrodynamics is the science that studies the motion of fluids and forces on solid bodies in fluids.

The more you understand why things happen in the water, the better you will swim, float, or move in the water. This chapter describes 10 scientific principles that apply to how you move in the water, as well as exercises to help you understand and get a "feel" for the principles.

WHY SOME THINGS FLOAT
Archimedes' Principle

Imagine that you have three glass bottles the same size. Each one weighs 1 kilogram (kg) and can hold 10 kg of water. Leave the first bottle empty, seal it, and put it in water. It floats high in the water, with most of the bottle above the surface. Now put 8 kg of pebbles in the second

bottle, seal it, and put it in water. This bottle also floats, but it is low in the water; most of it is submerged. Finally, put 11 kg of pebbles into the third bottle, seal it, and put it in water. It sinks even with air inside. However, if you lifted the third bottle while it was still under water, it would feel like it weighed only 2 kg (Figure 6-1).

What causes these three bottles to react as they do? The first floats because it weighs only 1 kg but would have to push aside 10 kg of water (the amount of water it could hold) for it to sink. This is called buoyancy, which means that the water exerts an upward force against an object equal to the weight of the water that would be pushed aside by the object. The amount of water pushed aside by the first bottle, called displacement, is more than the weight of the bottle; thus the bottle floats.

Buoyancy is the upward force a fluid exerts on bodies in it.

The second bottle also floats, and for the same reason. The 9 kg pushing down is still less than the force needed to push aside 10 kg of water. Since only 9 kg of the buoyancy is used to lift the 9 kg of glass and stone, part of this bottle ($^1/_{10}$ of it) floats above the water.

Even though the third bottle sinks, it still has buoyancy. The 10 kg of water displaced by the

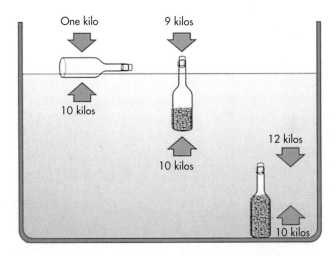

Figure 6-1. Archimedes' principle of buoyancy determines what objects float or sink.

sunken bottle is still pushing upward, so the bottle seems to weigh only 2 kg in the water, even though it weighs 12 kg out of the water.

The effect shown with all three bottles is called Archimedes' principle.

Archimedes' principle states that a body in water is buoyed up by a force equal to the weight of the water displaced.

How does this affect swimming and other water activities? This principle explains why most people float. Like the bottles, your body displaces water. You can see this when you lower yourself in a bathtub and the water level goes up. (In fact, this is just what Archimedes was doing when he discovered his famous principle!) When the weight of the water you push up is more than your weight, you float. The force of buoyancy in this case is greater than the force of gravity.

Because of buoyancy, you seem to weigh very little, if anything, in the water. You can put most of your energy into moving because you use very little energy to support yourself. This is especially valuable for persons with limited physical abilities (Figure 6-2). For example, those who find it hard to move on land or who depend on a wheelchair can get around in the water much more easily because the buoyancy of water does most of the work of carrying the person.

Figure 6-2. Often persons can move more easily in water because of buoyancy.

Specific Gravity

The two bottles with different weights floated at different levels in the water, even though buoyancy pushed both up. This is known as specific gravity. The ratio of the weight of a body to the weight of the water it displaces is its specific gravity. Water has a specific gravity of 1.0 and is the standard. A body with a specific gravity less than 1.0 floats; one with a specific gravity greater than 1.0 sinks. The first bottle, which weighs 1 kg but displaces 10 kg of water, has a specific gravity of 0.1 because it weighs 1/10 as much as the water it pushes aside. It floats high on the surface. The second bottle, which weighs 9 kg with its pebbles but displaces 10 kg, has a specific gravity of 0.9. It floats with only a small part above the surface. The third bottle, which weighs 12 kg but displaces 10 kg of water, has a specific gravity of 1.2, so it sinks.

Specific gravity is the ratio of the weight of a body to the weight of the water it displaces.

What does all this mean for being in the water and swimming? For one thing, it explains why some people float easily while others do not. A person's specific gravity depends mostly on how much muscle mass, fat, and bone density he or she has. People with lots of muscle and a heavy bone structure or those with little body fat do not float as easily as those with more body fat and less muscle. Because the average female has 21% to 24% body fat and the average male has 15% to 20% body fat, females generally float more easily than males.

Body composition also changes with age. For example, very young children tend to have more fat weight and less muscle. Their specific gravity is usually less than 1.0, and they float easily. Young adults tend to have more muscle and less fat, and in general they do not float very well. Older people often have more fat and less muscle and float more easily. The old saying that everyone can float is not entirely correct because a person cannot easily change his or her body composition.

You can use the jellyfish float to easily see how buoyant you are. When you try this skill, have a buddy swim with you. In chest-deep water, submerge to the neck, take a deep breath of air, bend forward at the waist, put your head in the water, and flex your knees slightly to raise your feet off the bottom (Figure 6-3). Hold your breath and relax as much as you can. If you sink, your specific gravity is greater than 1.0. If part of your head or back stays above the surface, you can learn to float. Your buddy can tell you how much of your head and back are out of the water during your float.

You can also use the jellyfish float to see how you can change your own specific gravity. Do the float the same way, but this time while floating exhale some air and see whether you start to sink or float lower in the water. With a friend, you can watch how high you each float when your lungs are full of air and how low you float (or whether you sink) with less air in your lungs.

This principle can also help you learn to float better. Remember that your specific gravity depends on your weight and the weight of the water your body displaces. You can't change your weight at will, but you can inhale deeply and lower your specific gravity. This helps you float. Wearing a personal flotation device (PFD) also increases your buoyancy because it displaces a lot of water without increasing your weight very much.

If you have great buoyancy, you can breathe normally when you float. If you have marginal buoyancy, you can stay afloat if you control your breathing. To keep your face above water when you float on your back, exhale rapidly and then inhale rapidly to keep your lungs full and your chest expanded as much as possible.

The water's specific gravity also affects how you float. Salt water has a slightly higher specific gravity than fresh water, so it has more buoyant force. If you float easily in fresh water, you will float even higher in salt water. If you have trouble floating in fresh water, you will float much better in salt water.

Centre of Mass and Centre of Buoyancy

Two other factors affect the position of a floating body in the water: the centre of mass (sometimes called the centre of gravity) and the centre of buoyancy.

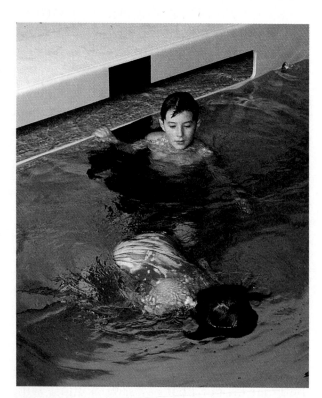

Figure 6-3. Use the jellyfish float with a buddy to check your natural buoyancy.

A body's centre of mass is the point around which its mass is evenly distributed. Imagine it as a single spot where all of the body's weight is concentrated. For a baseball, a body of even shape and density, the centre of mass is its centre. For the human body, the centre of mass is affected by the weight and positions of different parts of the body. One way to imagine the centre of mass of the human body is to see the body like a seesaw in every direction (from bottom to top, side to side, and front to back), with both sides of the balance point weighing the same. For most people, the centre of mass is somewhere in the pelvic region.

Centre of mass is the point around which the weight of the body is evenly distributed.

The centre of buoyancy is the point around which the body's buoyancy is evenly distributed. Its location is also affected by the buoyancy and position of all body parts. The centre of buoyancy is also affected by the lungs because they can expand and change a person's specific gravity. For most people, the centre of buoyancy is in the chest.

Centre of buoyancy is the point around which the buoyant properties of the body are evenly distributed.

When you are not in water, you keep your balance while moving by keeping your centre of mass balanced and supported. You usually do this without thinking, except when you move in an unfamiliar way or assume an awkward or unusual position. In the water, however, your position and motion also depend on your centre of buoyancy. When you float, your centre of mass is below your centre of buoyancy. Think of this like a hot-air balloon. The basket (where the centre of mass is) always hangs below the centre of the balloon (where the centre of buoyancy is) (Figure 6-4).

When a person of average build tries to float on his or her back with arms along the sides of the body, the centre of mass is nearly level with

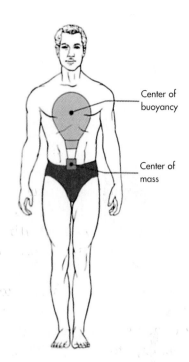

Figure 6-4. Centres of mass and buoyancy for the average person.

the centre of buoyancy. Most people have more body weight in their legs and hips because of the muscle tissue there, so their centre of mass is near the hips. Thus, when trying to float in a horizontal position, gravity pulls the hips and legs downward while buoyancy pushes the chest (centre of buoyancy) upward. The body rotates until the centre of mass is directly below the centre of buoyancy. At that point, the person should float motionless, except when the momentum of the legs moving downward causes the body to submerge.

A person's floating position (vertical or diagonal) in the water depends on how his or her centre of mass is positioned relative to the centre of buoyancy. A person with a specific gravity of 0.9 is likely to have more weight in the hips and legs and will float more vertically (Figure 6-5, *A*). It would be as difficult for this person to float horizontally as it would be to lift the basket of a hot-air balloon up alongside the balloon.

Someone with a specific gravity of 0.8 might float diagonally (Figure 6-5, *B*). This person's buoyancy is more nearly balanced between the upper and lower body.

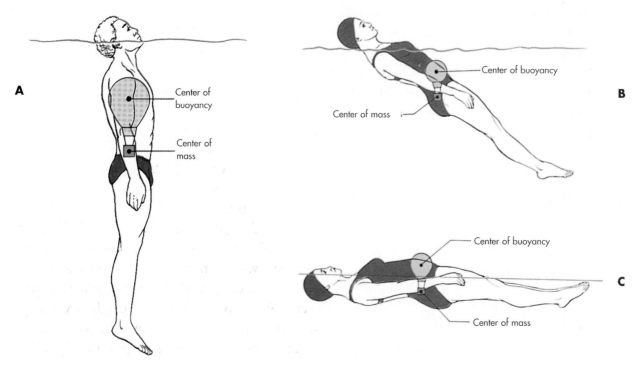

Figure 6-5, A to C. Three individuals with different specific gravity float in different positions.

A person with a specific gravity of 0.7 tends to float nearly horizontally because in that position the centre of mass is below the centre of buoyancy (Figure 6-5, *C*). A person with a specific gravity of 1.0 is suspended between the surface and the bottom, and neither floats nor sinks.

Although you cannot change your specific gravity much, you can move your centre of mass and the centre of buoyancy. You can shift the centre of mass by moving your arms and legs. You can change your centre of buoyancy by inhaling or exhaling. This means that if you float diagonally when your arms are at your side and your legs are straight out, you might be able to float horizontally with a few changes. To do this, you want to move your centre of mass toward your head and your centre of buoyancy toward your feet. Try these three things:

1. Slowly move your arms through the water above your head. This gives you more mass above your body, and your centre of mass thus moves up.

2. Bend your knees. This moves the mass of your lower legs closer to your head.

Figure 6-6. Changing the position of your arms, knees, and hands shifts your centre of mass and your floating position.

3. Flex your wrists to bring your hands out of the water (Figure 6-6). This makes your hands "heavier" because they are no longer held up by the buoyancy of the water.

To move your centre of buoyancy, inhale more air. As you fill your lungs, air moves downward in your body, moving your centre of buoyancy down also (Figure 6-7).

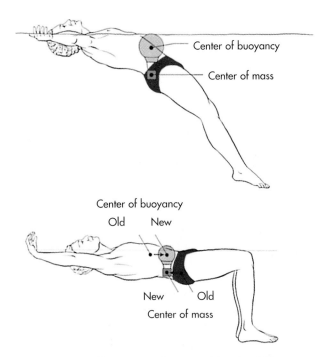

Figure 6-7. Filling your lungs with air shifts your centre of buoyancy and your floating position.

To test this and see how well you can float, start in a floating position on your back with your arms over your head, hands out of the water, and knees bent. Then bring your hands back into the water and move your arms to your sides. (Your legs will sink a little.) Next, straighten your legs. (Your lower body will sink more. You might have to control your breathing, as described earlier, to stay afloat.) If you are still diagonal, exhale some air until you are floating in a vertical position with only your face out of the water. Then slowly reverse these positions to go back to your original floating position.

MOVEMENT IN THE WATER
The Problem: Resistance

A person or object moving through water meets resistance from the water, called drag. There are three types of water resistance: form drag, wave drag, and frictional drag. All types of resistance work to slow you down when you swim, but you can do things to lessen their effects.

Form Drag

Form drag relates to the object's shape and profile in the water. A narrow shape has less form drag than a broad shape. Think of a sleek, narrow boat slicing through the water, compared to a wide tugboat pushing through. The narrow shape has to push less water aside. To feel this yourself, stand in waist-deep water and thrust your hands, fingers first, down to touch your knees (Figure 6-8, *A*). You can do this quickly and easily. Now bend forward and put both your arms, palms down, on the surface of the water. Try to touch your knees quickly by pushing your arms down through the water with your palms still flat. This is slower and much harder to do because your open hands have a much larger profile in the water and therefore create more drag (Figure 6-8, *B*).

Form drag is the resistance caused by an object's shape and profile as it moves through a fluid.

To reduce form drag, keep your body streamlined. To feel this for yourself, push off from the wall of the pool and try gliding in various positions: streamlined with your arms at your sides, less streamlined with your arms out to the sides, and much less streamlined with your knees flexed. As you become less streamlined, you increase form drag and you cannot glide as far (Figure 6-9).

When swimming strokes, the position of your body in the water can greatly affect the extent of your form drag.

Wave drag

Wave drag is caused by water turbulence, including the turbulence you generate as you swim. The faster you swim, the more wave drag you make. You can reduce wave drag if you use smooth, even strokes and avoid splashing with your arms. Reducing side-to-side and up-and-down body motion also reduces wave drag.

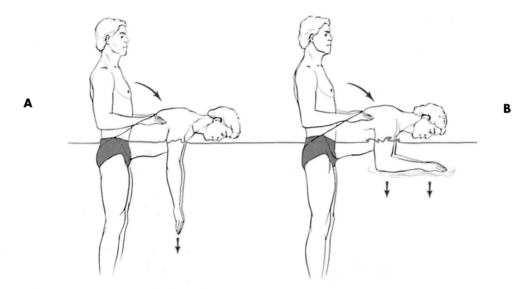

Figure 6-8, A and B. You can feel form drag by comparing the water resistance you feel when you reach to your knees with pointed fingers and with palms flat.

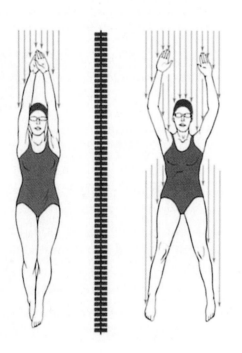

Figure 6-9. Streamlining body position decreases form drag.

Wave drag can be caused by other swimmers or activity in the water. Lane ropes are designed to reduce turbulence (Figure 6-10). Wave drag is also reduced when you move under water, such as during starts and turns and in underwater swimming.

Wave drag is the resistance caused by turbulence in a fluid.

Frictional drag

Frictional drag comes from the surface of the body as it moves through the water. A rough, uneven surface causes more drag, a smooth one less. To reduce frictional drag, swimmers wear swimming caps and smooth, tight-fitting swimsuits.

Frictional drag is the resistance caused by an object's surface texture as it moves through a fluid.

Some competitive swimmers even shave their body hair to reduce friction. You can feel frictional drag by wearing a tee-shirt when you swim and noticing how much it slows you down (Figure 6-11).

Bernoulli's Theorem and Laminar Flow

The basic principle of laminar flow is that as a fluid moves around an object, molecules that are split off on one side have to either speed up or slow down because they remain even with the molecules on the other side. Molecules that slow down create pressure against the object (drag), whereas those that speed up pull the object toward them with a force called lift.

These two forces, lift and drag, combine to move the object through a fluid or gas. In the air, lift on the upper side of an airplane's wing pulls the wing up. In swimming, lift helps the swimmer move forward through the water (Figure 6-12).

A simple way to experience lift is to stand in chest-deep water (or kneel in shallow water) with one arm extended forward from your elbow and your palm cupped and facing up.

First, relax your arm muscles. You will feel some buoyancy, making your hand drift upward. Next, bring your forearm back down to the horizontal position and, with your palm cupped, sweep your hand horizontally through the water. You will feel your hand pulled deeper into the water (Figure 6-13). Lift forces from the water passing over the back of your hand draw your hand down into the water. The faster you move it, the more it is drawn down. This is sometimes called the "propeller" effect because it acts in the same way that a propeller slices through the water to push a boat forward (Figure 6-14).

Figure 6-10. Lane ropes reduce water turbulence across lanes and thus reduce wave drag.

Figure 6-11. Wearing clothing in the water increases frictional drag.

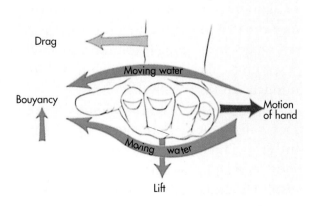

Figure 6-12. The result of lift and drag forces propels one through the water.

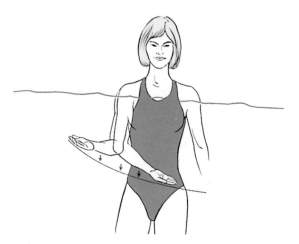

Figure 6-13. You can feel lift by swinging your cupped hand through the water.

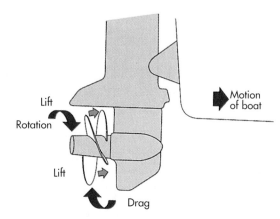

Figure 6-14. Lift forces created by your hand in swimming are similar to a boat motor's propeller forces.

This experiment with your hand in the water shows you that lift forces do not always act in an upward direction. Actually, they can act in any direction. A swimming stroke is made up of many different slicing motions, some outward and downward, some inward and upward. The lift from all these combine to make a horizontal force that moves you forward when you swim.

A second aspect of this principle is that the force of lift is proportional to the speed of motion. You felt this when you moved your hand faster and felt the pull downward get stronger.

Another kind of propulsion, called paddle propulsion, is demonstrated by oars propelling a rowboat through the water. Until recently, swimmers were thought to propel themselves best with paddle propulsion, pulling their body through the water with their arms and hands. However, the science of swimming has now shown that propeller propulsion is more effective for swimming. Paddle propulsion is used in some strokes, such as the arm stroke in the elementary backstroke (Figure 6-15, *A* and *B*). The combination of the two forms of propulsion is how we swim.

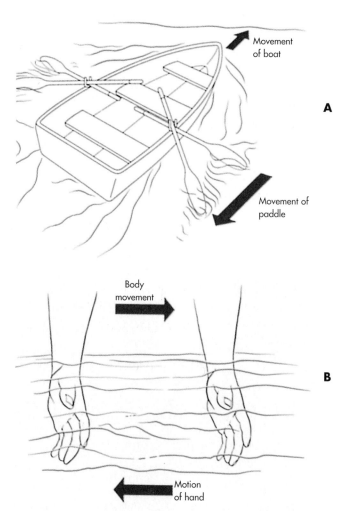

Figure 6-15, A and B. Paddle propulsion of the hands is like paddling a boat.

Newton's Laws of Motion and Swimming Efficiency

Isaac Newton discovered three laws of motion: the laws of inertia, acceleration, and action and reaction. These laws play an important role in efficient swimming.

The law of inertia

The law of inertia states that a force is needed to move a body at rest, to stop a body that is moving, or to change the direction of a moving body. All of these affect swimming in positive or negative ways.

> *Inertia is the tendency of a body at rest to stay at rest (static) and of a body in motion to stay in motion (dynamic).*

Static inertia is the tendency of a body at rest to stay at rest. You must overcome this every time you start to move or change position in the water. Dynamic inertia is the tendency of a moving body to keep moving. This principle helps you once you've started moving. If it were not for drag, dynamic inertia would keep a body moving through the water forever.

To experience the law of inertia yourself, push off on your back from the side of the pool and glide on your back as long as you can. As you push off, you feel that you need to exert a force to overcome static inertia. But once you are moving, you will experience dynamic inertia, which keeps you moving until drag forces slow you to a halt.

Inertia affects your swimming in two ways. First, you need more energy to start a stroke than to keep moving. It is easier to keep moving than to stop and start repeatedly. But dynamic inertia also lets you rest briefly during some strokes. With the sidestroke, breaststroke, and elementary backstroke, dynamic inertia keeps you moving forward and gives you some time to rest between strokes. But if you rest too long, you may slow down so much that you have to overcome static inertia with your next stroke.

The challenge is to balance the strokes with short rests to keep static inertia from increasing the energy you expend swimming.

Second, the more streamlined your body, the more you benefit from dynamic inertia. A swimmer who keeps a streamlined position uses less energy to keep moving than one who makes more form drag. This is true in all aquatic skills.

The law of inertia also states that force is needed to change the direction of a moving body. This has both positive and negative effects on swimming. When you are swimming in the direction you want, inertia helps keep you in line. This is true because force is needed to change your direction. The faster you are going, the more force it takes to push you off track. But this can work against you, too. If you are not swimming in the right direction or if your body is not aligned, you have to use energy to get back on course or to realign your body.

The law of acceleration

The law of acceleration states that the speed of a body depends on how much force is applied to it and the direction of that force.

If a certain force produces a certain speed, then twice that force will produce twice the speed. For example, if you push off from the wall with twice as much force as someone else, you will go twice as far, assuming that other factors are the same. Your speed right after pushing off, before drag starts to slow you down, will be twice as fast when you use twice the force.

> *The law of acceleration is the principle by which a body's speed depends on how much force is applied to it and the direction of that force.*

The law of acceleration also means that the effect of a force occurs in the direction in which the force is applied. For example, when you push a ball floating on the water, it moves in the direction you push it. With a body at rest, this principle is simple.

When the body is already in motion, the situation is more complicated. To understand it, imagine two billiard balls. If one ball is already moving and another one moving faster strikes it directly from behind, the first ball keeps moving in the same direction but faster. In this case, the force of the second ball acts in a direction in line with the first ball's direction, so that direction does not change (Figure 6-16, A). But if the force is applied in a different direction, the ball's direction is changed. The new direction combines the initial direction and the direction of the force. Imagine a moving billiard ball struck from the side by another ball moving at the same speed. In this case, the first billiard ball will not go faster, but it will go in a new direction (Figure 6-16, B).

This affects swimming in two ways. First, the more force you use in the direction of your stroke, the faster you will swim. Second, your swimming is more efficient when you stay in your chosen direction and when all your propulsive force is in that direction. When you turn, you use energy to correct your direction instead of to move forward. Likewise, if you exert force at an angle away from the direction you intend, you will push your body somewhat off course, and you will have to use more force to get back on track.

To feel this for yourself, swim the elementary backstroke across the pool, and then swim the same distance back with only one arm for each stroke. (Alternate arms, keeping the arm you are not using in the glide position along your body.) Note how much more effort and time it takes swimming with one arm at a time. You are applying less force, and your force is not in one direction because alternating arms creates a zigzag pattern. This exercise demonstrates both aspects of the law of acceleration.

The law of action and reaction

The law of action and reaction states that for every action there is an equal and opposite reaction. For example, if a moving billiard ball strikes one that is standing still, two things happen. The moving ball transfers some of its motion and direction to the one that is not moving. But the second ball, the one that was at rest, "pushes back" by transferring some of its static inertia to the first ball. This might even cause the first ball to stand still after the collision (Figure 6-17, A). When you dive from a diving board, the board reacts to the force of your feet acting against it, so you can take off for the dive (Figure 6-17, B). Likewise, during paddle propulsion in swimming strokes, as your arm pushes (acts) against the water, the water pushes back (reacts), providing resistance to let you move forward.

A 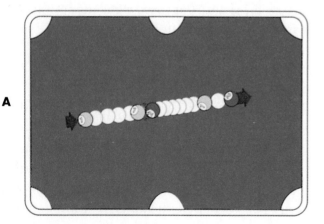 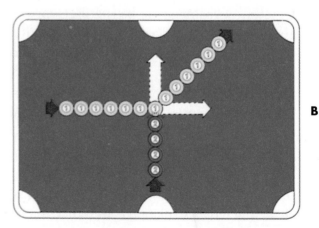 B

Figure 6-16, A and B. The law of acceleration can be seen in the way a billiard ball moves when struck by another ball. Both speed and direction depend on the force applied.

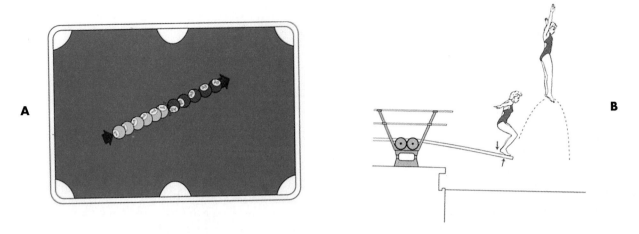

Figure 6-17, A and B. The law of action and reaction causes a billiard ball to stop when it strikes another and a diving board to react to the force of your jump by pushing you back up.

The law of action and reaction is the principle that for every action there is an equal and opposite reaction.

Conservation of Momentum

Conservation of momentum is based on Newton's laws. Circular stroke patterns are more effective than back-and-forth movements. When you use back-and-forth movements in your strokes, you first use force to stop moving in one direction (overcoming dynamic inertia) and then use more force to start moving again in another direction (overcoming static inertia). But movements in a circle keep going, so that you don't have to overcome either dynamic or static inertia.

To feel this, stand in waist-deep water and bend over to submerge your forearm. First move your forearm back and forth in a straight line so the water presses first against the palm and then against the back of your hand (Figure 6-18, *A*). Then make the same motion in a cir-

cular or oval path (Figure 6-18, *B*). This circular pattern takes much less effort because you are not starting and stopping your arm.

An application in swimming involves how you do the flutter kick. If you keep your ankles stiff, your kick will not be as powerful because they will be using a back-and-forth, linear motion. If you relax your ankles, they can follow a more efficient "rounded" path at the top and bottom of the kick.

The Law of Levers

The law of levers may seem complicated at first, but you don't have to deal with the math to improve your swimming stroke.

A seesaw illustrates the principle of the law of levers. A lever has a pivot point and one or two rigid arms. The pivot point is in the centre, and the arms extend on each side. The weights of two children riding the seesaw are the forces acting on the lever. The law of levers involves four components: the force applied (the weight

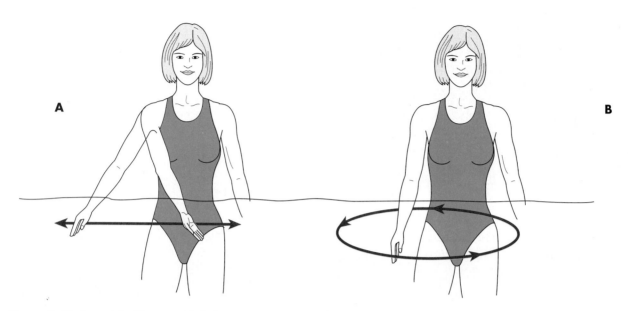

Figure 6-18, A and B. You can feel the conservation of momentum by noticing how moving your arm in a circular motion is easier (conserves momentum) than moving it back and forth.

of the first child), the resistance encountered (the weight of the second child), the force arm (the distance between the first child and the pivot point), and the resistance arm (the distance between the second child and the pivot point). The law of levers states that the product of the force and force arm is equal to the product of the resistance and resistance arm:

$$F \times FA = R \times RA$$

With a seesaw, if the two children weigh the same and sit at the same distance from the centre, the seesaw will be balanced and move only if the children push off the ground. If one child is heavier, the heavier child must sit closer to the pivot point for the seesaw to be balanced (greater weight × less distance = same effect) (Figure 6-19, *A* and *B*).

In practical application, the law of levers has relevance for how you do the arm stroke in the front crawl. Your shoulder is the pivot point. Your arm muscles supply the force. The force arm is the length of bone between the shoulder and where the muscle is attached. Resistance comes from the water acting on the arm. The resistance arm is the distance from the shoulder joint to the middle of the forearm (Figure 6-20, *A*).

The only practical way to improve your leverage and thus use less energy when swimming is to reduce the length of the resistance arm. With the front crawl, you can do this by bending the elbow (Figure 6-20, *B*). This reduces the force needed to move you through the water.

The law of levers has helped swimming researchers analyze strokes to find the best limb positions and motions for each. These are described with the swimming strokes in Chapter 9.

Figure 6-19, A and B. The seesaw illustrates the law of levers.

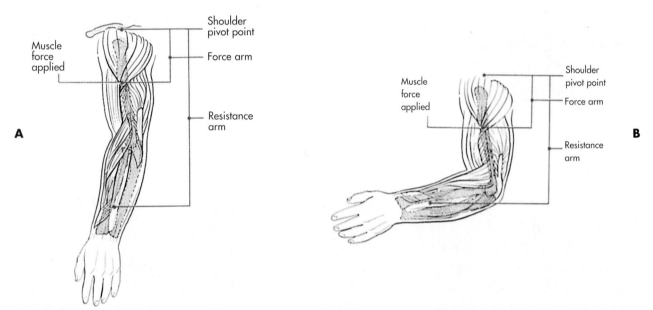

Figure 6-20, A and B. Bending the elbow in some strokes changes the leverage and reduces the force needed to move through the water.

SUMMARY

Even after reading this chapter, you might not be interested in the discoveries of Archimedes, Bernoulli, or Newton. Yet whether you are a beginner or an experienced swimmer, you probably are interested in swimming faster and more efficiently and not being as sore or tired afterwards.

Understanding the forces involved in swimming and knowing how to control them will help you improve your swimming skills. Consider one principle at a time and the way it applies to your strokes. Just as swimming researchers do, watch swimmers with proper technique to see how these scientific principles are working as they swim.

Entering the Water

Entering the water can be risky unless you first check the depth, clarity, and other conditions and choose the safest place to enter.

When you've decided the safest place to enter, choose a method of entry best suited for the water depth and your own abilities and skills.

To reach someone having difficulty in the water, you may need to enter the water fast or in a place not ideally suited for entry. The slip in, compact jump, or long shallow dive may provide you with the best entry for quick rescue.

You should be able to perform the following entries:

- Foot-first entry
- Forward roll
- Stride jump
- Dive

Should you find yourself in the water unexpectedly, you must be able to reorient yourself and recover to the surface of the water.

INTRODUCTION

When you think of swimming or other water activities, you often imagine yourself just *being* in the water—you may not think much about how you get into the water in the first place. Entering the water, however, can be just as much a part of the enjoyment—and the risk—as what you do once you are in it. You need only watch a group of children jumping and diving into a pool to realize or remember how much fun this can be. Learning to jump or dive correctly only heightens the enjoyment and ensures a safe experience.

Knowing how to enter the water the right way for the conditions at the time is a critical safety issue. Many aquatic injuries result from inappropriate water entry. A head-first entry into shallow water is the leading cause of head and neck injury resulting in death or permanent disability. Even feet-first entries can be dangerous in some conditions.

This chapter describes a wide range of feet-first and head-first methods of entering the water. With any entry you use, learn when it's safe to use it and when not, and practice in order to do it well.

PREPARING TO ENTER THE WATER

Before you enter the water, take a moment to check out the surroundings. For your safety and comfort, whether you're at a pool, river, lake, or ocean, you need to consider the water's depth and clarity, and your entry point into the water.

Water Depth

In different water environments the depth can vary considerably. From a beach or leisure pool you may be able to walk in from "zero depth"; in other environments you may be forced to enter immediately into deep water from a boat, cliff, dock, or diving tower. The time to think about your ability to swim and cope with the water depth is *before* you enter.

Water Clarity

Water clarity is another important factor to consider before entering the water. Even in a pool with filtration equipment, the clarity of the water can vary due to the effects of sunlight and algae and the level of sanitizing chemicals in the water. The clarity of natural bodies of water varies considerably and often can change rapidly. Lake water clarity is influenced by wind and rain, plant life, and minerals in the water. A river's clarity may change with the seasons, currents, rain runoff, and fluctuations in water level. Ocean water clarity is affected by plant life, tides, waves, and water flowing into the ocean. In any open water, debris such as weeds or garbage may be suspended in the water, making it nearly opaque. Moreover, water that is clear at one time can rapidly become cloudy or murky when people in the water stir up deposits on the bottom.

You should pay attention to water clarity for several reasons. If the water is not clear, you may not be able to see the bottom, and you may misjudge the depth. Cloudy water can hide underwater obstacles that may cause injury. If you are swimming or diving into murky water, you can more easily become disoriented because you can't see ahead of or beneath you. Your safety in the water may depend on your ability to see through it.

Entry Point

Along with checking the water depth and clarity, you should look for a safe point of entry. It is important to enter the water in a safe area when the environment is unfamiliar to you. At many pools or public beaches, safe entry points are marked with signs or buoy lines. If not, be especially careful. Talk to others familiar with the area and examine conditions carefully before going in. Do not assume a certain entry point is safe just because you see someone else there. Because we all have individual levels of ability, what one person can do, another may not be able to do safely. Check the safety points: water depth, water clarity, and entry point.

Entry Height

Walking or slipping into the water is always the safest way to enter. Aquatic environments vary widely, however, and in many areas your choice of where to enter may be restricted because of the surroundings or structures, such as a cliff, dock, or steep bank. If you must enter the water from a height, consider three factors first:

- Is the water deep enough for jumping or diving? (You will learn more about safe depth in the description of the jumps and dives later in this chapter.)
- If you are not familiar with the location, is the water clear enough that you can see the bottom and locate any potential hazards under water?
- Is there anything in the water you might strike during your entry, including people or underwater obstacles?

ADJUSTING TO THE WATER

Before you enter the water, pause to think about the different environment that you are about to enter. Usually the water is cooler than the air, which causes you to experience many different sensations. You will notice the effect of buoyancy and water pressure. At first this may be disorienting, particularly if you are not in the water frequently. Take the time to adjust.

Physical and Mental Adjustment

When you enter the water the first time, you may need to adjust gradually both physically and mentally. Swimming pool water is much cooler than bath water. Even relatively warm water (26° to 27° C) may feel cool and cause your breathing and pulse to speed up. When you are in up to your neck, either wading or crouching, breathing may seem harder because of the added pressure of the water on your chest. You may also feel somewhat lighter because of the effects of buoyancy (see Chapter 4). Take the time to get used to the effects of temperature, pressure, and buoyancy. As you become more comfortable and relaxed, you will no longer notice these effects.

Gradual Entry

Getting wet gradually helps your body get used to the cooler water temperature (Figure 7-1). Enter on the steps, ramp, or slope until you are thigh-deep, and then scoop water with your hands to wet your arms, chest, neck, and face. You may also sit on the edge of the pool and scoop water onto your body. Be sure you are comfortable with the water temperature before getting in all the way.

Unexpected Water Entry

Every year, Canadians who never expected to be in the water drown. They fall into water from a

The Old Swimming Hole

"Not too bad! The storm didn't do as much damage as I thought it would," said Joey to Jim as they reached their favourite swimming spot. They had been coming here for years, ever since Jim spotted the rock ledge on a canoe trip. The river was wide and deep here, and the place was very private. It was all the more special because it was hard reach. To make it "their place," they had built a fireplace for cookouts and made a swing of heavy rope from the high oak tree branches overhanging the water. They had great fun diving into the river from the ledge and swinging in with the rope.

"I thought the damage would be much worse," Jim said. Heavy storms that week had damaged the road to the site. Even with their four-wheel drive, it had been rough going, but the campsite and swimming hole looked pretty much the same as usual. A few tree limbs had blown down, and part of the bank had been washed away, but everything else looked okay.

"Last one in's a rotten egg!" they said almost at the same time. They had been playing this game since they were kids, anytime they got near water. Joey ran for the rock ledge, tearing off his tee-shirt and kicking off his shoes as he went. They were already in their swimming suits.

"No! Wait!" commanded Jim. His tone of voice told Joey this was not just a trick to slow him down. Joey stopped at the ledge and looked down at the murky water passing swiftly below. The river was muddier and much higher than usual.

Jim was making his way down the bank to the place they usually climbed out of the water, not in. He carried a long branch. Then he poked the branch into the water, starting in the area below the rope swing.

"You chicken!" Joey teased. He had always been more of a daredevil than his older brother, and he had the scars to prove it. But this time he had to admit that Jim had a point. He soon found a branch of his own and helped Jim search the murky water.

It didn't take long for them to find an old tree trunk, heavy from being in the water for years, that had washed down the river in the rains. It had come to rest just beneath the rock ledge. "Right where we would've dived in on it," said Jim. "I'm glad we checked."

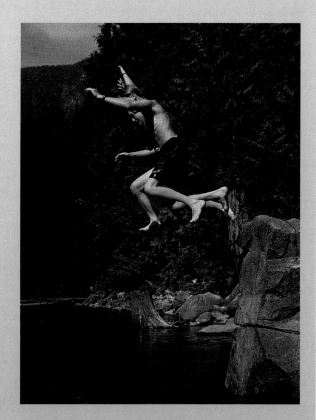

Figure 7-1. Enter the water gradually to get used to the temperature.

boat, dock, or shore. Although this chapter informs you how to enter the water safely, you may find yourself in the water unexpectedly. It is important that you be able to orient yourself to the surface of the water on submersion.

Once you enter the water, try to relax. Your body will naturally start to float to the surface. Slowly exhale into the water. The bubbles from your breath will float toward the surface and help reorient you.

TYPE OF ENTRIES

 There are many different ways to enter the water. Each is appropriate in some situations but may be dangerous in others. Either be sure the method you intend to use is safe for the water you are about to enter, or choose a different method. Some entries, such as dives, should be carefully practiced in a controlled setting before you start using them on your own.

Feet-first Entries

There are different ways you can slip or jump into the water. Your choice depends on the site, situation, and your abilities. Simply jumping in is not necessarily safe.

Slip-in and wade-in entries

At a beach or zero-depth pool deck, you can simply wade into the water. This method is almost always safe, although you should watch the bottom for possible hazards. Be especially careful in murky water.

Use a slip-in entry from a low dock or pool deck. Sit on the edge, turn to one side and put both hands on the wall on that side, and then turn your body and slip in (Figure 7-2). This method is often effective for persons with limited mobility.

Any time you are in unknown waters, you should enter by either the wade-in or slip-in method. Wait until you've reached a depth of 1 metre before swimming.

Stride jump

If the water is at least 2 metres deep, if you are not more than 1 metre above the water, and if there are no underwater hazards, you can enter with the stride jump. This jump allows you to enter deep water while keeping your head above the surface.

Figure 7-2. Use a slip-in entry from a low dock or pool deck.

Figure 7-3. Stride jump entry.

Approach the edge with one leg before the other, either standing or running if you must enter the water fast to rescue someone. If possible, curl the toes of your leading foot on the edge. Enter the water with your legs in a stride position, at an angle of about 45 degrees (Figure 7-3). Fully extend your hands and arms behind or to the side of your body at shoulder height.

After the entry, scissor kick with your legs and thrust your arms down to help you stay at the surface. Hold your head high and keep your eyes open. Usually you can keep your head entirely above the water.

Compact jump

Use the compact jump to enter deep water from a height more than 1.5 metres above the surface. Do not try this jump if there is a danger of unseen obstacles in the water. You may need to

use the compact jump from a pier, bridge, or bank when it is not safe to dive head-first into the water.

Lean forward to jump clear of the surface on which you are standing. Cross your arms over your chest or hold them down at your sides (Figure 7-4, *A*). Do not hold your arms out at right angles because this increases the risk of injury. Hold your legs close together or cross them at the ankles. Keep your knees and ankle slightly flexed (Figure 7-4, *B*).

During the descent, do not lean forward, because this may cause a forward rotation.

On entering the water, exhale through your nose, spread your arms, and bend or pike at the waist to slow the descent (Figure 7-4, *C*).

Head-first Entries

Entering the water head-first can be dangerous because the neck and spine are easily damaged if the head strikes the bottom or any obstacle under water. It takes so little force to injure the spine that many casualties of a broken neck do not even have a bruise on the skin from the impact. NEVER enter the water head-first unless the water is deep and you are completely certain there are no underwater obstacles. Other safety principles for diving are listed later in this chapter.

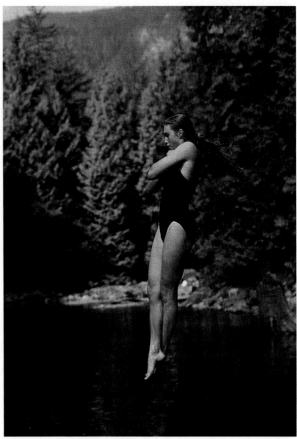

Figure 7-4, A to C. Compact jump entry (see text).

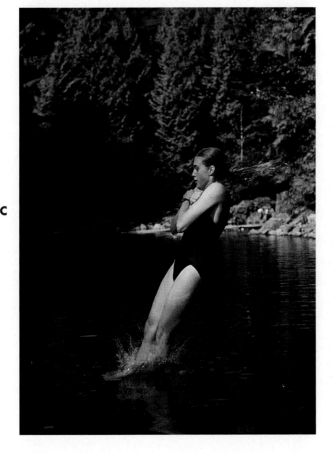

Forward roll

In the forward roll you simply roll forward into the water in a pike position (Figure 7-5), entering with shoulders and neck first. Keep your feet together through the roll. This entry is used when you do not need to move forward a distance into the water.

The simple dive

A simple dive has three parts: the stationary starting position, the moment of propulsion (the takeoff), and the entry into the water. You can use different starting positions, as you'll see in the following paragraphs, and the takeoff for a simple dive is quite easy, usually requiring only a slight push with one or both feet. Body alignment and entry point are important considerations for a clean entry.

To be sure you dive into the water at the correct point of entry, focus on a target (such as an imaginary point on the surface) until your hands enter the water.

Keeping proper body alignment is crucial for a safe and graceful dive. It reduces drag and the risk of straining muscles or joints. Head position is very important because it affects the position of the body in general. Moving the head may cause the body to arch or bend. The beginner who lifts the head too quickly may do a painful belly flop.

Try to stay in a streamlined position in flight (the passage of the body through the air) (Figure 7-6). A streamlined position helps you to control muscle and body tension and thus maintain proper body alignment.

Progression for a simple dive

Mastering the steps for learning a simple dive from the pool deck will give you self-confidence and a feeling of success. You may also use these steps to learn to dive from a dock. Remember to move through these steps at your own pace. Some of them might need lots of practice. If you have good coordination and body awareness, you may be able to move quickly through each step.

The step dive The step dive is useful for practicing correct head and arm position, body alignment, and muscle tension. You can do the step dive from a chair or bench in the water. Ensure that the chair or bench is secure and stable enough to stand on. The water should be at least shoulder deep. When you are on the step, the water level should be at your hips. Extend

Figure 7-5. Forward roll into the water in pike position.

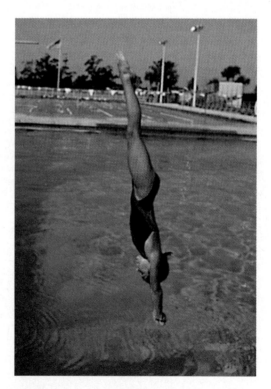

Figure 7-6. In a dive, maintain a streamlined position in flight.

your arms over your head, bend your knees slightly, and lean forward until you touch the surface of the water (Figure 7-7). Then push forward into the water with your legs so you are in the prone glide position.

Kneeling position While at the pool edge, kneel on one knee while gripping the pool edge with the toes of the other foot (Figure 7-8). The foot of the kneeling leg should be in a position to help push from the deck. Extend your arms over your head. Focus on a target either on the bottom about 1 metre out from the side or on the surface of the water about 0.5 metre from the side. The objective is to dive deeply. Focusing on a target helps you enter the water at the right place and at the correct angle, avoiding a belly flop. Lean forward, try to touch the water, and when you start to lose your balance, push with your legs. As you enter the water, straighten your body and extend both legs. Practice this skill until you feel comfortable with it and can do it without error.

Compact position You do this dive in much the same manner as the dive from the kneeling position. Put one foot forward and one back, with the toes of the leading foot gripping the edge of the deck. Start in the kneeling position. Then lift up so both knees are off the deck and flexed so that you stay close to the water. Extend your arms above your head. Focus on a target the same distance from the deck (as in the dive from a kneeling position) (Figure 7-9). Bend forward and try to touch the surface of the water with your hands. When you start to lose your balance, push off toward the water. Bring your legs up and together before entering the water.

Stride position After several successful dives from the compact position, you should be ready for a dive from the stride position. Stand upright with one leg forward and one leg back. The toes of the forward foot should grip the edge of the pool. Extend your arms above your head. Focus on a target on the bottom of the pool about 1.5 metres out from the side or on the surface about 1 metre out. Bend your legs only slightly as you bend at the waist toward the water. Try to touch the surface of the water with your hands and, as you lose your balance, lift your back leg until it is in line with your torso (Figure 7-10). The forward leg should stay as straight as possible.

Figure 7-7. Step dive position for learning to dive.

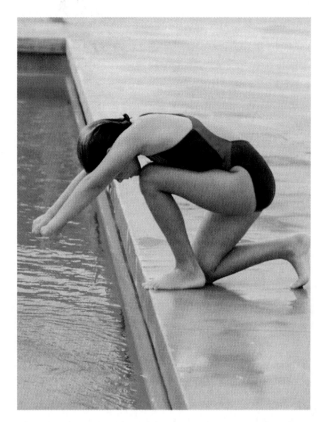

Figure 7-8. Kneeling dive position for learning to dive.

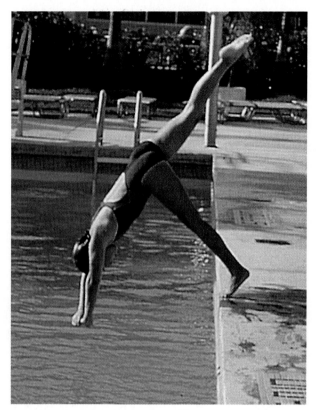

Figure 7-10. Stride position for learning to dive.

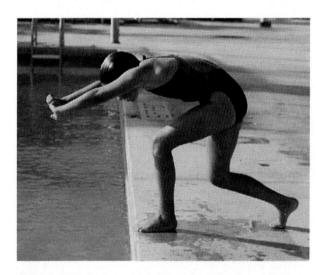

Figure 7-9. Compact position for learning to dive.

Standing dive The final dive from the deck is the standing dive. Stand with your feet about shoulder-width apart, with the toes of both feet gripping the edge of the deck. Extend your arms above your head. Focus on a target at the same distance as in a dive from the straddle position. Bend at the knees and angle your hands down toward the target (Figure 7-11, *A*). Push off the deck, lift the hips, and extend your legs so they are in line with your torso (Figure 7-11, *B*). As you gain confidence, you may move your feet closer together.

Shallow dive

The shallow dive is used when you need to start out fast. For example, you may need to use the shallow dive to quickly reach someone in the water who needs urgent help. The shallow dive is also used by competitive swimmers to start a stroke and is described in detail in Chapter 10.

Figure 7-11. Standing dive. **A,** Starting position. **B,** Enter the water in streamlined position.

A shallow dive is a dive for entering the water head-first at a shallow angle with great forward momentum.

Diving from a diving board

When you are skilled at diving at the water's edge into deep water, you are ready to learn to dive from a diving board. At swimming pools you may find diving boards of various heights. Usually there is a diving board 1 metre high and sometimes a high board 3 metres high. Some competitive pools also have diving towers with heights of 5, 7.5, and 10 metres. You may try diving from a 1-metre board using a standing dive. You should never use the higher boards or towers without competent diving instruction and supervision.

Figure 7-12. A movable fulcrum on a diving board is positioned forward for greater stability.

Diving boards should never be considered "pool toys" or a climbing structure. They are made for a specific purpose and should be used only for diving or to practice jumping from a height. Injuries can occur when diving boards are used for other purposes.

You can use the same progression as you used to learn to dive from the deck. The surface of the diving board may be rough and scrape your knee in the kneeling position, so you may want to put a towel or wet pad over the end of the board. If the diving board has a movable fulcrum (Figure 7-12), move it all the way forward to make the diving board more stable. Once you have learned the standing dive from the 1-metre diving board, you are ready to start learning some basic springboard diving skills. To learn springboard skills properly, take instruction from a qualified instructor.

SURFACE DIVING

Surface diving is used to go under water when you are already in the water and at the surface. Surface diving is used to retrieve objects from the bottom, to rescue a submerged casualty, and to go under water in activities such as skin diving. Surface diving is the quickest way to accurately descend under water.

*A **foot-first surface dive** is a technique for moving under water from the surface with the feet leading.*

A surface dive can be either foot-first or head-first. The head-first dive may be in a tuck (curled) or pike (bent at the hips) position. To avoid injury from an object in the water, keep your eyes open and arms in front of your head. In all surface dives, exhaling while you go down prevents water from entering your nose and decreases your buoyancy.

*A **tuck surface dive** is a technique for moving head-first from the surface to under water initially with the hips and knees flexed and later with the hips and knees extending.*

*A **pike surface dive** is a technique for moving under water from the surface by bending at the hips and descending head-first with legs kept straight the entire time.*

While performing any surface dive, you may feel ear pain or discomfort as you go deeper or swim under water. This is due to the pressure of the water. To alleviate the pressure, hold your nose and try to blow air out through the nose. This will cause your ears to "pop." If this does not relieve the pressure, you must swim to shallower water or to the surface to prevent damage to your ears.

Foot-first Surface Dive

A foot-first surface dive is the only safe way to go into murky water or water of unknown depth. Start in a vertical surface support position in the water (see Chapter 8). Simultaneously press both hands down vigorously to the sides of the thighs and do a strong scissors or breaststroke kick. These movements help you rise in the water so you will have a better descent. Take a deep breath at the top of the rise (Figure 7-13, *A*). As you start down, keep your body vertical and in a streamlined position. When your downward momentum slows, turn your palms outward, and then sweep your

hands and arms upward (Figure 7-13, *B*) to get more downward propulsion (Figure 7-13, *C*). When you are as deep as you want, tuck your body and roll to a horizontal position. Then extend your arms and legs and swim under water.

A

B

C

Figure 7-13. Foot-first surface dive. **A,** Rise in the water to start a deeper descent. **B,** Sweep arms and hands upward for more downward propulsion (**C**).

Head-first Surface Dive—Tuck Position

The tuck surface dive is a head-first surface dive. First, get forward momentum with a swimming stroke or glide. Take a breath, sweep your arms backward to the thighs, and turn your palms down. Tuck your chin to your chest, bend your body at a right angle at the hips, and draw your legs into a tuck position (Figure 7-14, A). Roll forward until you are almost upside down (Figure 7-14, B). Then extend your legs upward quickly while pressing the arms and hands forward, palms down, toward the bottom (Figure 7-14, C). For greater depth, do a breaststroke arm pull. If you do not know the depth of the water or if it is less than 2 metres, keep one arm extended over your head as you move toward the bottom.

Head-first Surface Dive—Pike Position

The pike surface dive is similar to the tuck surface dive, except that you keep your legs straight and use the pike position. Use a swimming stroke or glide to gain forward momentum. Sweep your arms backward to your thighs and turn them palms down. Tuck your chin to your chest and flex at the hip sharply while your arms reach forward and downward toward the bottom (Figure 7-15, A). Lift the legs upward, straight and together. Your body is now fully extended, streamlined, and almost vertical (Figure 7-15, B). The weight of your legs and the forward momentum usually take you deep enough without more arm movement.

A

B

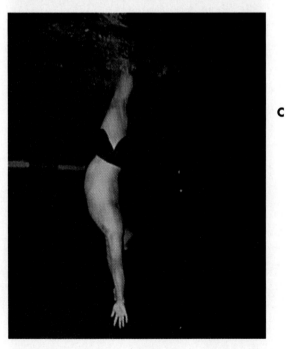

C

Figure 7-14, A to C. Head-first surface dive. Tuck position.

Typical Diving Injuries

Who is the average spinal cord injury casualty?
- Male, 17 to 22 years old, and athletic
- No formal training in diving
- First-time visitor to the location
- Making his first dive in the location
- Was not warned, by word or sign, about dangers
- Had been using alcohol and/or drugs

How does a diving injury occur?
- Diving into shallow water (95%)
- Diving from a deck or adjacent structure into an in-ground pool
- Diving without supervision or training from starting blocks into shallow water

What is the situation?
- There is no lifeguard on duty.
- Water depth where the casualty hit the bottom is less than 1.5 metres.
- The water is cloudy or murky.
- The bottom has no markings.
- No warning signs prohibit diving.

What happens then?
- Your head hits the bottom, and you stop instantly with an injured spinal cord.
- Even if you're conscious, you may be unable to move and may drown before someone reaches you.
- Even if someone reaches you, he or she may not know how to move you, and any movement of your head may worsen the injury.
- Even if you're rescued and reach the emergency room, you have just begun to suffer. Your life is saved, but you are paralyzed.

Imagine living the rest of your life unable to move your arms and legs or control when you go to the bathroom.

Imagine how your relationships with friends and family will change.

Now think:
- Is it worth it to make one careless dive?
- Is it worth it to allow your friends to dive recklessly?

Figure 7-15. Pike surface dive (see page 107).

STAY SAFE WHILE DIVING

The following guidelines are recommended for safe diving:

- Learn how to dive properly from a qualified instructor. The self-taught diver is much more likely to be injured.

- Follow safety rules at all times—never make exceptions.

- Do not wear earplugs; they can add dangerous pressure as you descend.

- Obey "No Diving" signs. They are there for your safety (Figure 7-16).

- Be sure of water depth. The first time in the water, ease in or walk in; do not jump or dive.

- Never dive into an above-ground pool or the shallow end of any in-ground pool.

- Never dive into cloudy or murky water.

- In open water, always check first for objects under the surface, such as logs, stumps, boulders, and pilings.

- Check the shape of the pool bottom to be sure the diving area is large enough and deep enough for the dive you plan to make.

- Remember that the presence of a diving board doesn't necessarily mean that it is safe to dive. Pools at homes, motels, and hotels might not be safe for diving.

- Dive only off the end of a diving board. If you dive off the side of a diving board, you might hit the side of the pool or other swimmers.

- Bounce only once on the end of a diving board. You could miss the edge or slip off the diving board if you bounce repeatedly.

- Walk on a diving board and do not attempt to dive a long way through the air. The water might not be deep enough at your point of entry.

- Swim away from the diving board. Don't be a hazard for the next diver.

A

B

Figure 7-16, A and B. Check signs before entering the water.

If you own a backyard pool or supervise others at an apartment, condominium, or hotel pool, be responsible. Make sure that your own children, your friends, and even strangers follow these guidelines too. Watching children dive into shallow water and saying nothing is like letting a child play with a loaded gun. Chapter 3 lists other guidelines for water safety in all settings.

Risks and Causes of Diving Injuries

Trauma is a physical injury caused by a violent action. Most spinal injuries result from diving into shallow water. Injuries occur from diving into ocean surf, lakes, rivers, quarries, and swimming pools. Of these diving injuries, the great majority occur in water 1.5 metres deep or less. Only a small percentage of diving injuries occur during supervised diving or from diving off diving boards into water 2.5 metres or deeper. Some injuries involve the use of alcohol and/or drugs.

Even an experienced diver can be seriously injured by diving improperly, diving into shallow water of unknown depth, diving into water, sliding down a water slide head-first, falling off a diving board, or diving from starting blocks without proper training and supervision. You may hit the bottom, an underwater object, or another swimmer. A spinal injury can also happen in the deep end of a pool. Injuries have been associated with dives or falls from diving boards, starting blocks, 3-metre stands, and from the deck into spoon-shaped pools or hopper bottom pools. Many diving incidents result in quadriplegia—total paralysis from the neck down. However, when we generalize any situation, there are always exceptions. In 1993, for example, three of five deaths due to diving were in a water depth over 2.5 metres.

SUMMARY

Jumping and diving into the water is fun but does present risks. Keep your own aquatic experiences safe by entering the water appropriately for the conditions. Check the depth and clarity to select the best entry point. With unknown conditions, always start out feet-first. When you have learned how to dive safely, practice your technique and have fun. Do not use alcohol around the water. The safe diving guidelines help ensure that you survive to keep diving in the future!

Basic Aquatic Skills

Before learning to swim or participate in aquatic sports and activities, you must master basic flotation and movement skills in the water. Developing the skills described in this chapter will help prepare you for safe activities in and around the water.

Many drownings happen to people who had never planned to be in the water. Everyone should know how to float and move to a safer position in the water. These basic skills will help you stay safe if you find yourself in deep water.

• Many of the skills in this chapter form the foundation for swimming stroke development and as such are not safety standards themselves. Surface support is an important safety skill. You should be able to stay at the water surface in a relaxed manner for a minimum of 5 minutes.

When you think of swimming, you often think of moving through the water smoothly with powerful arm strokes and kicks. But becoming a good swimmer doesn't happen overnight. Most swimmers begin by learning basic aquatic skills, such as rhythmic breathing, floating, gliding, and supporting themselves at the water's surface. They gradually progress through these skills as they become more comfortable in the water.

This chapter describes these basic skills, starting with learning to control your breathing and bobbing. As you become comfortable in the water, you will learn skills in water movement skills. Surface support techniques, gliding, and sculling are basic ways to hold and change your position and to move you in the water.

You need not try to learn all the skills in this chapter immediately. Take your time and enjoy the water. When practicing these skills, ask a friend who is a competent swimmer to assist you. The safety skills here are important both in themselves and as learning tools for more advanced strokes.

BREATH CONTROL AND BOBBING

You must be able to control your breathing to swim well. You don't need to be able to hold your breath for a long time, but you should be able to breathe rhythmically and steadily while swimming. Often beginning swimmers do not take the time to work on breath control before they try to master their arm and leg strokes, and they may never become efficient swimmers because their breathing interrupts the stroke. One good method used to practice breath control is bobbing.

Bobbing is the skill of submerging, exhaling underwater, and pushing off from the bottom to return to the surface.

To bob, hold onto the side of the pool in chest-deep water. Take a breath, bend your knees, and submerge your head. As you go down, gently exhale and then straighten your legs to return to the surface (Figure 8-1). Inhale when your mouth rises above the surface of the water. Exhale through your mouth and nose, and make the bobbing movement smooth and steady. Repeat this movement over and over until you are comfortable, and then move to chin-deep water away from the wall and practice more.

Figure 8-1. Exhale underwater when bobbing.

Deep-water bobbing is good to know as a skill for rescuing yourself. If you are suddenly in water over your head, you can keep breathing as you bob, pushing off the bottom at an angle toward shallow water, until you are out of the deep water.

STAYING AFLOAT

Everyone needs to feel confident and safe in the water. Confidence helps you prevent panic and think clearly. One of the first lessons the beginner or nonswimmer must learn is to stay on the surface and move calmly to safety.

Floating is an easy way for many people to stay near the surface. Chapter 6 explains the principles that make people float. Learning to float is easier if you think about these principles and if you feel comfortable in the water. Remember that not everyone floats in the same manner. Some people float horizontally, while others float in a more vertical position.

Front Floats

There are three ways to float on your front: the jellyfish float, the tuck float, and the prone float.

Jellyfish float

In chest-deep water, submerge to the neck and take a deep breath of air. Bend forward at the waist, put your head in the water, and flex your knees slightly to raise your feet off the bottom. Let your hands and feet hang loose from your body (Figure 8-2). Hold your breath and relax. Chapter 6 describes how you can use the jellyfish float to see how buoyant you are and to feel how water can support you.

Tuck float

The tuck float is similar to the jellyfish float, except that you flex your hips and knees and hold onto your legs at mid-calf. (This is the tuck position.) You can also use this float to see how buoyant you are (Figure 8-3).

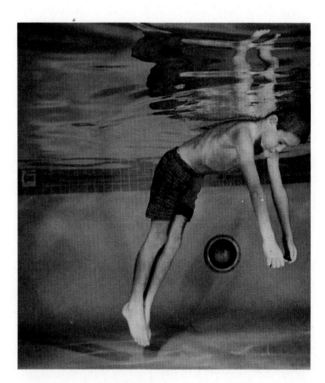

Figure 8-2. The jellyfish float.

Figure 8-3. The tuck float.

Prone float

The prone float helps you become comfortable in a position that involves holding your breath. It is easy to learn this skill where the water is shallow enough for you to put your hands on the bottom. Start by lying face down with your hands on the bottom. Take a breath and place your face in the water until your ears are covered. Relax and slowly lift your hands off the bottom. Extend your arms in the water above your head. To keep your nose from filling with water, lift your chin slightly and blow some air gently out through your nose. If your toes are still on the bottom, relax your legs and gently push up off the bottom to see if they will rise (Figure 8-4). Do not be alarmed if your toes return to the bottom. This only means that the water is not deep enough for your body to rotate to its normal (diagonal or vertical) floating position.

To recover, lift your head, bend your hips, and press your arms down until your hands and feet touch bottom.

You can also learn the prone float in chest-deep water. Flex your knees until your shoulders are submerged, extend your arms on the surface, take a deep breath, place your face in the water, lean forward, and gently push your toes up off the bottom. If your normal floating position is near vertical, your toes will return to rest on the bottom.

To stand from this floating position, pull your knees under your body and move your arms toward the bottom. Lift your head and stand up.

To check your buoyancy, you can combine several face-down floats. In chest-deep water, begin with the jellyfish float, move to the tuck float, and extend to the prone float. Then reverse the process and recover to a standing position.

Back Float

You can learn the back, or supine, float if you let your body rise to its natural floating position. Stand in shoulder-deep water. Take a deep breath, lay your head back, arch your body gently, relax, bend your knees, and hold your arms out from the shoulders, palms up. The water will support your body as you lie all the way back. Do not push off the bottom, but let your feet rise to the floating position that is normal for you—vertical, diagonal, or horizontal (Figure 8-5, *A*, *B* and *C*). As you float, breathe in

Figure 8-4. The prone float.

and out through your mouth every few seconds. As you learned in Chapter 6, filling your lungs will help you float.

If your natural floating position is diagonal or vertical, you can float more horizontally by moving your arms in the water above your head, lifting your hands out of the water, and bending your knees (see also Chapter 6). If you cannot float motionless, sculling motions can help you stay on the surface with only a little effort. See page 120 for a more detailed description of the sculling action.

> **Sculling** *is a technique for moving through the water or staying horizontal, using only the arms and hands.*

To recover to a standing position, exhale, tuck your chin toward your chest, drop your hips, and bring your knees forward. Sweep your arms back, down, and forward in a circular motion to bring your body back to vertical position, and then stand. This motion is like pulling a chair up underneath you.

Side Float

After you have learned the front and back floats, try floating on your side. This float helps you develop stability in the breathing position for the front crawl stroke.

Ease into the position as if you are gliding into it (Figure 8-6). The arm of the side you are lying on should be fully extended above your head. Rest your ear on your shoulder and look up. This is the breathing position for the front crawl stroke, and you should be able to breathe

A

B

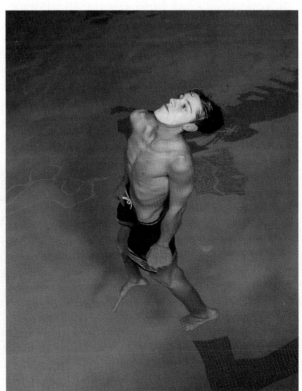

C

Figure 8-5, A to **C.** People float differently on their backs.

without moving in this floating position. Your other arm should remain at rest along your body. Be sure to practice floating on both sides.

Although you may at first feel as if you are sinking, once you've learned to stay stable in the side float position, you will find it is easy to do.

Experiment with putting your arms and legs in different positions while floating on the front, back, and side. This will help you get a feel for your own buoyancy related to position.

Turning Over

As you become more comfortable floating in different positions, learn to roll from one side to another (Figure 8-7). Rolling over while floating, especially from the front to the back float, is an important safety skill. If you find yourself unexpectedly in the water due to a fall, you will want to roll onto your back where breathing and relaxation are easier. Rolling is also how you will change from swimming one stroke to another. If you become tired while swimming on your front, you can roll over and float on your back to rest or catch your breath.

To roll over from a front float to a back float, start on your front with your body straight and your arms in front of you (at the 12 o'clock position). To roll to the right, pull back with your right hand until it touches your right thigh. At the same time turn your head to the right, and drop your left shoulder until you are floating on your left side. Keep your right hand moving across the body, keep your head turning until you face straight up, and pull back with your left hand until it is by your left thigh (with arms in the 6:30 clock position).

To turn from your back to your front, start in a back float or glide. To roll to the left, move your right arm across your body and put it in the water by your left shoulder. At the same time take a deep breath, drop your left shoulder, and turn your head quickly to the left and put your face in the water. Extend your arms and legs into the front glide (prone position).

A

B

Figure 8-6. The side float.

Figure 8-7, A and B. Moving from the front float to back float.

MOVEMENT IN THE WATER

Once you feel comfortable floating, you can learn how to move in the water. The following sections describe basic skills to help you move or change direction in the water without actually swimming. When you are ready to learn swimming strokes, go on to Chapter 9.

Gliding

Gliding is a fun way to learn to streamline your body for efficient movement in the water. You can glide by pushing off from either the bottom or side of the pool.

Start with the front glide in shallow water, with your arms in front of you in the 12:00 o'clock position (Figure 8-8). Stretch out from finger to toe and try to hold the glide as long as you can, even after you think you have stopped. Then try the glide with your arms back at your sides in the 6:30 clock position.

As you practice gliding, feel free to shift the position of your legs to try to reach the most balanced, streamlined position. Make it your goal to slip through the water like a torpedo.

When you are familiar with gliding face down, try gliding on your back with your arms both out in front of you and held close along your sides (Figure 8-9). Then try a side glide (Figure 8-10). Mastering the side glide will help

you feel more comfortable as you learn to breathe in the front crawl swimming stroke.

Kicking

When you develop your swimming strokes, you will learn different kinds of kicks for the different arm strokes. The propulsion from kicking is important for all strokes. You can begin to learn to kick by starting to kick while gliding on your back, your front, and your side. Chapter 9 describes these kicks in detail.

- Try kicking on your back first, because you can breathe easily while you practice. This position helps you gain confidence in the water because, if you become tired when swimming in deep water, you can roll over onto your back and kick leisurely to shallow water (Figure 8-11).

Figure 8-9. The back glide.

Figure 8-8. The front glide.

Figure 8-10. The side glide.

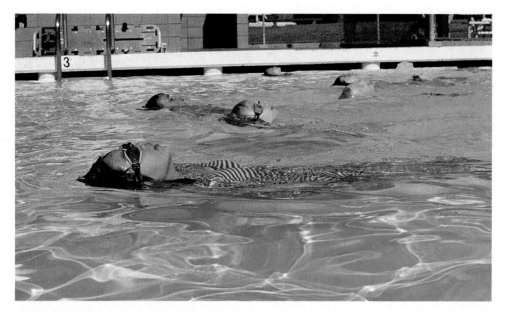

Figure 8-11. The position for kicking on your back.

Practice kicking on your front. The most common kick is the flutter kick. You will get the feel for keeping your whole leg straight in this kick, pointing your toes rather than bending your knees (Figure 8-12). Keep your ankles loose and floppy.

Side kicking is good preparation for the breathing phase of the front crawl stroke.

Sculling

Sculling is a way to move through the water using only your hands and forearms. You can also use sculling to stay in position while floating on the back or supporting yourself at the surface. On your back, you scull with your arms extended along the sides of your body, palms down under the surface of the water. Exert equal and constant pressure with continuous hand movements.

The easiest way to scull is to stay still when floating supine. From the starting position, rotate your hands slightly to put the thumb down, and move your hands outward just beyond shoulder width. Keep your elbows

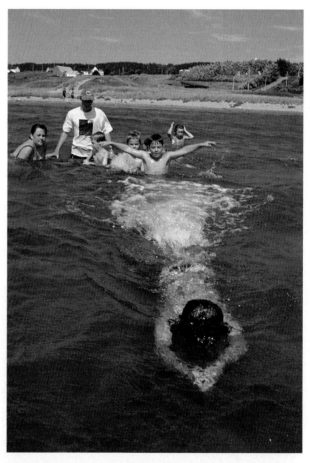

Figure 8-12. Keep your legs straight and ankles floppy when kicking on the front.

slightly bent the whole time. Then rotate your hands to put the thumbs up and palms facing inward. Move your hand toward your hips. The hands lead, and the forearms follow. Make the motion into a smooth, continuous figure-eight pattern (Figure 8-13). As you sweep each hand from side to side, water passing over the back of the hands creates lift that raises your hand in the water (see Chapter 6). This force, combined with the leverage of your shoulder, helps you stay in one position in the water.

To move forward (head-first) in the water, change the pitch of your hands. Force water outward away from your body and inward toward your feet. Extend your wrists so your fingers point up slightly. Do the sculling motion with the thumb side of each hand pitched slightly toward the feet during the inward press and the little finger of each hand pitched slightly toward the feet during the outward press (Figure 8-14).

SURFACE SUPPORT

Surface support techniques keep you upright in deep water with your head out of the water. Surface support is an important personal safety skill for all swimmers. You can support yourself in the water using arms only, legs only, or arms and legs together. Use the scissors, breaststroke, or rotary kick along with sculling movements of the arms and hands, as described in the following paragraph. You should learn surface support techniques in a relaxed way with slow movements. Move the arms and legs only enough to keep your body vertical.

*A **rotary kick** is a kicking technique used for surface support; sometimes called the eggbeater kick.*

To support yourself in the water, stay nearly vertical with your upper body bent slightly forward at the waist (Figure 8-15). Make continu-

Figure 8-13. Hand movement for sculling.

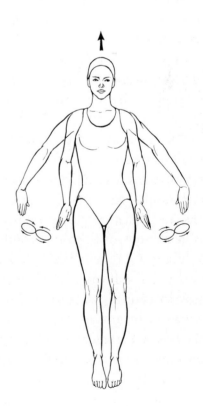

Figure 8-14. Hand movement for sculling in forward direction.

ous broad, flat, sculling movements with the hands a few centimetres below the surface in front of the body. Keep the elbows bent. Do the sculling movements with a much wider reach than you use to hold your position when floating on your back. Do the scissors or breast-stroke kick with just enough thrust to keep your head above water (Figure 8-16).

The rotary or "eggbeater" kick is also effective for surface support. It gives continuous support because there is no resting phase. This strong kick is used in water polo, synchronized swimming, and lifeguarding.

To support yourself with the rotary kick, stay in the same position for surface support as with other kicks. Your back should be straight. Keep your hips flexed so your thighs are comfortably forward (Figure 8-17, *A*). Flex your knees so your lower legs hang down at an angle of nearly 90 degrees to the thighs. With your knees slightly wider than hip distance apart, rotate your lower legs at the knees, one leg at a time. The left leg moves clockwise and the right counterclockwise. Make a large circular movement with the foot and lower leg. Reach as far sideways and backward as you can while keeping your body position. As you move each foot sideways and forward, extend it sharply (Figure 8-17, *B*). The power of the kick comes from lift forces created by the sweeping action of the leg and foot (Figure 8-18). As soon as one leg completes its circle, the other starts. Kick just hard enough to keep your head out of the water.

CHANGING DIRECTIONS

It is important to know how to change directions while moving in the water, and, if you unintentionally fall into the water from a boat or dock, it is important to be able to turn to face safety (the place from which you fell).

If you are kicking or sculling in shallow water, simply stand up to change directions. In deep water, stop propelling yourself forward and start vertical surface support. By pushing the water (sculling) harder with one arm, you can rotate your body. Rotate into the desired position and start moving forward again.

If you fall into the water unintentionally, start surface support immediately after surfacing. Rotate your body toward safety and begin movement toward it.

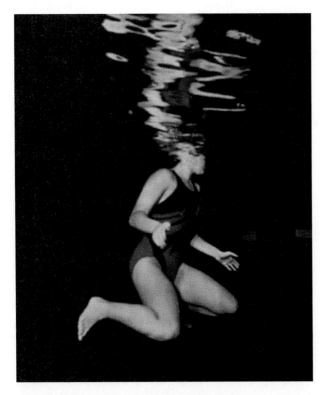

Figure 8-15. Surface support technique.

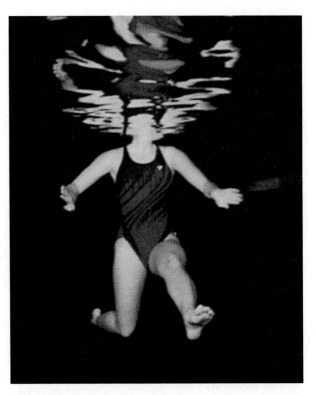

Figure 8-16. Scissors kick for surface support.

A

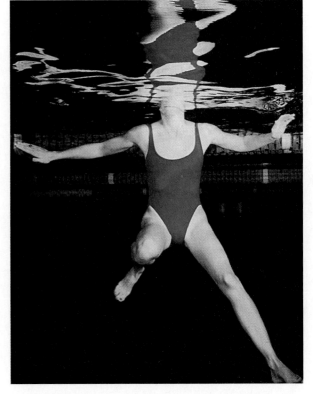

B

Figure 8-17, A and **B.** Rotary kick for surface support. Alternating-leg circular kick of the rotary kick for surface support.

Taking a Chance—a Drowning

On holiday with friends, James Howard has spent the day swimming at a lake with friends. Though they were rather tired, he and two others decided to continue to swim after they returned to their hotel that evening. The heated hotel pool was unsupervised, with signs stating that no lifeguard was on duty.

James was not concerned with the lack of a lifeguard. After all, he was an excellent swimmer and in fact was in training to become a swim coach. He saw no risk in swimming now with his friends.

After an hour of swimming, the three boys started competing to see who could hold his breath longest underwater. One of them later remembered James claiming that his record was over 4 minutes.

When it was his turn, James swam several pool lengths underwater, came up for several deep breaths, and then went under and stayed on the bottom. One of his friends became concerned and went under to check on him. James pushed him away, so his friend left him there. On the deck, they joked that James was just showing off, and they decided to ignore him.

After a time, they realized he had been underwater much too long, and a friend dove in and brought him to the surface, bluish and unconscious. One friend started CPR while the other called an ambulance, the ambulance personnel arrived and then took over the efforts to resuscitate James.

It was too late. His breathing and heart never started again. He had drowned.

His family and friends were shocked. No one thought that such a good swimmer in such good physical shape could be at risk for drowning. What they didn't realize was that staying safe in the water also means knowing and staying within your limits, regardless of what they are. James had pushed too far beyond his limits, and he became unconscious while underwater. He took a risk and lost.

SUMMARY

When you swim, you use various water skills. If you are a beginner, first get used to being in and moving in the water. Progress gradually from feeling comfortable in the water to bobbing, to gliding, to kicking, to sculling, and to surface support. You will become increasingly independent in the water as you develop the skills needed to be safe and to go on to learn swimming strokes. If you are a more advanced swimmer already, review these techniques to improve your own basic skills. As you begin to learn the strokes in the next chapter, you will see how these skills are even more useful.

9

Strokes

Your ability to swim efficiently not only helps you enjoy swimming but is an important safety skill as well. Learning to swim helps you be prepared for any activity in or around the water. Almost anyone can learn to swim, regardless of personal abilities. Even if you do not plan to swim regularly, knowing how to swim well is a valuable safety skill because you may end up in deep water even when you do not intend to be. Most drownings occur to people who fell into deep water unintentionally.

Research shows that a person in distress in the water uses up to 10 times the amount of energy he or she would normally use to swim a distance to safety. Most drownings also occur within 50 metres of the shore, dock, boat, or other safe area. Therefore you should learn to swim at least 500 metres in any stroke that is comfortable and effective for you. To be safe around the water, all Canadians should achieve this standard.

Throughout history, swimmers have developed many strokes to improve their speed and mobility in the water. Although new developments still occur, swimming research continues to focus on improving the basic swimming strokes that have endured over time. The science of stroke mechanics has led to more efficient ways to propel ourselves through the water.

This chapter describes the six basic swimming strokes. Most of the illustrations used show competitive swimmers, and the descriptions of movements are precise, as one would use in competitive swimming. You don't need to duplicate exactly what you see here to use these strokes for recreational and fitness swimming. No two people swim exactly the same, and most people end up with two or three preferred strokes with which they are most comfortable.

All strokes have three characteristics:

- The goal is efficiency of motion.

- The stroke depends on principles of hydrodynamics.

- Stroke components, such as body position, arm and leg action, and breathing, are critical for success.

All strokes are "feel strokes" in that the more you "feel" the water, the better you swim. You feel the resistance from lift forces (propeller propulsion) and action-reaction forces (paddle propulsion) of your arms and legs.

Recovery is the stage of the stroke when the arms and/or legs relax and return to the starting position.

*The **catch** is the stage in a stroke when the swimmer first engages the water in a way to start moving, the start of the power phase.*

*The **power phase** is the stage when the arm or leg stroke is moving the body in the desired direction.*

The six basic strokes are the front crawl, the elementary backstroke, the breaststroke, the sidestroke, the back crawl, and the butterfly. Each stroke is described in simple terms for the beginner but in enough detail also for an experienced swimmer to benefit. Each stroke is described in the same way, with an analysis of the different movements that make up each:

- Body position/motion
- Arm stroke
- Kick
- Breathing and timing
- One or two hydrodynamic principles involved in the stroke

This chapter is designed to help you improve your strokes. Whether you swim for leisure or competition, propelling yourself easily and efficiently through the water is one of your goals. Thus this chapter focuses on how to do strokes efficiently. To understand the scientific principles involved in the strokes described here, first read Chapter 6, The Science of Swimming. Because your size, strength, body composition, and flexibility all influence how you perform your strokes, there is no one "perfect" way to swim a stroke. You can adjust the basics you will learn here for yourself.

Obviously, one can learn only so much from a book. When you've read and thought about the movements described here, get in the water and try them out! You might then come back to the book and study these strokes more carefully. Then keep practicing in the water. A water safety course under the expert guidance of a Red Cross Water Safety Instructor will help you progress through all strokes and provide you with useful learning tips.

Front Crawl

The front crawl, sometimes called freestyle, is for most people the fastest stroke. Many people learn this stroke first.

Body Position/Motion

In the front crawl, you keep your body prone (face down) and straight. The front crawl uses much body roll. Body roll helps you use a relaxed and high elbow recovery and improves arm propulsion. Body roll helps you keep good lateral body position (your position in relation to the midline) and helps you breathe rhythmically and keep an overall rhythm in your stroke.

Head movement also is critical. As is commonly said, "Where the head goes, the body follows." If your head moves from side to side, as often happens if you move it improperly for breathing, your body will move sideways. If your head bobs up and down, your hips will do the same. In both cases, the resulting body motion slows you down. Most swimmers keep the waterline between the eyebrows and hairline, depending on their bouyancy.

Finally, help yourself maintain a good body position with your legs. Poor body position can cause a poor kick, and a poor kick can cause poor body position. With an effective kick, your heels just break the surface of the water. Your legs roll with the rest of your body.

Arm Stroke Power Phase

To begin the power phase of the stroke, bring your hand into the water in front of your shoulder, index finger first. With the elbow partly flexed, the hand enters about three-fourths as far as you could reach forward with your arm straight. Use a smooth entry, with your elbow higher than the rest of your arm and entering the water last. Think of it as your forearm going through a hole that your hand makes in the water's surface.

Angle your hand out and down as you extend your arm fully under water to start the catch. (It is called the catch because you feel as if you've grabbed a semi-solid mass of water.)

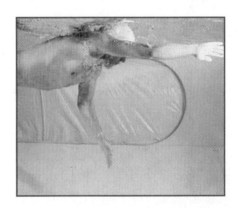

As seen from below, trace an S-shaped pattern in the power phase. Start the power phase with the catch. With arm extended and wrist slightly flexed, sweep your hand down and slightly out to just outside the shoulder (the top of the S shape). Keep your elbow higher than your hand throughout the pull. (The catch feels like a natural motion to make to move forward. It happens naturally if your hand is pitched well and you let your shoulder roll. You will feel tension in your wrist and pressure on your palm. This part of the power phase is dominated by lift forces.)

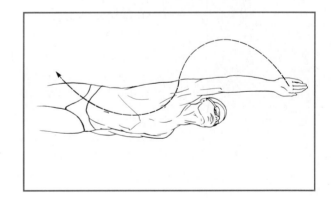

Continuing the power phase, bend your elbow to a maximum of 90 degrees and sweep your hand and arm back toward your feet and up toward your chest. (This is the diagonal part of the S-shape.) Do not let your hand cross the midline of your body. Pitch your hand in instead of out and keep your wrist nearly flat. Move your arm and hand from the deepest point of the stroke (at the end of the catch) to the shallower mid-pull phase. (The sweep of your hand from deep to shallow produces lift forces. The press of your arm and hand against the water in the backward direction produces propulsion with action-reaction forces.)

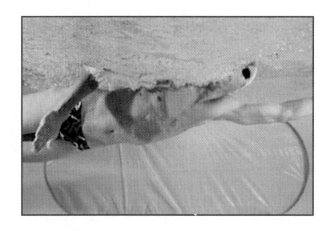

In the finish of the stroke, straighten your arm and press your hand straight back toward your feet while moving it to the side of your body. (This is the bottom of the S-shape, which is not as broad as the top.) Extend your wrist (bend it back) to keep your palm pressing toward your feet. Keep this pull going to the full extent of your reach, until your thumb brushes your thigh. (Your hand has accelerated from the catch through the finish of the stroke and is at its highest speed. The finish is dominated by action-reaction forces, which create the greatest acceleration.)

Recovery

The recovery does not propel you, but it does put your hand in a position to pull again. The recovery should be relaxed, letting the muscles rest. If you don't let your arm, hand, and fingers relax briefly in the recovery, you'll tire more quickly. Make a smooth transition from the finish of the power phase to the beginning of the recovery.

Lift your elbow high out of the water. Turn your palm toward your leg so that your hand exits the water little finger first.

Keep your body roll at a maximum. Lift your elbow high and relax your arm with your forearm hanging down.

As your hand passes your shoulder, let it lead the rest of your arm until it enters the water. At this point your arms are not completely opposite each other. Instead, the recovering arm starts to catch up with the stroking arm.

Body roll is a rotating movement around an imaginary midline from head to feet dividing the body into left and right halves. With it, the whole body rotates, not just the shoulders, making arm recovery easier.

Kick

The way you hold your ankles is important in the flutter kick used with the front crawl. They must be relaxed and "floppy" to be effective. Even if you move your legs perfectly, the kick will be ineffective if your ankles are stiff (with toes pointed) or flexed. With loose and relaxed ankles, the kick will be effective. You can use different cadences or "beats" in the front crawl. The number of beats is measured by the number of kicks per arm cycle: from the time one arm starts to pull on one stroke to the time it starts to pull on the next stroke. Cadences vary from a six-beat kick to a two-beat kick. No one way is best. Different cadences are used at different times and at different speeds. Usually more beats are used for shorter distances, fewer for a longer swim. The kick should have a rhythm corresponding to the arm stroke, however, and most swimmers fall into a cadence that suits them.

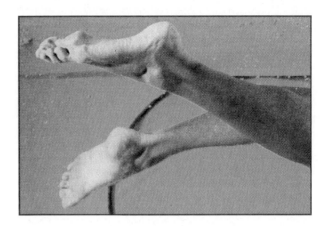

The power part of the kick is the downbeat. Start the motion at the hip, moving your thigh downward even while your calf and foot are still moving upward. For most of the downbeat, keep your knee slightly flexed.

Straighten your leg to give the propulsive force. Continue this motion through the whole leg, and follow through with the feet. Turn the feet slightly inward (pigeon-toed). Snap your foot downward, completing the motion as though you were kicking a ball.

In the upbeat (recovery), raise your leg straight toward the surface with little or no flexion in your knee, until your heel just breaks the surface. Keep your leg straight in the recovery. Flex your knee for most of the power phase, but extend it forcefully at the end of the kick.

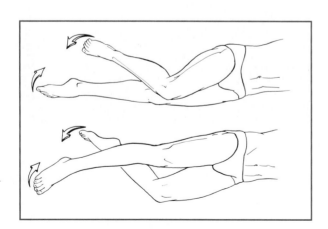

Generally, do not move your leg up and down too much. Depending on how tall you are, move only 30 to 37 cm.

Breathing and Timing

Most swimmers breathe each arm cycle (eg., each time their right arm recovers) or every 1¹/₂ arm cycles (alternating the side on which they breathe, often called bilateral breathing). Either method can work for you, although most people learn this stroke by breathing every cycle. Coordinate your breathing so that you do not pause in the stroke to breathe. You can practice your breath control with bobbing exercises. You do not need to inhale a large amount of air with each breath because the next breath is coming soon.

Start turning your head to the side as that arm starts its pull. Your mouth clears the water at the end of the pull, and you inhale just as the recovery starts. Body roll makes it easier to turn your head to the side. Look to the side and slightly back, keeping your forehead slightly higher than your chin. The opposite ear stays in the water. In this way you breathe in a trough made by your head as it moves through the water.

After inhaling, return your face to the water.

Good head motion for breathing helps you keep your head low in the water for good body position. Return your face to the water as you move your arm forward. Exhale slowly through your mouth and nose between breaths. Exhale completely under water so you are ready to inhale at the next breath.

FRONT CRAWL Arm Stroke Sequence

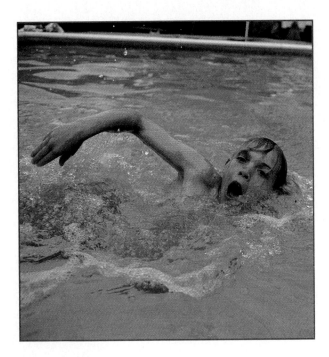

Hydrodynamic Principles Involved

Almost all hydrodynamic principles are involved in the front crawl, but two stand out. First, the lift propulsion of sweeping arm motions is more important than pushing arm motions, which use action-reaction forces.

Second, be sure to keep your body aligned in this stroke because of Newton's laws of inertia and acceleration. Proper body alignment makes strokes much more efficient. Any sideways movement of parts of the body away from the midline increases the resistance of the water. The body position caused by holding your head too high is also ineffective because it increases frontal resistance (form drag). In either case you expend energy to correct your body position instead of using it to propel yourself forward.

Efficient Front Crawl

BODY POSITION

☐ Keep body prone and straight

☐ Rotate whole body with arm movements

☐ Keep the head from bobbing or moving laterally

ARMS

☐ Keep elbow high upon water entry

☐ Use S-shape pattern during the power phase

☐ Relax arm, hand, and fingers during recovery phase

KICK

☐ Relax ankles during the power phase

☐ Move legs from slightly bent to straight during power phase

☐ Keep legs straight during recovery

BREATHING

☐ Do not pause to breath

☐ Breathe with body roll keeping one ear in the water

☐ Complete the exhale under water

Elementary Backstroke

The elementary backstroke is used for recreation, for survival swimming, and for exercising muscle groups not used in other strokes. You can also use this stroke to recover from strenuous effort while still making slow but effective progress through the water. Breathing is easy because your face stays out of the water.

Body Position/Motion

This stroke uses symmetrical and simultaneous movements of the arms and legs.

Most swimmers keep their head submerged to the ears only, with the face always out of the water. Keep your back almost straight, with hips and legs slightly lower than head and shoulders. Extend your arms along the body with palms against the thighs, with legs fully extended and together. The hips stay near the surface at all times in this stroke.

Arm Stroke Recovery

Begin the recovery gliding with your body in a streamlined, supine (face up) position. Move your arms continuously and smoothly.

From the glide position, recover your arms by bending your elbows so your hands, palms down or in, slide along your sides to near your armpits.

Power Phase

Point your fingers outward from your shoulders with palms facing back toward your feet. With fingers leading, extend your arms out to the sides until your hands are no farther forward than the top of your head. Imagine a clock with your head at 12:00 and your feet at 6:00; your hands should extend no farther than 10:00 and 2:00.

Without pause, press your palms and the insides of your arms, at the same time and in a broad sweeping motion, back toward your feet. Keep your arms straight or slightly bent in the propulsive phase. Keep your arms and hands just below the surface throughout the power phase. End this motion with arms and hands in the glide position.

Kick

In the kick for the elementary backstroke, bend both legs at the knee and move them around in a kind of circular whipping action. Thus this kick is called the "whip kick." Kick in a continuous and smooth movement, without a pause between the recovery and the power phase.

In the glide position keep the legs together and straight, toes pointed.

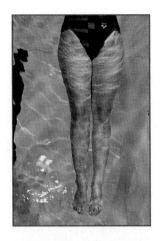

Recover your legs by bending and slightly separating your knees and drawing your heels downward to a point under and outside your knees. Spread your knees as wide as your hips or slightly wider. Recover your legs in an easy, rhythmical motion, keeping back, hips, and thighs nearly straight. At the end of the recovery, rotate your knees inward slightly while flexing your ankles and rotating your feet outward.

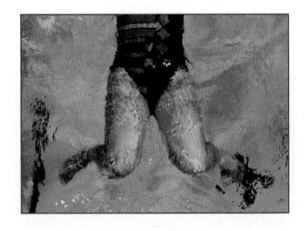

Start the propulsive action by pressing your feet backward with a slightly rounded motion, ending with legs in the glide position. In this action, move your feet into a pointed position. Start the pressing action of this kick slowly and speed up to completion where the feet touch.

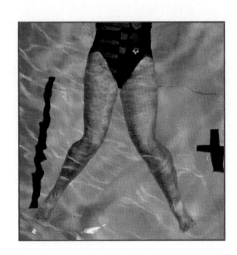

Breathing and Timing

Breathe during each arm stroke. Since your face is always out of the water, breathing is very easy.

Exhale as you move your arms and legs through the power phase. (Exhaling in the power phase keeps water from entering your nose during the forceful part of the stroke.) Remember to relax and to slowly exhale throughout the arm action.

Glide with your body streamlined. Start the next stroke as your momentum slows, before coming to a complete stop.

Start to recover your arms just ahead of your legs. However, because of their shorter movement and greater strength, the legs finish their thrust at the same time as the arms.

ELEMENTARY BACKSTROKE Kick Sequence

A

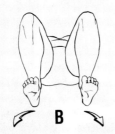

B

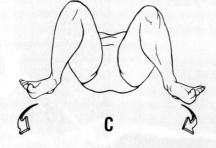

C

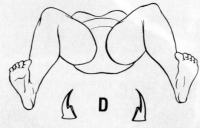

D

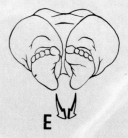

E

Hydrodynamic Principles Involved

The most obvious feature of the elementary backstroke is how the arms function as levers. The resistance on the whole surface of the arms and hands is overcome by the muscles rotating the arm at the shoulder, using action-reaction propulson to power the body forward. You also use leverage when you extend the knees and when you move the ankles from flexed to toes pointed.

Efficient Elementary Backstroke

BODY POSITION

☐ Keep back straight with face out of water

ARMS

☐ Keep arms and hands below the level of the water

☐ Extend arms (bent or straight) from the "10 to 2" clockface position to the glide position

KICK

☐ Recover legs by bending knees spaced slightly apart

☐ Rotate legs and squeeze them together into the glide position

TIMING

☐ Start moving arms out of the glide position first, but return arms and legs to the glide position together

Breaststroke

The breaststroke is the oldest known swimming stroke. For many centuries it was the first stroke beginners learned. It is one of four competitive strokes, but it is also very popular for leisure swimming because you can keep your head up to see around you and breathe easily, and because you can rest momentarily between strokes. You can use it for survival swimming and in modified form in some lifesaving situations.

Body Position/Motion

In this stroke, the arms and legs move symmetrically. In the glide, your body is flat, prone, and streamlined, with legs together and extended. Extend your arms in front of your head. Keep your palms down and 15 to 20 cm below the surface. Position your head with the water line near your hairline. Keep your back straight and your body nearly horizontal, with hips and legs just below the surface.

The stroke uses a rocking action that comes from lifting your hips as you extend your hands in front and then lifting your upper body as your hands finish and start to recover. The final lift from the kick adds to this rocking action.

Arm Stroke

From the glide position, angle your hands slightly downward and turn your palms outward at 45 degrees to the surface of the water. With your arms straight, press your palms directly out until your hands are wider apart than your shoulders.

From this catch position, bend your elbows and sweep your hands downward and outward until they pass under your elbows with forearms vertical.

Rotate your wrists and sweep your hands inward, upward, and back slightly toward your feet.

Move your arms until your palms are below the chin, facing each other and almost touching. Throughout the power phase, keep your elbows higher than your hands and lower than your shoulders. Point your elbows outward, not backward, and do not pass them back beyond your shoulders.

Start to recover your arms immediately after the power phase. After you sweep your hands in together, keep squeezing your elbows toward each other. Then, with palms angled toward each other, extend your arms forward to a glide position below the surface and rotate your wrists until your hands are palms down.

Kick Recovery

The kick is like the whip kick used in the elementary backstroke. From the glide position, start to recover your legs by bending slightly at your hips and knees and bringing your heels up toward your buttocks.

With that action, gradually separate your knees and heels until your knees are hip-width apart and your feet are outside your knees. Keep your heels just under the surface. At the end of the recovery, flex and rotate your ankles outward to engage the water with your soles when you start the propulsive action.

Draw your feet as far forward as you can for strongest propulsion without upsetting good body position. (The ideal distances between the knees and between the heels and buttocks at the end of the recovery vary among swimmers.)

Power Phase

With a continuous whipping action, press your feet outward and backward until your feet and ankles touch. Extend your ankles and lift your legs and feet slightly. Start the pressing action slowly, and speed up to the completion of the kick. (Lift forces on your feet moving outward give some forward propulsion. The pressing action also gives your feet some momentum for their thrust backward. Propulsion results from the pressure of the water against the soles of your feet and the insides of your feet and lower legs.)

Breathing and Timing

As your arms and hands start to pull backward, start lifting your head to breathe. Near the end of the arm pull, with your jaw jutting forward, your mouth just clears the water and you inhale. As your arms start to recover, lower your face into the water. Exhale in a slow, steady manner, mostly through your mouth, from the arm recovery until just before the next arm pull. At that point, explosively exhale the last of your breath and start lifting your head for the next breath. Breathe during each armstroke.

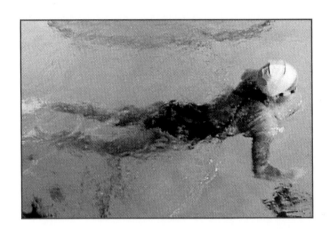

From the glide position, start the propulsive phase with your arms.

Near the end of the arm pull, take a breath and start to recover your legs.

Without pause, put your face in the water, start to recover your arms, and start the kick with your feet positioned properly.

Reach about two thirds of arm extension forward when you start to press backward with your feet. Reach full arm extension just before your kick ends. Glide briefly and start the next stroke before losing forward momentum. Remember the timing of this stroke with the phrase, "Pull and breathe, kick and glide."

BREASTSTROKE SEQUENCE

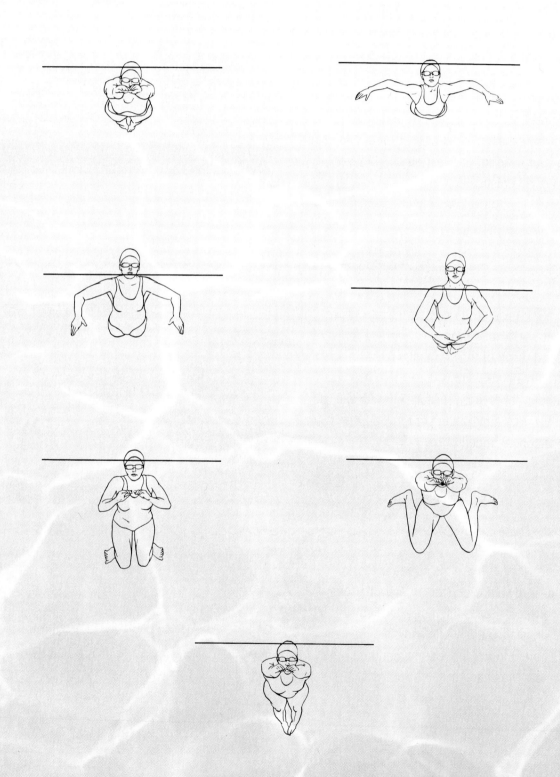

BREASTSTROKE Kick Sequence

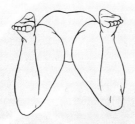

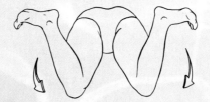

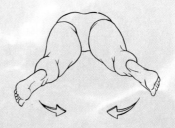

BREASTSTROKE Breathing and Timing Sequence

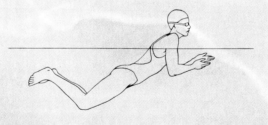

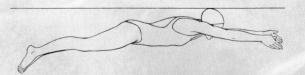

Hydrodynamic Principles Involved

Proper body alignment is important for all strokes. It is easier to keep aligned with the strokes that involve symmetrical movements (breaststroke, elementary backstroke, and butterfly) because of the law of acceleration. Because the arm and leg actions of both sides are performed together, forces that would otherwise push the body out of line are counteracted by the same forces from the other side of the body.

More than in any other stroke, the propulsive force of this stroke is almost all from lift.

Efficient Breaststroke

BODY POSITION

☐ Use a rocking motion during the stroke

☐ Keep the glide prone and streamlined

☐ Move arms and legs symmetrically

ARMS

☐ Keep elbows higher than hands and lower than shoulders during the power phase

☐ Do not pass the arms back beyond the shoulders

☐ Squeeze the hands together

KICK

☐ Rotate and squeeze legs together to glide position

☐ Recover legs by bending knees spaced slightly apart

BREATHING

☐ Position head with water near the hairline

☐ Exhale during arm power phase

☐ Let head enter water during recovery

SIDESTROKE

In the sidestroke, the body position reduces frontal resistance and lets the face and one ear stay out of the water. Propulsion comes mainly from the kick. The arms give some propulsion but mainly just stabilize the body in the side-lying position. The sidestroke is easy to learn because the breathing is simple. Because it is a resting stroke, it requires less energy than other strokes, and you can use it for long distances without tiring.

Body Position/Motion

In the glide, your body is nearly horizontal on its side. Keep your head, back, and legs in a straight line, your legs fully extended and together, and your toes pointed. Extend your leading arm (or bottom arm) in front of you, parallel to the surface, palm down and in line with your body, 15 to 20 cm below the surface of the water. Fully extend your trailing arm (or top arm) toward your feet, palm resting on top of the thigh. Your lower ear rests in the water close to your shoulder. Keep your face just high enough to keep your mouth and nose above the water for easy breathing. In general, you face out to the side, but you can occasionally glance to the front to see where you're going. Keep your head and back aligned throughout the stroke

Arm Stroke Leading Arm

In the power phase, use a shallow pull with your leading arm. Keep your hand about 20 cm deep. From the glide position, rotate your leading arm slightly to put your palm down and angled slightly outward (the way you are facing).

From this catch position, bend your elbow and sweep your hand downward slightly and then back toward your feet, until your hand almost reaches your upper chest.

Without pausing after the power phase, recover your leading arm by rotating the shoulder and dropping the elbow. Pass your hand under your ear until your fingers point forward.

Thrust your leading arm forward, rotating it palm down for the glide position.

Trailing Arm

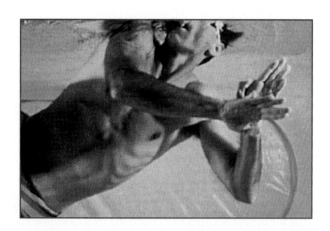

During the power phase of the leading arm, recover your trailing arm by drawing your forearm along your body until your hand is nearly in front of the shoulder of your leading arm. Keep the palm down and angled slightly forward. (This creates lift to help keep your face above water.)

In the power phase, sweep your trailing hand downward slightly and then backward close to your body to the glide position.

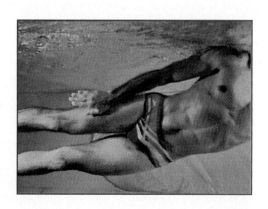

Start this phase with your wrist flexed but finish with it extended, so that your palm is always toward your feet.

Kick

The sidestroke uses the scissor kick. When done well, this kick is propulsive enough to give a good rest between strokes. In the kick, the legs move smoothly in a plane nearly parallel to the surface. Avoid rolling your hips forward and backward as you recover and kick. This kick and its alternate, the inverted scissor kick (in which the top leg moves backward), are also used for lifesaving carries, treading water, and underwater swimming.

From the glide position, recover your legs by flexing your hips and knees and drawing your heels slowly toward your buttocks. Keep your knees close together in this movement.

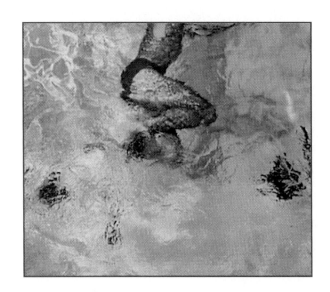

At the end of the recovery, to prepare for the kick, flex your top ankle and point the toes of your bottom foot.

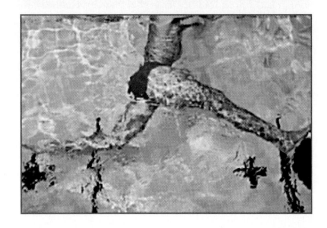

Move your legs to their catch positions, top leg toward the front of your body, bottom leg toward the back. When extended, your top leg is almost straight. When recovered, your bottom leg extends the thigh slightly to the rear of your trunk, with that knee flexed.

Without pause, press your top leg (which stays straight) backward while extending your bottom leg (like kicking a ball), until both legs are fully extended and together in the glide position. Push the water with the bottom of your top foot and the top of your bottom foot. As you move your top foot backward, move that ankle from a flexed position to a toes-pointed position to let the sole of the foot press with greatest pressure against the water. Do not let your feet pass each other at the end of the kick. Keep your toes pointed in the glide to reduce drag.

Inverted Scissor Kick

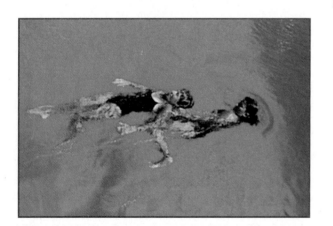

This kick is identical to the scissor kick, except that it reverses the top and bottom leg actions. Move the top leg (with toes pointed) toward the rear of the body and the bottom leg (with ankle flexed) toward the front of the body. This kick is often used during water rescue.

Breathing and Timing

Breathe with each stroke. Inhale through the mouth while you recover your trailing arm, and exhale in the power phase of your trailing arm.

From the glide position, start the stroke with the sweep of your leading arm. Then recover your trailing arm and your legs.

Initiate the power phase of your kick and trailing arm as your leading arm recovers.

Fully extend your arms and legs when you complete the kick and arm stroke. Glide until your momentum slows. (Remember not to glide too long, since it takes more energy to stop and start than to keep moving.)

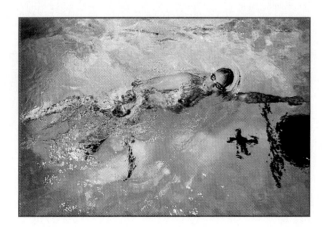

SIDESTROKE Arm and Leg Stroke Sequence

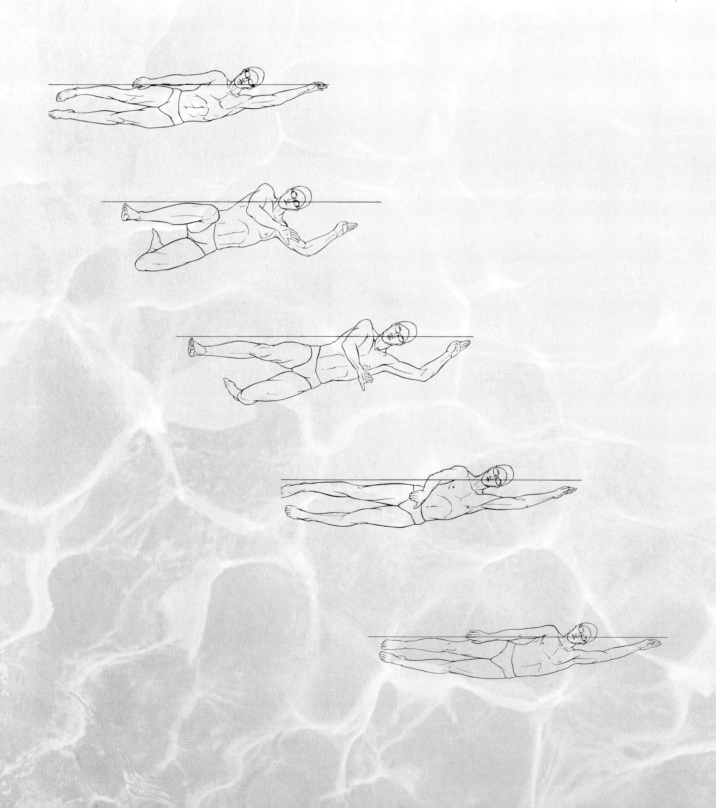

Hydrodynamic Principles Involved

The sidestroke was developed from the breast-stroke to reduce form drag. Two principles are important for this stroke. Your smaller profile moving through the water, with part of your head and one shoulder out of the water, reduces the water resistance.

Second, remember the relationship between dynamic inertia and static inertia. If you glide too long and lose almost all of your dynamic inertia, your stroke loses efficiency because of the effort needed to start moving again. This principle is important for all strokes with a glide.

Efficient Sidestroke

BODY POSITION

☐ Fully extend body during the glide

☐ Keep head and back aligned during the stroke

☐ Stay nearly horizontal on the side

ARMS

☐ Have hands meet near the chin

☐ Sweep the trailing arm from chin to side during power phase

KICK

☐ Move top leg forward, bottom leg back (alternate position: top leg back, bottom leg forward is acceptable).

☐ Keep legs fully extended during the glide

☐ Squeeze legs together to create the power

TIMING

☐ Start arms and legs moving together

☐ Finish moving arms and legs at the same time

Back Crawl

The body position of the back crawl generally allows unobstructed breathing and clear vision above the water. It is one of the four competitive strokes and is the fastest stroke on the back. It is often called the backstroke.

Body Position/Motion

In the back crawl, lie on your back in a flat, streamlined, horizontal position. As in the front crawl, use a lot of body roll. Keep your head still and aligned with your spine. Because your face is out of the water, you do not have to roll your head to breathe. For most swimmers, the water line runs from the middle of the top of the head to the tip of the chin, with the ears under water. The best head position depends on your proficiency, speed through the water, body composition, and buoyancy. Keep your back as straight as you can. Flex your hips slightly to let your feet churn the surface.

Except for differences of speed between the power phase and the recovery, each arm is generally opposite the other arm.

Arm Stroke

Move your arms continuously in constant opposition to each other; one arm recovers while the other arm pulls.

~~~~~~

The arm stroke in back crawl is called opposition rhythm and looks like a windmill.

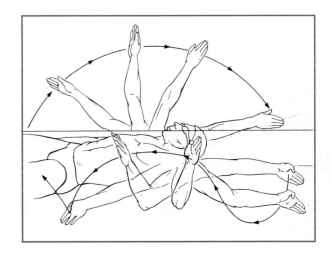

Power Phase

With the arm straight, enter the water with one hand just outside the shoulder, little finger first. Keep the palm to the outside and the wrist angled slightly down. Keep your body streamlined. With your head steady, roll your body to the side of your entry arm just before your hand enters the water. At the same time, lift the other arm toward the surface to start its recovery.

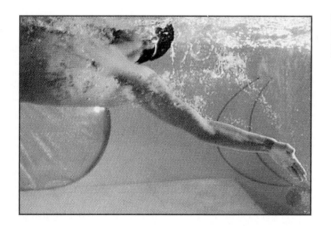

With your entry hand, slice downward 20 to 30 cm and slightly outward to the catch, where the propulsive action starts. Sweep your hand outward and downward as you start bending the elbow. (This elbow must point down toward the bottom of the pool for the same reason that it is held high in the front crawl. "Dropping" the elbow toward your feet and letting it lead the hand greatly reduces the propulsive forces.)

About one quarter through this sweep, start the mid-pull. Keep bending your elbow and rotate your wrist slightly so your hand presses upward and inward. Bend your elbow most (about 90 degrees) at the midpoint of this movement as your forearm is passing your chest.

For the finish of the power phase, speed up your hand as you sweep it downward and toward the feet, with wrist extended so your palm faces your feet. This phase ends with your arm straight and your hand below your thigh. (The finish gives propulsion and helps overcome the tendency of the body to sink from the weight of the recovering arm.)

Recovery

Start the recovery by lifting your arm from the water, shoulder first, palm inward. Relax your wrist so that your thumb and the back of your hand leave the water first. (This position of the arm when it leaves the water allows the large muscles on the back of your upper arm—the triceps—to relax more.)

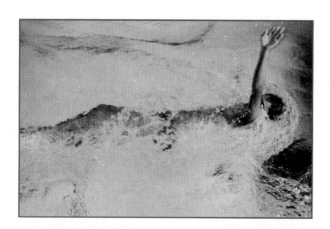

In the recovery, move your arm almost perpendicular to the water. Body roll makes this easier. Keep your arm straight but relaxed in the recovery.

Rotate your hand so the little finger enters the water first. Remember to rest your arm muscles in the recovery.

Kick

The kick is like the flutter kick as used in the front crawl but is a little deeper in the water. It is a continuous, alternating, up-and-down movement that starts from your hips. Keep the ankles loose and floppy, your feet slightly pigeon-toed, and your legs separated slightly so that your big toes just miss each other. Most of the propulsive force comes from the upward kick, which is like punting a football with the tip of your foot. The downward movement of the sole of your foot against the water also helps propel you. The kick also helps stabilize you by counteracting the motion of your arms and the rolling of your body.

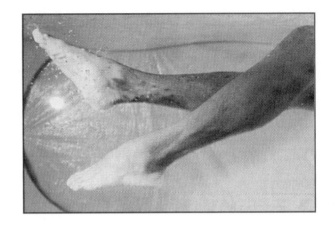

At the start of the upward kick, flex your knee to gain the most propulsion from the upper surface of your lower leg and foot.

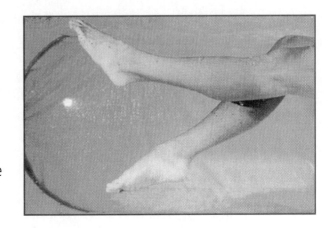

Bring your thigh and knee near the surface, but keep whipping your foot upward until your leg is straight and your toes reach the surface. Keep your leg nearly straight in the downward kick. At the end of the downward movement, bend your knee and start your upward kick. Your thighs should pass each other, and your knees should stay relaxed. The depth of your own kick depends on the length of your legs, your hip and ankle flexibility, your pace with the stroke, and the amount of body roll. (Remember that, if you kick too deep, the greater form drag will cancel out the kick's added propulsion.)

Breathing and Timing

Use a regular breathing pattern during each stroke. Inhale when one arm recovers and exhale when the other arm recovers.

Start your body roll to the side of your entry arm as it starts to enter the water. Your body continues to roll as the entry hand reaches the catch and the other arm lifts toward the surface to start its recovery. (The propulsive action of one arm and the recovery of the other arm start at the same time. Keep an opposition rhythm.)

This stroke uses a continuous kick. Although most swimmers use a six-beat kick for each full arm cycle, the beat is an individual matter. Find your own best timing by adjusting your stroke until it is smooth and effective.

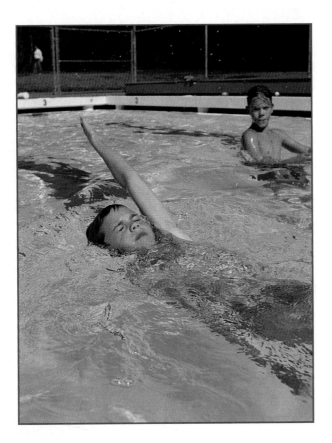

Hydrodynamic Principles Involved

The flutter kick in the back crawl, as in the front crawl, takes advantage of the conservation of momentum. The loose ankles in the upsweep and downsweep actually travel in circular patterns that efficiently maintain momentum. Holding the ankles stiff would force the feet to use an ineffective linear start-and-stop motion that has to overcome inertia with each kick.

Efficient Back Crawl

BODY POSITION

☐ Keep body prone and straight

☐ Keep head still and aligned with back

☐ Rotate whole body with arm movements

ARMS

☐ Move arms continuously

☐ Move arms in opposition

☐ Bend elbows during power phase

☐ Have little finger enter water first

KICK

☐ Keep ankles relaxed

☐ Flex knee during the power

☐ Keep leg nearly straight during downward action

☐ Kick continuously

TIMING

☐ Roll body with arm entry

☐ Use an opposition rhythm throughout the arm stroke

Butterfly

Many people think of the butterfly as a difficult stroke used only for competition. Thus many swimmers, even those good at other strokes, do not try to learn it. But even beginning swimmers can learn the butterfly stroke by practicing timing and technique. The key is relaxing and using your whole body in a flowing motion. This stroke gives you a rewarding feeling of power and grace.

Body Position/Motion

Leg and body motions give this stroke a unique dolphin-like feeling. In a prone position, the body moves in a constantly changing, wave motion in which it rolls forward through the water. The wave motion starts with the head and continues to the ends of the feet. The kick, breathing, and pull are very closely related. For this reason, body motion is described in the section on breathing and timing, after you understand how the kick and pull are done.

Arm Stroke Power Phase

The power phase of the butterfly arm stroke consists of the catch, the mid-pull, and the finish. The arm stroke is like that of the front crawl, except that the arms move together and the sweep out and in are exaggerated, tracing a pattern like a key hole. The press back is very much like that of the front crawl. The sweep in and out create lift forces, which give most of the propulsion of this stroke.

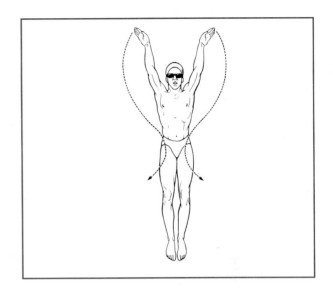

Start the catch, an outward sculling motion, with your arms extended in front of your shoulders. End the catch with your hands spread slightly wider than your shoulders. Flex your hands slightly down and pitch them to the outside in this phase.

In the mid-pull, continue the sculling action and sweep inward and backward from the end of the catch to a point near the midline of your body. Change the pitch of your hands from outward to inward. Start to bend your arms after the catch to a maximum of about 90 degrees at the finish of the arm pull.

As your arm reaches this maximum bend, have your hands very close together under your shoulders. As your hands sweep together, keep your elbows higher than your hands, as in the front crawl. (Action-reaction forces increase in this phase, but most of the propulsion still comes from lift.)

End the inward sweep of the hands and start a backward press toward your feet in the finish of the power phase.

Continue to press your hands back toward your feet, past your hips to near the sides of your thighs. As in the front crawl, speed up this motion from the start of the stroke to the finish, especially here at the end. (Action-reaction forces are dominant in the end of the power phase.)

Recovery

A relaxed arm recovery is important but takes more effort than in the front crawl because you can't roll your body to help and your arms stay nearly straight. The recovery is easier if you accelerate hard through the finish of the stroke and then lower your head as your arms recover.

Start the recovery as your hands finish their press toward your feet and your palms turn toward your thighs. Bring your elbows, slightly bent, out of the water first.

S wing your arms wide to the sides with little or no bend in your elbow.

M ove your arms just above the surface to enter in front of your shoulders. Keep your wrists relaxed and your thumbs down through the recovery.

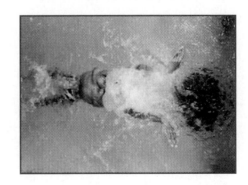

E nd the recovery with the entry. With your elbows still slightly flexed, your hands enter the water directly in front of or slightly outside of your shoulders. After the entry, extend your elbows to prepare for the next arm stroke. Pitch your hands out and down for the catch of the next stroke.

Kick

The power of the dolphin kick, the kick used in this stroke, comes from the same dynamics as the flutter kick. Use the same leg action as in the front and back crawl, but move both legs together in the dolphin kick. Start the kick at the hips and make the same whiplike motion as in the front crawl. Most of the power comes from the quick extension of the legs.

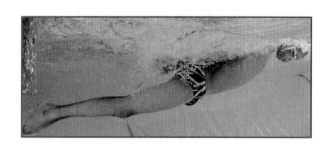

Bend the knees slightly through most of the downbeat and straighten them on the upbeat. Relax your ankles. Let your heels just break the surface at the end of the recovery.

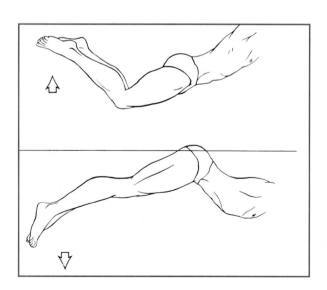

Compared to the front and back crawl, you use your hips much more, moving up and down in the stroke. (Raising your hips at the right time in the stroke makes the follow-through of the legs a natural continuation of the motion. Thus the dolphin kick involves your whole body, not just your legs.)

Breathing and Timing

The butterfly uses two kicks at specific moments in each arm stroke. With the right timing, this stroke is graceful and looks effortless. With the wrong timing, the stroke is very difficult. The timing of the butterfly depends on the relation of the kicks to the entry and finish of the arm stroke.

As you move your hands into the water to start the catch, raise your hips and start the downbeat of the first kick.

As you press your hands through the finish of the power phase, start the downbeat of the second kick.

End the second kick just as you finish the pull.

Inhale at the end of the second kick, before your arms start their recovery. To be ready, exhale fully during the underwater pull and raise your head as your hands press toward your hips.

Thrust your chin forward (not upward) as your face just clears the water.

As soon as you inhale and start your arm recovery, lower your head to return your face under water. Some swimmers learn to breathe only every two or more strokes to gain efficiency in the stroke.

Hydrodynamic Principles Involved

Many hydrodynamic principles make the butterfly work. Dynamic inertia is one of the important ones. The power of each stroke maintains the speed and momentum of the body. In the wave motion, the separate actions of the head, torso, hips, and legs each build on the dynamic inertia of the preceding part in forward progress. If the swimmer does not use this inertia well, the stroke becomes awkward or does not work at all.

Efficient Butterfly Stroke

BODY POSITION

☐ Move the body with a wave-like motion

ARMS

☐ Move arms together

☐ In the water, sweep arms out and then in

☐ Accelerate arm motion through end of power phase

☐ Relax arms in the recovery phase

KICK

☐ Keep legs together

☐ Move hips up and down with the stroke

☐ Quickly extend hips on the downbeat

TIMING

☐ Use two kicks per arm cycle

☐ Drop hips as head lifts

☐ Breathe as the arms start the recovery phase

UNDERWATER STROKES

Although no one stroke is always best for underwater swimming, a modified breaststroke is generally used. You can modify the breaststroke for underwater swimming in several ways. Use a breaststroke kick or flutter kick. Extend the arm pull backward to the thighs for a longer and stronger stroke. Another method is to use the arm pull and kick together followed by a glide with arms at the sides. If you cannot see very far in the water, shorten the arm pull or do not use it at all. Keep your arms stretched out in front to feel for obstructions.

To change direction or depth while swimming under water, raise or lower your head and reach your arms in the desired direction while pulling. Flexing or extending the hips directs the body up or down.

SUMMARY

We have come a long way since our ancestors found they could propel themselves safely through the water. New swimming techniques have been invented, improved, adapted, and sometimes abandoned. Swimmers, coaches, and researchers constantly examine new ways to swim. No doubt the continuing study of biomechanics, using the latest technology, will lead to faster and more efficient strokes in the years to come.

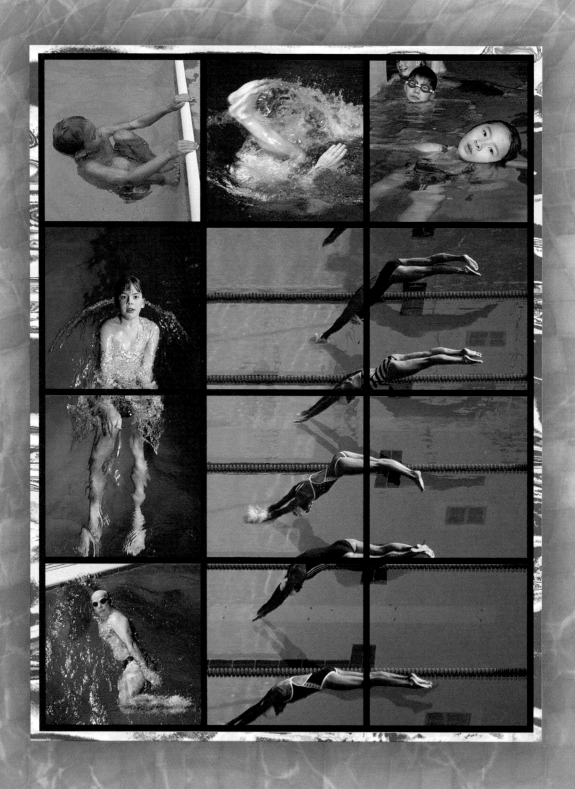

10

Starting and Turning

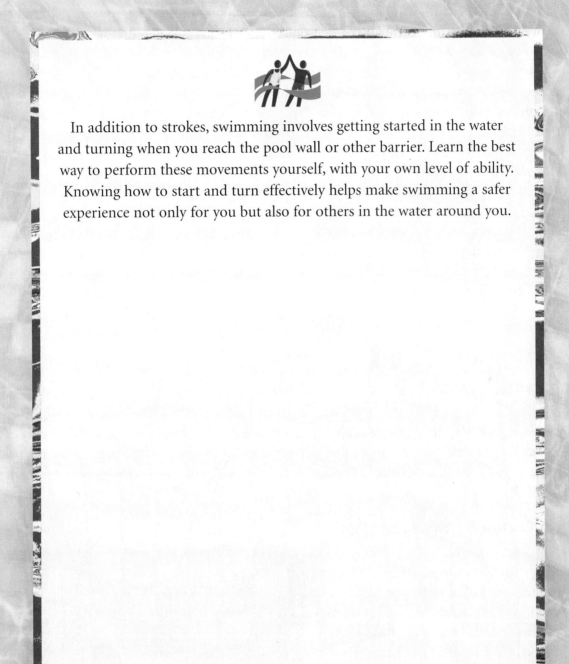

In addition to strokes, swimming involves getting started in the water and turning when you reach the pool wall or other barrier. Learn the best way to perform these movements yourself, with your own level of ability. Knowing how to start and turn effectively helps make swimming a safer experience not only for you but also for others in the water around you.

When you swim, you use various water skills. You begin by simply becoming familiar with being in and moving in the water. If you swim for recreation or fitness, you may want to learn how to swim more efficiently. If you swim competitively, you may want to learn techniques to swim faster. Most of us also want to improve our skills to have more fun. This chapter describes different ways to start your movement in the water and to turn when you reach the pool wall or other barrier. Knowing these moves also helps you become safer and more confident in the water. As you become more accomplished, you will begin take many of these skills for granted.

This chapter begins with basic ways to start and turn in the water that anyone can learn to use. The second half of the chapter focuses on the starts and turns used in competitive swimming (see page 191).

BASIC STARTS AND TURNS
Starting in the Water

When first learning strokes, most people prefer to start the stroke while already in the water. For an effective start, begin from a position at the pool wall.

Starting face down from pool edge or dock

To start face down, grasp the overflow of the pool wall or the pool side with one hand. If holding on with the left hand, rotate your body and lean forward slightly so that your right shoulder and arm are under the surface. Your hand should point in the direction you want to travel. Hold your feet together and place them against the pool wall, with the left foot closer to the surface (Figure 10-1). As you push off the wall with both feet, lift your left hand up and extend your arm above the head. As your left

arm extends, rotate your body face down and submerge so that both arms are under water and extended over your head. Interlock your thumbs or index fingers, or overlap your hands, to glide in a safe and streamlined manner. Glide until your momentum slows to your swimming speed, start your kick, and follow with your first arm stroke. You can use this technique for the front crawl, the butterfly, and the breaststroke. This start is better than just plunging forward in the water because it puts you in a streamlined position for starting the stroke. You can use this start regardless of the pool depth.

Starting face down from shallow water

Use the front glide to start from a standing position in open water or when you are not near poolside. Begin as you would for a prone float (see Chapter 8), but push off the bottom with your feet so you move forward in a face-down, streamlined position. Then begin your swimming stroke.

Starting on your side

To start a sidestroke, use the same body position as for face-down strokes, but do not rotate your body. Extend before you the arm closer to the bottom of the pool. Push off with both feet and

Figure 10-1. Starting face down from the wall.

rest your other arm against your thigh. Glide until your momentum slows and then start the sidestroke.

Starting on your back

To start swimming a back crawl, hold the pool wall with both hands about shoulder-width apart. Tuck your body and put your feet about hip-width apart against the wall just under the surface. Bend your arms slightly and put your chin on your chest (Figure 10-2, *A*). Pull your body closer to the wall, take a breath, and lean your head backward to slightly arch your body. Then, all in one motion, let go, bring your hands close to your body, reach your arms over your head with hands touching, and push strongly off the wall (Figure 10-2, *B*). Keep your body stretched and streamlined as it pushes into the water. As soon as your face submerges, tuck your chin slightly and start to lift your arms toward the surface. Glide just under or at the surface of the water until your momentum slows. Then start the flutter kick followed by the first arm pull.

For an elementary backstroke start, hold the pool wall as described in previous paragraphs for the back crawl. Push gently off the wall, floating on the surface with your hands at your side. Glide until your momentum slows. Then start the kick and arm movements together.

Starting out of the Water

The long shallow dive is a low-projecting dive done in a streamlined body position from the pool deck. You enter the water at a controlled, shallow angle with great forward momentum. It is used to dive in shallow areas and in rescues when speed is urgent. You should use this dive only in clear water of known depth. Do not try to learn this dive in shallow water, because you may go deeper than you intend. Once you learn it, also never dive in shallow water. Misjudging the depth or angle of your entry could lead to hitting the bottom and becoming seriously injured.

Before diving the first time, learn to enter the water head-first through a gradual progression of steps. These are described in Chapter 7, Entering the Water.

For the long shallow dive, start on the edge of the pool with your feet about shoulder-width apart and your toes gripping the edge. Flex your hips and knees, and crouch with your back nearly parallel to the pool deck. To gain momentum for the dive, start by drawing your arms backward and upward, letting the heels rise as your body starts to move forward (Figure 10-3, *A*). Immediately swing your arms down and forward. As you lose balance, push out with your hips, knees, ankles, and toes forcibly to dive out nearly horizontal over the water

A   B

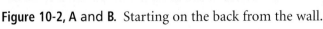
Figure 10-2, A and B. Starting on the back from the wall.

(Figure 10-3, *B*). Keep your body stretched and your hands interlocked and out in front of you.

During the flight, lower your head between your outstretched arms, which should be angled downward slightly (Figure 10-3, *C*). Enter the water at a shallow angle to avoid a painful flat landing. Once under water, steer upward toward the surface with your hands and head. Keep your body fully extended and streamlined as you glide. When your speed slows, start the leg kick to rise to the surface and start swimming.

Turning While Swimming

Being able to change directions while swimming is an important safety skill. When using the front crawl, reach an arm in the desired direction, look toward that arm, and pull slightly wider with the other arm in the new direction. To change directions while swimming on your back, tilt your head in the desired direction and stroke harder with the opposite arm.

Turns

Most people swimming for general fitness swim in pools. Since you usually swim back and forth, being able to turn easily at the wall is important. This chapter describes basic turn methods called open turns. Flip turns, used by more advanced swimmers, are described later.

Front crawl turn

As you approach the wall, reach out with your leading arm and grab onto the edge of the pool (Figure 10-4, *A*). Bend that elbow, drop the shoulder, and turn on your side (Figure 10-4, *B*). Tuck your legs up and rotate away from the wall until you are one your other side. Your trailing arm has now become your leading arm (pointing toward the opposite end of the pool), and your feet are against the wall, one above the other (Figure 10-4, *C*). (If the right hand is the leading hand, the right foot will be on top.) Take a breath with your head to the side and return your face to the water as you let go of the wall and your leading hand recovers over the surface (Figure 10-4, *C*). Keep both arms in front of you as your legs push off. Stay streamlined on one side. Rotate in the glide until you are face down. As you slow, start kicking to rise to the surface and start your arm stroke.

A

B

C

Figure 10-3, A to C. Starting with the long shallow dive.

A B C D

Figure 10-4, A to D. Open turn for the front crawl.

Sidestroke turn

For a sidestroke turn, vary the front crawl turn slightly. Touch the wall with your leading (bottom) arm, and do the whole turn as for the front crawl. In the glide, stay in the side-lying position from the push-off and pull your trailing arm to the thigh ready for the next stroke.

Breaststroke turn

As you come to the wall, reach to touch the wall with both hands (Figure 10-5, *A*). Tuck your legs into your body, turn your head in the chosen direction, and swivel your hips to bring your feet to the wall, one above the other. (With a spin to the right, your head turns right and your left foot is on top.) Push off with your hand to help the spinning action (in this case, the right hand), and raise the other hand over the surface toward the other end of the pool. Submerge your hands, arms, and head as you strongly push off the wall with your body in a side-lying position (Figure 10-5, *B*). This turn is deeper and the underwater glide longer than in the front crawl turn. Rotate your body face down, and glide with arms and legs outstretched until your speed slows. Do a full arm pull to your thighs, followed by a breaststroke kick and glide. Then raise your head and return to the surface and start your strokes.

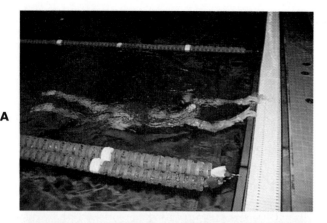

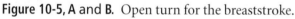

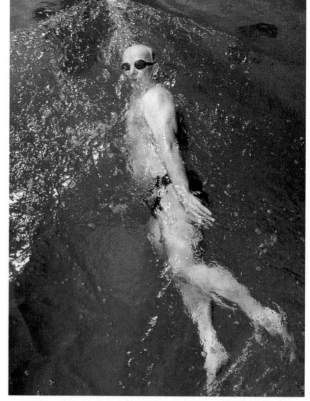

Figure 10-5, A and B. Open turn for the breaststroke.

Back crawl spin turn

With the elementary backstroke or back crawl, plan your approach to the wall by glancing backward. In some pools there are backstroke flags, or the lane lines change colour as you near the wall. Fully extend one arm behind your head and take a breath as your palm touches the wall (Figure 10-6, *A*). Bend the elbow of the leading arm and let your head come near the wall as you tuck your body and spin the hips and legs toward the wall (Figure 10-6, *B*). You can keep your head above water if you choose, although submerging it allows for a smoother turn. Sweep the trailing hand toward your head to spin faster, and put both feet on the wall, assuming a sitting position in the water.

Push off with the top of your head facing the other end of the pool. Breathe out slowly through your nose during the push-off to keep water from entering the nose. Fully extend your

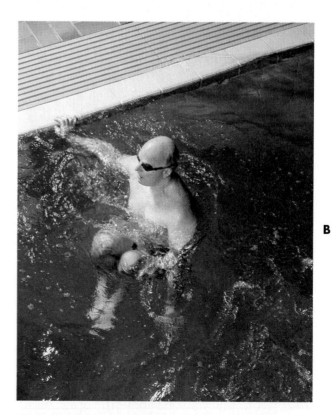

Figure 10-6, A to C. Back crawl spin turn.

Figure 10-6, A to C—cont'd.

arms over your head to be streamlined (Figure 10-6, *C*). As you lose speed, tuck your chin, angle your hands and arms slightly toward the surface, and start kicking. As you come to the surface, start the first arm pull.

COMPETITIVE STARTS AND TURNS

You can use the simple starts and turns described so far to start your strokes and turn around in a pool. However, if you want to swim laps more efficiently or swim competitively, use the more advanced starts and turns. You have probably seen other swimmers working out with fast, smooth flip turns. These turns take some practice but will help you improve your swimming skills.

If you are racing competitively, you must follow rules for starts and turns set by FINA. These rules are changed periodically, so check with race officials to find out what is current. Even a slight variance from the rules can lead to a race disqualification.

> A **starting block** is a platform from which competitive swimmers dive to start a race. A bar or handhold is usually attached for backstroke starts.

You need proper training and supervision when learning or practicing these starts and turns, or you may have the following problems:

- If you try to use a starting block without proper training, you face the risk of neck or head injury.
- Using a starting block not anchored securely or not over water that is deep can lead to injury.
- If you misjudge your distance from the wall, you could be hurt by swimming into the wall or by hitting your head in the backstroke.
- You may hit your heels on the wall during a flip turn.
- You might push off at the wrong angle and may hit the bottom of the pool or other swimmers.
- Because these skills can be very tiring and require more strength and stamina than the basic starts and turns, you might experience disorientation or fatigue or swallow or breathe in water.

THE GRAB START

Most swimmers think the grab start is the fastest start for competition, for all strokes but the backstroke. Before trying the grab start, you must be able to do a long shallow dive safely.

*The **grab start** is a competitive start often used from starting blocks for the fastest takeoff.*

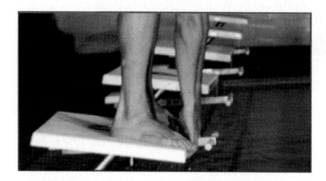

To position for the start, curl your toes around the starting block with your feet about shoulder width apart.

Grasp the front edge of the starting block. Put your hands either inside or outside your feet, whichever feels more comfortable. Lower your head and bend your knees slightly.

Pull against the starting block and bend your knees more, so your body starts moving forward. Look forward, release the block, and quickly extend your arms forward to lead your body's flight; at the same time, bend your knees still further and then push off by driving your feet against the block and forcefully extending your hips, knees, and ankles.

As your feet leave the block, focus your eyes on and aim your arms and hands at the entry point.

Just before hitting the water, lock your head between your arms and enter smoothly, as if going through a hole in the water.

Once in the water, start to angle your hands up toward the surface to decrease your downward motion.

Glide in a streamlined position, hands out in front, until you start to slow. For the front crawl, start your kick and follow immediately with your first arm pull. Do not take a breath until you finish your first arm cycle.

For the breaststroke, do a full arm pull to your thighs, followed by a breaststroke kick and glide. Then raise your head and return to the surface and start your strokes.

BACKSTROKE START

To get in position for the backstroke start, grasp the starting block with both
hands and put your feet parallel on the wall. Move your feet a comfortable
distance apart.

Bend your arms and pull your body up and out
of the water into a crouched position. Bring
your head close to your knees and tuck your body
as much as possible.

Thow your head back and push your arms out
and around with palms outward.

Push forcefully with your legs as you arch your
back and drive your body, hands first, up and
out over the water.

Tip your head back and look toward your entry
point.

Your whole body should enter smoothly through a single point in the water.

Once in the water, adjust the angle of your hands for a good glide. When you start to slow down, kick and use your first arm pull to come to the surface. Then start stroking.

Alternative: Many swimmers prefer to do several quick dolphin kicks after the start and after each turn instead of the flutter kick. If you have a strong dolphin kick, you may want to try this.

FRONT CRAWL FLIP TURN

The flip turn is usually used in competition for the front crawl.

*A **flip turn** is a fast and efficient turn done in a tuck position, used in lap swimming and in the freestyle and backstroke events in competition.*

Watch the bottom markings to help judge your distance from the wall. When you are one stroke from the wall (1 to 1 $^1/_3$ metres, keep your trailing arm at your side while you take the last stroke with your lead arm.

Keep both hands at your thighs. With both arms straight, turn your hands palms down and use a dolphin kick to push your hips forward and upward.

Drive your head downward and go into a tuck position so your body does a somersault. During the somersault, flex both elbows so your palms push toward your head; this helps complete the rotation.

Plant your feet on the wall with your toes pointed up or slightly to the side and your knees bent.

Push off in a face-up or side-lying position. (Some swimmers prefer to rotate into a side-lying position as they plant their feet on the wall, but the push-off on the back is generally considered to be the faster method of turning.)

Rotate to a face-down position in the glide. Your initial speed when you push off is faster than your swimming speed. When you slow to swimming speed, take one or two kicks and resume the arm stroke.

FLIP TURN SEQUENCE

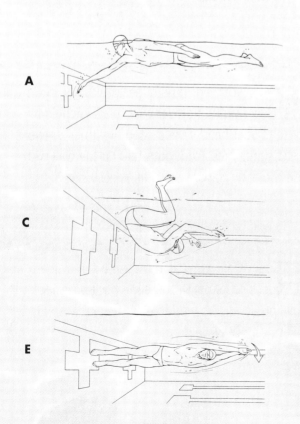

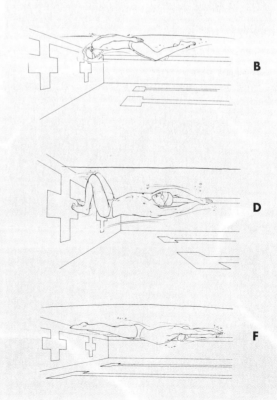

A

B

C

D

E

F

SPEED TURNS FOR BREASTSTROKE AND BUTTERFLY

The turns used for the breaststroke and butterfly are faster variations of the open turns described earlier.

Time your last stroke so that you are fully stretched as you reach the wall. As both hands reach to touch the wall, dip the shoulder on the side to which you will turn. (The example used here starts with dipping the left shoulder to turn left.) Touch the wall with both hands and tuck your hips and legs tight as they continue to move toward the wall.

As your hands touch the wall, move your head away from the wall, bend your left elbow, and move your left arm backward as close as possible to your body.

When your legs pass under your body, move your right arm over your head, keeping it close to your head. Take a deep breath before your head submerges. Plant both feet on the wall with toes pointing toward the side, knees bent.

Extend your arms as you push off in a side-lying position. Rotate to a prone position while gliding about $1/3$ metre below the surface. This helps reduce wave drag.

Breaststroke Push-Off

Push off slightly downward for a longer glide.

When you slow down, take a complete underwater breaststroke pull to the thighs, and glide again.

Then kick upward as your hands recover close to the body. This brings you to the surface to resume stroking. The underwater pull for breaststroke differs from the usual pull because you pull all the way past the hips and recover the hands close to the body.

Butterfly Push-Off

After the turn, glide a short distance, and then dolphin kick to the surface and start stroking.

BREASTSTROKE Turn and Underwater Pull Sequence

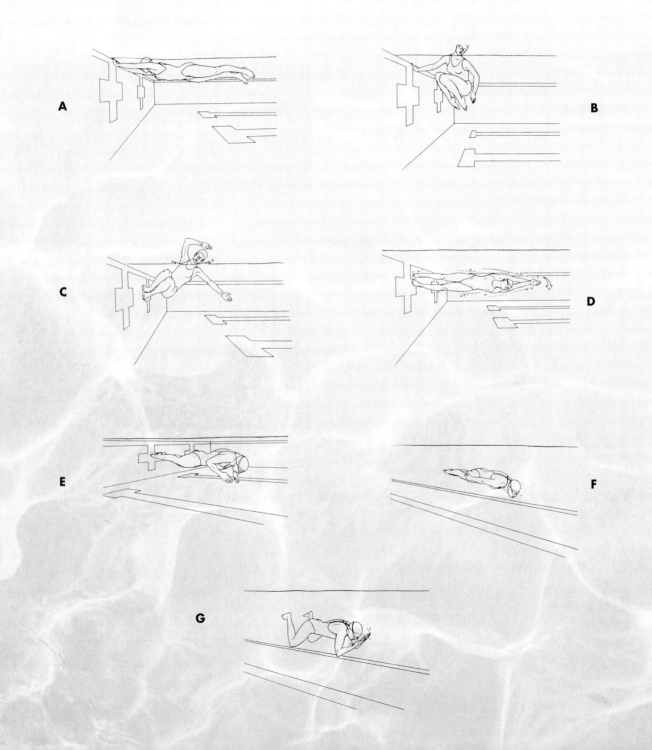

BACKSTROKE FLIP TURN

Rules for the competitive backstroke turn now allow a swimmer to touch the wall with any part of the body. (Previously a hand touch was required.) During the turn, the shoulders may turn past vertical as long as the motion is part of a continuous turning action. You must return to a position on the back before yout feet leave the wall. Properly done, this turn may improve your swim time by as much as one-half second per turn.

Your motion in the turn must be continuous. Any hesitation, dolphin kicks, or extra strokes after turning onto your stomach may disqualify you in a competition.

After you pass the backstroke flags, accelerate toward the wall. Start the flip one stroke from the wall by turning your head and looking toward your pulling arm as it does the catch.

As you pull, rotate onto your stomach, drive your head downward, and stop your pulling hand at your hips. At the same time, your other arm recovers across your body, enters the water in the same position as in the front crawl, and pulls to the hips.

Drive your head down and start the somersault while tucking your knees tightly to your chest. During the somersault, turn both palms up and sweep them toward your head to complete the flip.

Keep your legs tightly tucked until your feet contact the wall, toes pointed upward.

While still on your back, push straight off forcefully and go into a streamlined position as you leave the wall.

BACKSTROKE Flip Turn Sequence

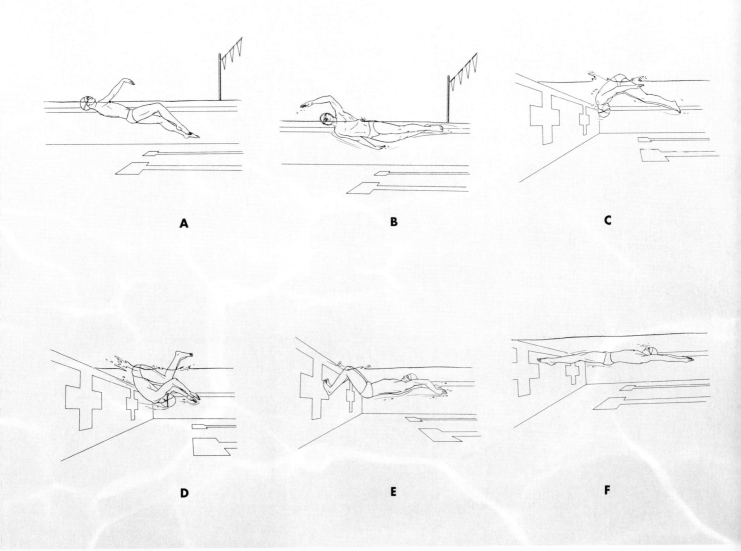

A

B

C

D

E

F

SUMMARY

You do not have to learn all the skills in this chapter now. As you develop as a swimmer, your goals change. If you do fitness swimming, for example, learning more efficient turns helps you swim longer and makes your strokes smoother. If you plan to compete, good starts and turns are essential.

Everyone who swims, whether for leisure or competition, develops a personal starting and turning style. For help learning or improving your skills, ask a coach at your local swim team for pointers. Always follow the safety guidelines for learning or practicing these skills.

11

Lifetime Fitness

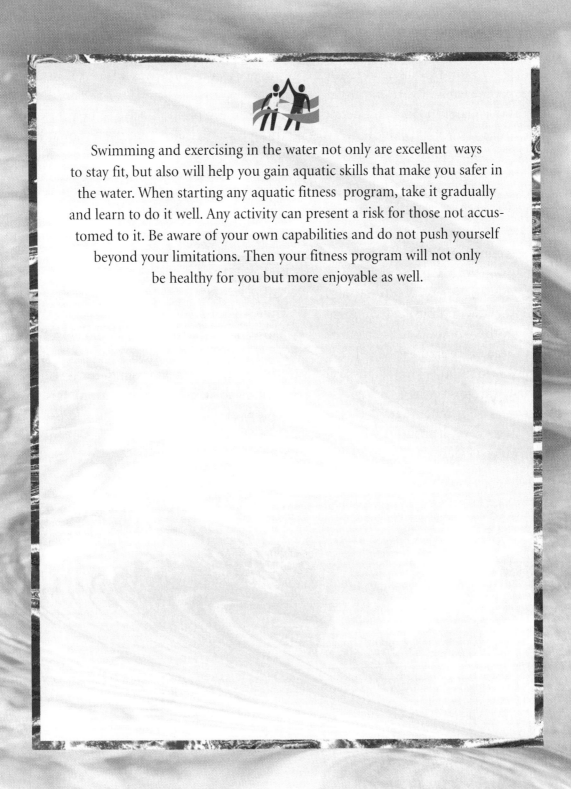

Swimming and exercising in the water not only are excellent ways to stay fit, but also will help you gain aquatic skills that make you safer in the water. When starting any aquatic fitness program, take it gradually and learn to do it well. Any activity can present a risk for those not accustomed to it. Be aware of your own capabilities and do not push yourself beyond your limitations. Then your fitness program will not only be healthy for you but more enjoyable as well.

In modern times most of us are far less physically active in our daily lives than people who lived in the past. At work many people are not physically active enough to maintain health and fitness. Inactive people are more prone to serious health problems such as heart disease, obesity, high blood pressure, diabetes, and muscle and joint problems (Figure 11-1). Far fewer people would die from cardiovascular disease if they participated in moderate exercise. Now more than ever, people need physical activity in their daily lives. And the good news is, even if you have not exercised much in the past, starting an exercise program now will help you live a longer, healthier life.

Physical fitness is important for good health. Physical fitness is not just the absence of disease. Fitness is a means to reach optimal health.

This chapter describes fitness swimming and water exercise. Fitness swimming is a swimming program in which the workouts are organized and sustained to reach a desired level of fitness. It is an excellent way to improve overall physical wellness, especially cardiovascular health.

Water fitness exercise is water activity that is generally done in a vertical position with the face out of the water (Figure 11-2). You walk,

jog, and dance in shallow water or run in deep water, sometimes using a flotation device (Figure 11-3). For example, you may push or pull your limbs against the resistance of the water by standing in neck-deep water and flexing your elbow to bring your fist toward your shoulder (biceps curl). Some water fitness programs focus on cardiovascular fitness; others emphasize muscular strength and flexibility.

As with any physical activity or fitness program, see your health care professional before you begin your program. This is especially true if you have not exercised for a long time.

You may be interested in competition. Thus you be interested in a training program, which is a physical improvement program designed to prepare for competition in a sport. Exercise is at a higher intensity. Before starting a training program, you should already have a basic level of fitness.

This chapter will help you develop fitness through swimming or water exercise. If you are just beginning a fitness program or if you want to include aquatics in your program, this chapter is for you. It also describes how to use swim training for greater levels of fitness or for competition.

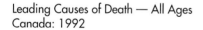

Leading Causes of Death — All Ages
Canada: 1992

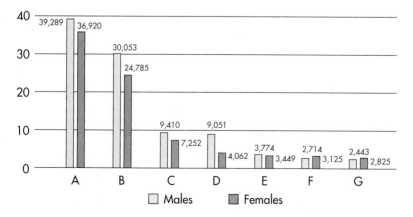

A Diseases of the circulatory system
B Cancer
C Respiratory diseases
D Fatal injury
E Diseases of the digestive system
F Endrocrine diseases
G Diseases of the nervous system

☐ Males   ■ Females

Figure 11-1

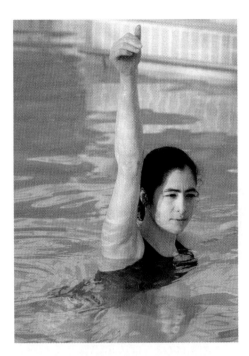

Figure 11-2. Water fitness exercise.

Figure 11-3. Use of flotation device during water fitness exercise.

BENEFITS OF AEROBIC EXERCISE

Aerobic exercise is sustained, rhythmic, physical exercise that requires additional effort by the heart and lungs to meet the increased demand by the skeletal muscles for oxygen.

Frequent aerobic exercise improves your health by developing or increasing your—

- Cardiovascular endurance.
- Muscular strength and endurance.
- Flexibility.
- Weight management.

Cardiovascular Endurance

The cardiovascular system supplies oxygen and nutrients to the body through the blood. Cardiovascular diseases cause more than half of the deaths in Canada. The most common type is coronary artery disease. This results from the narrowing and hardening of the coronary arteries, which carry needed oxygen-rich blood to the heart (Figure 11-4).

With the right exercise, cardiovascular efficiency (aerobic capacity) is improved. The heart becomes stronger and can pump more blood with each beat. Circulation improves, and the blood vessels stay healthy. Other benefits include the following:

- Lower heart rate at rest and in moderate exercise
- Shorter recovery time (the time it takes for the heart to resume its regular rate after exercise)
- Improved blood circulation to the heart muscle
- Increased capacity of the blood to carry oxygen
- Increased ability of muscles to use oxygen
- Less muscle soreness and fatigue due to decreased lactic acid production in the muscles
- Lower blood pressure (especially in people with high blood pressure)
- Lower cholesterol levels

Figure 11-4. **A**, The coronary arteries supply the heart muscle with blood. **B**, Build-up of materials on the inner walls of these arteries reduces blood flow to the heart muscle and may cause a heart attack.

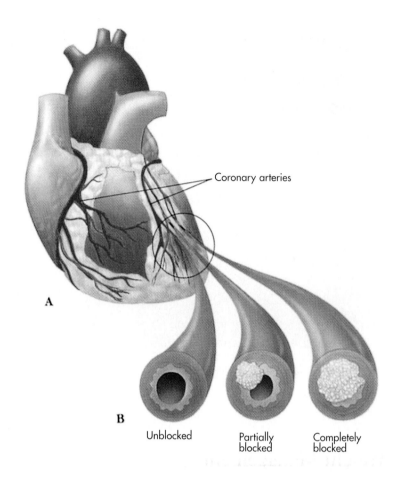

Coronary arteries

A

B

Unblocked   Partially   Completely
                   blocked   blocked

Muscular Strength and Endurance

Muscular performance involves both strength and endurance. Muscular strength is the ability of muscle to exert force. Strength leads to endurance, power, and resistance to fatigue. Muscular strength protects against joint injury and helps the body maintain good posture.

Weakness in some muscles causes an imbalance that can impair normal movement and cause pain. For instance, weak abdominal muscles combined with poor flexibility in the lower back and other muscles can lead to lower back pain. Lower back pain is a major problem in Canada that causes many people discomfort and limits activity. Muscular imbalances cause up to 80% of all lower back problems. Thus muscular strength is an important factor for staying healthy, and aquatic activity is a popular, effective way to develop this strength.

Muscular endurance is the ability of muscle to keep working over an extended period of time. Greater muscular strength often improves muscular endurance. For many people, muscular endurance, which helps to delay fatigue, is more important than strength for athletic activity.

Muscular strength and endurance generally decrease as you age or become less active. You may be less able to do everyday chores and enjoy recreation. For this reason, you should perform muscular development exercises two to three times per week.

Aerobic exercise, together with strength and flexibility exercises, offers the following benefits:

- Improved range of motion and function
- Increased strength and endurance
- Increased strength of tendons and ligaments
- Improved muscle tone
- Improved posture
- Reduction of lower back pain and other disorders caused by inactivity

Flexibility

Flexibility is the range of motion in a joint or group of joints.

Flexibility can vary from joint to joint in the same person. Even if you are flexible in some joints, you may not have overall flexibility in your body. Good flexibility helps prevent injuries to the bones, muscles, tendons, and ligaments. Stretching is an important part of any exercise. If your workout includes a muscular development set, be sure that, at the end of the session, you stretch the muscles you were working.

> *Ligaments are strong elastic tissues that hold bones in place at joints.*

> *Tendons are strong tissue that attach muscles to bone.*

Weight Management

As many as one half of the adults in Canada are thought to carry excessive fat. This means that the percentage of fat in their bodies is higher than recommended. This is not the same as being overweight. A person is overweight if his or her weight is more than the average based on sex, height, and frame size, as you may have seen in standard printed tables. However, because muscle is heavier than fat, a person with large muscles may be classified as overweight even though he or she has a normal percentage of body fat. Thus actual body fat, not just weight, must be considered. For information on how to have your body fat measured, ask your health care professional or a fitness specialist.

Individuals with a higher percentage of fat are at greater risk for many chronic health problems, such as diabetes, high blood pressure, heart disease, stroke, and cancer. They may also have low self-esteem. A person is considered obese if body fat exceeds 20% of total body weight for males or 30% for females. Obese people are $2^1/2$ times more likely to die of cardiovascular disease than people with normal body fat. For these reasons, proper body weight and percentage of body fat have become a national health priority.

Regular exercise is necessary for long-term weight control. Exercise increases the basal metabolic rate (the amount of calories the body burns at rest). Moderately intense exercise also improves appetite and mood. A person who exercises can eat more than an inactive person and still not gain weight. However, everyone should ensure that his or her diet does not contain an excessive amount of calories from fat.

Aerobic exercise helps control body weight in the following ways:

- Increases the rate at which the body burns calories
- Decreases body fat
- Maintains lean muscle tissue when losing weight or dieting
- Increases the ability of the body to use fat as fuel

Benefits of Exercising in Water

Exercise in water, whether in water exercises or fitness swimming, has unique benefits. Buoyancy lessens the impact and stress on the joints and thus reduces the risk of injury. Because water helps cool the body during exercise, workouts in cool water are refreshing, a benefit for those prone to heat stress. On the other hand, exercise in warm water increases blood circulation and promotes healing of injured tissues. Warm water eases muscle spasms, relaxes tight muscles, and increases joint motion.

Exercise in the water is also a popular form of aerobic activity. Water resistance helps improve muscular strength and endurance. Moving in and through the water helps maintain and improve flexibility. Because you can control water resistance by your speed and motions, you can design your workout to meet your own needs, regardless of your fitness level.

ADJUSTING EXERCISE LEVELS

Your body is affected by any exertion: pulse and breathing rates speed up, you may start to sweat, and you begin to burn calories. Physical fitness can come from exerting your body in certain ways. To reach or maintain a certain level of fitness, your exercise must stress the cardiovascular system at the right level, without too much or too little work, and it must be of sufficient duration. To become more fit, you must work harder than normal so that the muscles and cardiovascular system are forced to adapt. This is called overload. You must also exercise regularly to maintain the same level of fitness.

The FIT Principle

To reach and stay at a good level of fitness, you should design and follow an exercise program based on three factors: frequency (F), intensity (I), and time (T). This is called the FIT principle.

Frequency refers to how often you do the exercise. You should exercise 3 to 5 days a week. Exercising more than 5 days does not lead to better results. Your frequency depends on your own goals. For example, to lose fat, it is better to exercise 5 days a week rather than 3.

Intensity refers to how hard you work out when you exercise. This is the most difficult of the three factors to measure. Results are best with medium intensity. Very low–intensity exercise has less cardiovascular benefit. High-intensity exercise is difficult to sustain; thus your workouts are shorter, and the resulting benefit to the cardiovascular system is limited.

The *time* you spend exercising also affects the benefits. You should spend at least 15 minutes at the recommended level of intensity, not counting the warm-up or cool-down.

A typical aerobic workout lasts 20 to 30 minutes. Going beyond 60 minutes is not necessary, but more exercise time can help when you are training for a specific activity.

Target Heart Rate Range

The ideal heart rate to maintain during exercise for greatest cardiovascular benefit is called the target heart rate range.

The simplest way to know if you are exercising at the right intensity is to measure your heart rate, since heart rate is a measure of physiological stress. The more intense the exercise, the higher the heart rate.

In general, a workout should raise your heart rate to between 60% and 85% of your predicted maximum heart rate. Table 11-1 shows sample water fitness target heart rates for different age groups.

Regardless of your target heart rate numbers, if you experience any of the following problems, slow your workout immediately, notify your instructor if you are in a class, and consult your health care professional:

- Inability to talk, sing, hum to music
- Shortness of breath
- Excessive redness or splotchy skin colour
- Excessive sweating
- Excessive fatigue
- Weakness
- Dizziness
- Consistently taking a long time to recover after exercise

If your heart rate remains within your target range when you exercise, you will progress safely toward fitness if you exercise frequently and long enough. The 60% to 85% range is appropriate for most people. The cardiovascular health of a sedentary person may begin to improve with an intensity level as low as 50%. Very fit athletes might not reach their training goals with less than 85% intensity.

You can measure your heart rate during exercise with a pulse check (Figure 11-5). Feel your pulse at the carotid artery in the neck or the radial artery in the wrist (Figure 11-6). It will

Aquatic Heart Rate

People who exercise both on land and in the water often find their heart rates to be lower when exercising in the water. Researchers have developed several theories to explain why this is so:

- *Heat* produced in the body during exercise is dissipated more quickly in water than in air; therefore the body does not work as hard in the water.

- The effect of *gravity* is reduced in the water, making it easier to jump up high in the water and making it easier for the heart to pump blood "uphill" and back to the heart.

- *Hydrostatic pressure* of the water supports the compression of veins and arteries, which facilitates bloodflow and supports the body overall.

- *Blood-oxygen partial pressure* is higher in the water, making it easier for blood to absorb oxygen, thus reducing the workload on the heart.

The minimum and maximum working heart rates are on the average 13 beats per minute lower in water exercise than in the equivalent land exercise. Table 11-1 gives the target rates in these lower numbers for water exercise.

Table 11-1

Sample Water Fitness Target Heart Rates

Age	Minimum Working Heart Rate (60%)	Maximum Working Heart Rate (85%)
20-29	124	179
30-39	119	161
40-49	114	152
50-59	108	143
60-69	103	134
70+	98	125

drop fast when you pause to do this, so find the pulse quickly. Count the beats for 10 seconds and multiply by 6 to calculate your heart rate in beats per minute. Or you can count the beats for 6 seconds and add a zero to this count, which is more accurate because the heart rate drops rapidly once you stop to take your pulse. However you determine your heart rate, this number should fall within your target heart range.

To check your pulse, start timing on the first beat and count "0." Count "1" on the second beat and so on.

If your heart rate is below the target range, you should increase the intensity of your workout. You can move faster or, in water fitness, make wider arm and leg motions. If your heart rate is above the range, decrease the intensity. Make smaller movements, slow down, or take rest breaks more often. If you are often above or below your range but still think that you are at the right intensity, you can instead set your intensity by the method of perceived exertion, which is described in the next section.

Figure 11-5. Check your pulse during aquatic exercise and fitness swimming.

Rate of Perceived Exertion

Many factors, such as stress, illness, and fatigue, can affect the heart rate. It is also difficult to measure the heart rate accurately during exercise. You may want to use another way to monitor the intensity of your workouts, called the Rate of Perceived Exertion (RPE). It is based on how hard an individual thinks that he or she is working. RPE correlates with the heart rate (Figure 11-7).

A

B

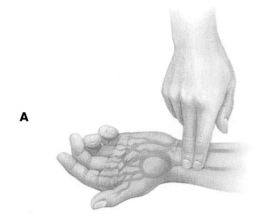
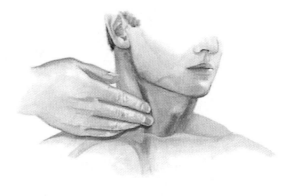

Figure 11-6. You may check your pulse at **A**, the radial artery, or **B**, the carotid artery.

In the initial phase of an exercise program, RPE is often used with the heart rate to monitor intensity. Identify a number on the RPE scale that corresponds with your perceived intensity, and then check your heart rate to see how the two numbers relate. Once you understand the relationship between heart rate and RPE, you can rely less on heart rate and more on the way you feel.

Stay Safe in Your Fitness Program

 For most people, a fitness program is not risky. However, some people cannot start a program at 60% intensity and continue for 15 minutes. If you have not exercised in a long while, this intensity can even be dangerous. A general health assessment to measure your level of fitness is in order whenever you begin an exercise program.

A health assessment can be as simple as a physical examination or as complex as an exercise stress test (Figure 11-8). Consult your health care professional. Once you know how fit you are, you can choose an exercise level that is safe for beginning your program.

Knowing your swimming ability is also important. With less skill, you use more energy, even at slow speeds. Swimming even one length of the pool can be exhausting for the beginning swimmer. Rest as often as you need and use resting strokes such as the sidestroke and the elementary backstroke when starting your program. Check your heart rate at each break to make sure it is within your target range. Your goal is to increase the time you spend continuously swimming and gradually decrease the rest breaks.

Always watch out for exercise warning signals. The following signals tell you to stop the workout:

- An abnormal heart action (such as a heart rate that stays high for some time after you stop exercising)

Borg's Perceived Exertion Scale

Perceived Exertion	% Workload
20	100%
19-Very, Very Hard	90%
18	
17-Very Hard	80%
16	
15 Hard	70%
14	
13-Somewhat Hard	60%
12	
11-Fairly Light	50%
10	
9-Very Light	40%
8	
7-Very, Very, Light	
6	

Figure 11-7. Borg's Perceived Exertion Scale.

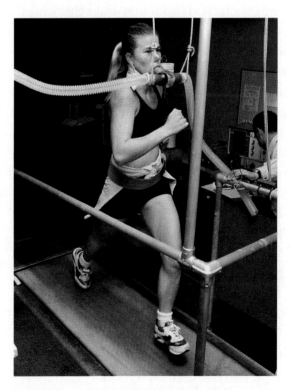

Figure 11-8. An exercise stress test may include using a treadmill while being monitored.

- Pain or pressure in the chest, arm, or throat
- Dizziness, light-headedness, or confusion during or immediately following the workout
- Breathlessness or wheezing

If you feel any of these, tell the instructor or lifeguard. If conditions persist, see your health care professional.

COMPONENTS OF A WORKOUT

Your workout should be designed to meet your own fitness goals. A safe, effective workout has a warm-up, stretching, aerobic set (the main part of the workout), followed by a cool-down. A muscular development set may follow the aerobic activity.

Warm-Up

The warm-up prepares the body for the increased work. It raises deep muscle temperatures, increases blood flow, and helps you adjust to the workout environment. Since pool water is often 8° to 11° celsius cooler than skin temperature, you may want to spend some time warming up at poolside before you enter the water. A good warm-up helps prevent injury to muscles and joints. The warm-up should last 5 to 10 minutes or about 15% to 20% of the total workout time or distance. It may consist of slow walking, jogging, or low-intensity swimming (Figure 11-9). A person with a disability may need a longer, more gradual warm-up.

Stretching

Stretching makes joints more flexible and improves your range of motion (Figure 11-10). Stretch during the warm-up or right after it. Stretching can prevent soreness and help you perform better. It can also reduce your risk of injury.

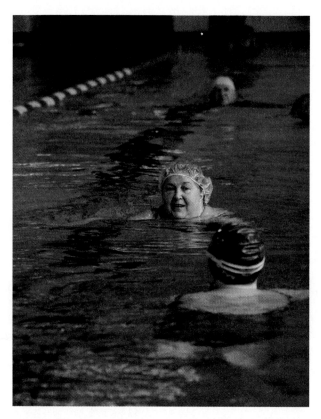

Figure 11-9. Low-intensity swimming is an effective warm-up technique.

Figure 11-10. A synchronized swimmer stretches at the beginning of a workout.

Proper stretching requires slow, gentle movements, holding the stretch for 10 to 30 seconds. Do not force a joint beyond the normal range of motion. You should feel no pain or discomfort during the stretch.

Aerobic Set

To benefit from an aerobic workout, your heart rate must remain in your target range for at least 15 minutes. At a lower level of intensity, you will not increase your fitness level as much. The aerobic set should make up 50% to 70% of the workout time and distance.

Muscular Development Set

A fitness program generally should include some exercise for muscular development. Probably the most popular form of exercise for muscular development is resistance training (weight lifting). The muscles are overloaded by using barbells, dumbbells, or a weight machine (Figure 11-11). Try to overload muscles from each muscle group rather than to focus on a few muscle groups. It is best to use one or two exercises for each muscle group.

First, identify the proper weight for each exercise. This usually happens by trial and error. It is recommended that a beginner use a weight that can be lifted 12 to 15 times in one set. If you cannot lift the weight at least 12 times without a break, the weight is too heavy for that exercise.

Once you have established the weight you will use for each exercise, you may begin your strength training program. A standard program

Figure 11-11. Resistance training for muscular development.

for beginners is to lift the selected weight 10 times (repetitions) for three sets. The more often you resistance train, the easier the selected weight will be to lift. As you improve, try each exercise with the next heavier weight to maintain the overload. Do this strength training two or three times per week as part of your regular fitness program. For more information on safe strength training techniques, consult a coach or a trainer at a health club.

Strength training with water fitness is another way for fitness swimmers to improve muscular strength and endurance. Because it is hard to calculate the resistance of the water in water fitness, performing only three sets might not provide the overload needed to increase strength and endurance. The overload for strength improvement may mean increasing the number of sets and the number of repetitions per set.

Cool-down

The last part of your workout is a cool-down period, during which you taper off to let the heart rate, blood pressure, and metabolic rate return to their initial levels. A proper cool-down helps return the blood from the working muscles to the brain, lungs, and internal organs. The cool-down helps you recover from fatigue and may prevent muscle soreness later.

Metabolic rate is the amount of energy produced by the body in a given period of time.

Cool-down activities are like warm-up activities (Figure 11-12). You may change to a resting stroke so you can slow down the workout gradually and keep blood from collecting in the muscles. You may stretch in a stationary position toward the end of the cool-down, but not immediately after strenuous activity in the aerobic set or the muscular development set. A typical cool-down lasts 5 to 10 minutes or 10% of the total time or distance of the workout.

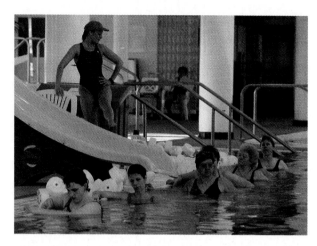

Figure 11-12. Cool down at the end of your workout.

PHASES OF A FITNESS PROGRAM

Your fitness will improve when you gradually increase the exertion of your workout. As your body adapts to a workload, the work level should gradually increase. This is referred to as progression. You can increase the workload by increasing the frequency, intensity, or time of your workouts (the FIT principle). In general, increase the time first, then the intensity or frequency. Remember that you cannot become more fit unless you increase the stress of the exercise on your body.

> *Progression is gradually increasing frequency, intensity, and/or time of exercise so that an overload is produced.*

How fast your condition improves depends on how fit you are when you begin your program and other factors. For safe and effective exercise, increase the overload gradually in three phases: the initial phase, the improvement phase, and the maintenance phase. It is possible for your condition to decline if the workload decreases or stops.

Initial Phase

This phase should include exercise of a very low intensity. If you have not exercised in a long time, this phase helps increase your workload slowly and comfortably. Move on to the improvement phase when you can comfortably maintain 60% intensity for at least 15 minutes. Be patient. You may need up to 10 weeks before going to the improvement phase.

Improvement Phase

The improvement phase begins when you reach the minimum level to attain cardiovascular fitness: exercising three times per week for at least 15 minutes at a level of at least 60% intensity. Your fitness will then improve by increasing frequency, intensity, or length of time. For example, exercising five times a week leads to improvements sooner than exercising only three times a week, if all else is the same. You will improve more rapidly in this phase than in the initial phase, but be sure to stay well within your target heart rate range. *Remember to increase the time before you increase intensity or frequency.*

Maintenance Phase

This phase begins when you reach your fitness goals. Your goal now is to sustain your fitness level rather than to increase your workload. You exercise at a comfortable level and set different goals. For example, now that your cardiovascular system is more fit, you might work on learning a new stroke or explore other activities to vary your program. This will help keep your workouts interesting.

Reversibility of Training

The physical fitness you gain from exercise can be lost. If you stop exercising regularly, your fitness level will decrease and you will gradually return to your original physical condition at the beginning your exercise program. It is better to maintain your current level of fitness than to let it decline and then try to regain it. Having once been physically fit does not make it any easier to get back into shape, even though you may know the proper technique for an effective workout. Fitness declines quickly but can be maintained with as few as two workouts a week. The key is to develop fitness habits you can use for a lifetime.

FITNESS SWIMMING

Fitness swimming is a swimming program in which the workouts have a specified level of intensity and are sustained for a set period of time.

You should design your fitness swimming program carefully. This means starting at the right level and following an effective progression in your exercise plan. This section will help you design a program to progress from an inactive lifestyle to your desired fitness level. Depending on your current fitness, you may move through the initial phase quickly or even skip it. Remember, your success depends on having a comfortable, practical plan you enjoy enough to continue the rest of your life.

Use a warm-up, stretching, an aerobic set, and a cool-down in each workout. You should also include a muscular development set in two or three workouts each week.

Check your heart rate before, during, and after your workout to ensure that you are at the right intensity. Also, check your resting heart rate every few weeks because exercise gradually lowers it.

Initial Phase

Following are examples of specific exercises for designing your own program. They are based on these assumptions:

1. The pool is 25 metres long (a common length for indoor pools in Canada). If the pool you use is longer or shorter, make adjustments for your workout.

2. You can swim 1 length of the pool using any stroke.

3. You do your workouts on three nonconsecutive days per week.

4. You have done a gradual warm-up, including stretching exercises, before the aerobic set.

Between lengths, rest or walk or jog in the water for 15 to 30 seconds (Figure 11-13). Try to keep a continuous effort without becoming too tired. To find a safe level to start, swim 1 length and check your heart rate. If it is above your target range, start with Step 1. If your heart rate is well within the target range, start with Step 3. If the water is too deep for walking or jogging, use a life jacket or stay in water no deeper than your shoulders. Remember that using a life jacket does not substitute for knowing how to swim.

Figure 11-13. Walk or jog in the water between swimming lengths in the initial phase of your fitness program.

In this phase of your program, you need not reach the target heart rate range of 60% intensity. If you have not exercised in a long while, you may begin at 50% for the progression.

Proceed with each step of your workout until you can do it easily, keeping your heart rate close to the lower limit of the target range. The initial phase can take as long as 10 weeks, so don't try to rush through it at an uncomfortable pace.

Step 1. In chest-deep water, walk 5 minutes and exercise your upper body with an underwater arm stroke such as the breaststroke. Check your heart rate after each length. If you can walk 5 minutes without your heart rate rising above the target heart rate range, rest 15 to 30 seconds and do the 5-minute walk two more times. Gradually decrease the rest period until you can walk 15 minutes continuously. Be sure your heart rate does not go past the upper limit of the target range.

Step 2. In chest-deep water, walk 1 length using the arm stroke as in Step 1, then jogging 1 length. Rest 15 to 30 seconds after the jogging length. Continue this pattern for 15 minutes. Check your heart rate at each break. Over a period of weeks gradually decrease the rest breaks until you can walk or jog 15 minutes continuously. Check your heart rate every 5 minutes in the workout.

Step 3. Swim 1 length and then rest by walking or jogging 1 length. Continue this pattern for 5 minutes. Check your heart rate to be sure that it is not too high. If it is, rest another minute. If your heart rate is within the target range, continue alternating swimming lengths with walking or jogging lengths. Check your heart rate every 5 minutes. Gradually decrease the rest breaks until you can swim or jog continuously for 15 minutes.

Step 4. Swim 1 length, rest 15 to 30 seconds, and swim another length. Use a resting stroke on the second length or just swim more slowly. Check your heart rate. Continue this sequence for 15 minutes. Gradually decrease the rest break to 10 seconds.

Step 5. When you can swim 15 minutes continuously or with minimum rest as in Step 4, recalculate your target heart rate range at 60% and repeat Step 4. When you can swim continuously for 15 minutes at an intensity of 60% you have completed the initial phase. Move on to the improvement phase.

There are several ways to check your progress. One way is to check your resting heart rate every 3 to 4 weeks. As you become more fit, your resting heart rate will drop. Another indication of progress is that your heart rate returns to its resting rate more quickly as your fitness improves.

Improvement Phase

People have very different improvement phases. If you were not very fit when you began, you may progress more slowly than someone who was more fit.

The steps in this phase move in 2-week increments. Do not move to a more difficult step until you can do the prior step easily. You might not need the full 2 weeks for some steps, or in some cases more than 2 weeks may be required.

Weeks 1-2. Swim 2 lengths. Rest 15 to 30 seconds. Repeat for 15 minutes. Check your heart rate during the breaks.

Weeks 3-4. Swim 3 lengths followed by a slow length or resting stroke. Rest 15 to 30 seconds. Continue for 20 minutes. Through this period, gradually shorten the rest breaks to 10 seconds.

Weeks 5-6. Swim 5 lengths followed by a slow length or resting stroke. Rest 15 to 30 seconds. Check your heart rate. Continue for 20 minutes. With each successive workout, gradually decrease the rest breaks to 10 seconds.

Weeks 7-8. Swim continuously for 20 minutes. Rest only when needed but not longer than 10 seconds. If possible, use resting strokes instead of breaks. Check your heart rate every 10 minutes in the workout.

Weeks 9-10. Swim continuously for 20 minutes. With each successive workout, add 1 or 2 lengths until you can swim continuously for 30 minutes.

Weeks 11-12. Swim 30 minutes continuously without rest. In the last week of this progression, test your progress by swimming a timed 12-minute swim.

After you reach the 30-minute goal, you can continue to increase the overload by raising the intensity or lengthening the workout. When you do this, be sure to change only one variable (frequency, intensity, or time) at a time. Keep your progression gradual.

Maintenance Phase

Once you reach your fitness goals, you might not wish to increase your workload any more. Consider your original goals and either set new ones or maintain your current fitness level by staying with your present workout. Most important, keep at least at a minimum level of fitness.

If your goal is to train for competition, take a look at the methods described in the next section.

Swimming Etiquette

You may feel frustrated in your swimming workout when you have to share the pool with other swimmers. Cyclists do not have to share their bikes, and runners can usually find a quiet road, but fitness swimmers rarely get a lane to themselves. Proper swimming etiquette helps ease this problem.

To share a lane you need to be organized, cooperative and know your swimming level. You must first know your exercise speed. Your workout will be better in a lane where other swimmers are doing a similar type of workout (pulls, kicks, repeat short distances, long continuous swims) at a speed similar to yours. Most pools have lanes for fast, medium, and slow swimmers, but swimmers still vary a great deal in speed within a lane.

Once you find the best lane, use circle swimming so that all swimmers can enjoy the workout. Circle swimming is swimming in a pattern around the line on the pool bottom in the centre of the lane. With the correct etiquette, a faster swimmer overtaking a slower swimmer in the lane signals

to pass by tapping the lead swimmer's foot. The lead swimmer should stop at the wall or pull over to let the faster swimmer pass. It is common courtesy to allow the new lead swimmer at least a 5-second lead before following. Although this may seem to disrupt your workout, such short breaks will not affect the intensity.

SWIMMING IN OPEN WATER

Triathlons and cross-training techniques have led more and more people to swim in open water. Open-water swimmers must consider the psychological and physical differences of open water. A swimmer may feel fear of being disoriented, of hazards in open water (rocks, sandbars, bites and stings from marine life), or of being overpowered by the water. The fear itself is probably more dangerous than the actual situation. Open water swimming often takes place outside a supervised area. Therefore never swim in open water alone.

Anytime you swim in open water you may be at risk for hypothermia. This life-threatening situation happens when the body loses so much heat that the core temperature drops below normal. Be alert to the possibility of hypothermia if the water temperature is below 21° C. Temperatures below 15° C pose an immediate threat of hypothermia. Constant shivering is an important warning signal. An even more critical signal is loss of judgment, which can quickly worsen the effects of the cold.

Following certain precautions helps prevent hypothermia. First, practice in cold water. Repeated exposure to cold water acclimates the body. Second, insulate yourself. Most heat is lost through the head. Wearing multiple swim caps or a neoprene swim cap helps hold the heat in.

TRAINING TECHNIQUES

Following are training techniques you can use in your workouts to meet your fitness and training goals. You can use them alone or in combination. The distances you swim, the time it takes you to swim them, and the duration of rest periods depend on various factors, such as the time you have for training, your training goals, and the observations of your coach or trainer, if you have one. Using different techniques also adds variety to your workouts.

Over Distance

This method involves swimming long distances with moderate exertion with short or no rest periods. Over-distance training is used to improve your endurance. Your heart rate stays in the low to middle level of the target range for the whole swim. You can also use this for a warm-up activity.

Fartlek

This method gets its name from the Swedish word that means "speed play" and was popularized by runners. It breaks swims into slow and fast lengths of the pool, using the same stroke. It can make long swims more interesting and is good for developing speed and endurance at the same time.

Interval Sets

This is one of the most common swimming training methods. Intervals are a series of repeat swims of the same distance and time interval. They give you a specific rest period between the time spent swimming (Figure 11-14).

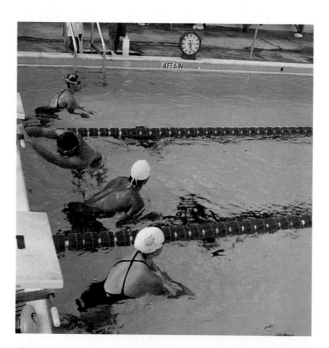

Figure 11-14. Swimming in interval sets.

An example of an interval set is "8 × 100 on 1:30." The first number represents the number of times you repeat the distance. The second number (100 in this case) is the distance of each swim in meters, and the 1 minute and 30 seconds is the total amount of time for the swim and rest. If you swim the 100 in 1:15, you have 15 seconds to rest. This short rest period keeps your heart rate within the target range without dropping back to your resting rate. Used in the aerobic set of a workout, interval swimming is the best all-around method to develop both speed and endurance.

Repetition

This technique uses swim sets of the same distance done at close to maximum effort (up to 90% of maximum), but with rest periods as long as or longer than your swim time. Repetition sets develop your speed and anaerobic capacity. Use this training method after you have developed an effective aerobic base. It is usually used after the aerobic set as a muscular development set.

Sprints

These are short, fast swims (100% effort) to simulate race conditions. The rest between sprints is usually long enough to let the heart return to its resting rate. Like repetition swims, sprints improve your anaerobic capacity.

Straight Sets

With this method you swim at a steady speed throughout the set. Monitoring your time helps you keep an even pace. This method is often used by distance swimmers.

Negative Split Sets

Negative-splitting involves swimming the second half of each swim period faster than the first half. For example, if you swim 200 meters four times, the second 100 should be faster than the first 100 in each repetition.

Descending Sets

Often confused with negative splitting, descending sets refers to decreasing the time on successive swims. To swim 200 metres four times in a descending set, each 200 would be faster than the 200 preceding it.

Ladders

Ladders are several swims with regular increases or decreases in distance. For example, you swim 25, then 50, and finally 75 metres.

Pyramids

A pyramid is a swim of regular increases and decreases in distance. For example, you swim a 25, then a 50, then a 75, then a 50, and finally a 25. A variation of both pyramids and ladders is to increase the number of times you repeat the distance as the distances get shorter, for example, 1 × 500, 2 × 400, 3 × 300, 4 × 200, and 5 ×100.

Broken Swims

Broken swims are timed swims that are faster than your racing speed and are interrupted by short periods of rest (for example, 10 seconds). Such a swim is followed by a long rest. On completing the entire swim, you subtract the total time of rest from the final time to determine your swimming time. Broken swims are a highly motivating method of training because they simulate stress conditions of competition while yielding a swimming time that may be faster than your racing time for an actual event. Broken swims are often combined with other variations, such as negative splits and descending swims.

Dry Land Training

Dry land training is the use of training techniques done out of the water to improve swimming skills. These techniques fall into two areas, flexibility and strength training. Done properly, resistance training builds both strength and flexibility. A half hour of resistance training 3 days a week, combined with 15 minutes of stretching, can produce favourable results. Although most coaches prefer dry land training before a swimming workout, you can do it before or after your swim, depending on your schedule.

WATER FITNESS EXERCISE

Water fitness is water activity generally done in a vertical position with the face out of the water. Water fitness grew in part from athletics. Coaches wanted to rehabilitate injured athletes in a way that was safe but also good for cardio-vascular conditioning. Water exercise was the perfect activity.

Not only are water fitness programs a rehabilitation method, but they have become a new physical fitness avenue for health-conscious people. Facilities now offer many equipment options and programs flexible enough to meet the needs of people in all walks of life.

Water fitness varies in many ways. The water temperature and depth used, the style of aerobic dancing or calisthenics with range-of-motion activities, and the specific motions used all vary from program to program. Different programs exist for different age groups (Figure 11-15). People participate in water fitness to manage weight, relieve stress, feel better, and generally become more fit. Another advantage of water fitness is that even individuals with limited swimming ability can participate.

People with disabilities may get a special benefit from water fitness. Aquatic activity may

Figure 11-15. Water fitness classes are available for different age groups.

improve your level of fitness, range of motion, and muscular strength and endurance.

You can develop your own water fitness exercise routine, or you can join a class. Check in your area for available classes. Specialty classes may include beginning water walking or aerobics, bench aquatics, prenatal or postnatal classes, cardiac classes, arthritic classes, children's programs, circuit training, and other specialty classes.

Physiological Benefits of Water Fitness

Water fitness exercise helps you increase your fitness level in three ways:

- Greater cardiovascular and respiratory efficiency
- Greater flexibility, balance, and coordination
- More muscle strength and endurance

Water fitness exercise is often safer than land exercises because the movements are less likely to produce injury, impacts are reduced, muscle groups are less subjected to overuse, and the range of motion of joints is increased.

Factors That Affect Your Workout

In water fitness, you maintain the proper intensity by adjusting your body position and by moving in the water. Intensity is affected the most by buoyancy, resistance the working muscles must overcome, speed of movement, and type of movement.

Buoyancy and water depth

Buoyancy reduces the pull of gravity on the limbs and trunk. The deeper the water, the more support it gives. Exercise in water that is only ankle-, knee- or waist-deep has little support against the impact of the feet landing when jogging or dancing. In deeper water, the body has more buoyancy, but in neck-deep water it is hard to keep balance and control. Increased buoyancy also reduces the workload, so you may have trouble getting your heart rate into the target range.

Exercise in chest-deep water may be best because the arms stay submerged (Figure 11-16). Using your arms also helps you keep balance and proper body alignment. The effort of pushing the water improves upper body strength and endurance and helps make the exercise aerobic. Arm work under water improves the muscles that stabilize the trunk. These muscles, particularly the abdominal muscles, become stronger and help reduce stress in the lower back.

Figure 11-16. Exercising in chest-deep water helps make the exercise aerobic.

Obese people may need to adjust their workouts if their hips and thighs cause the centre of buoyancy to be lower. The legs then tend to rise toward the surface, making it hard to keep balance. Obese people may want to exercise in shallower water, but it should still be deep enough to support and protect the body from hard landings.

The way you exercise also affects the intensity of the workout. With bouncing and bounding movements (such as those commonly associated with aerobics done out of the water), the heart rate might not reach the target range, since the body has a short rest while it drifts back to the bottom. However, movements involving walking, jogging, or aerobic dance in the water can be of value as you progress to workouts of higher intensity. Water fitness helps avoid problems that are associated with the impact of landing.

Resistance

Exercise intensity is greater when the surface area of the body presented to the water is larger. By choosing which limbs to manoeuvre in which ways, you can adjust the resistance your body encounters when it pushes against the water. For example, a biceps curl uses more effort with an open hand than with a fist (Figure 11-17). Moving a longer body segment, such as the whole arm kept straight from the shoulder, uses more effort than a shorter body segment, such as the forearm during a biceps curl. You may also increase resistance by using equipment designed for this purpose.

Speed of movement

The speed of movement in the exercise also affects the intensity of the workout. Faster movements cause greater resistance and use more effort. In water fitness, this principle applies more to the speed of moving the limb than to the speed of moving the whole body from one point in the pool to another.

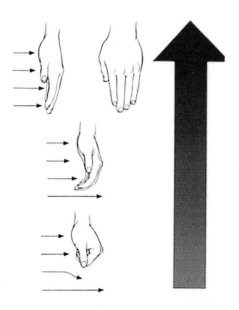

Figure 11-17. Changing the position of your hands changes their resistance to the water.

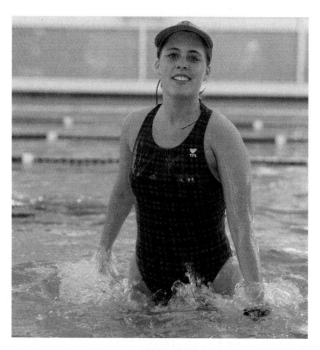

Figure 11-18. Rebound movement.

Type of movement

Some types of movement require more effort than others. When your limbs move through the water in water fitness, the water behind the limb is set in motion and stays in motion. Generally, there are three ways you can move during water fitness exercise:

1. **Neutral** movement involves pressing lightly and lifting off the bottom of the pool with tapping and sliding motions. As you keep more of your body submerged, you neutralize gravity and mimic the buoyant state. Increase the intensity of the exercise by adding more power and force in the movement.

2. **Rebound** movement involves pressing forcefully off the bottom of the pool (Figure 11-18). As you rebound higher, you feel more gravity. Increase the intensity of the exercise by pressing more forcefully off the bottom to gain more height out of the water.

3. **Suspended** movement uses the buoyant state. The feet occasionally touch the bottom. You stay suspended in the water by your treading movements. Stabilize and balance yourself by contracting abdominal and trunk muscles.

Workout Design

A water exercise workout should have the same components as a fitness swimming workout. The warm-up lasts 5 to 10 minutes and consists of walking, slow jogging, and slow aerobic activities, in the water or at poolside if the water is not warm enough. You can add stretching after the warm-up. If you chill early in the workout, you may be more comfortable stretching after the aerobic set.

The aerobic set should be rhythmic and continuous and use both arms and legs. Monitor your heart rate several times during this set to be sure it stays in the target range.

To increase the intensity of your movements—

• Move faster.

• Increase your frontal surface area to increase water resistance.

• Make larger movements.

- Press against the water.
- Stay in water depth where you can keep control.
- Exercise for a longer time.
- Keep hands cupped, wrists stiff.

To decrease the intensity of the exercise—

- Move more slowly.
- Decrease your frontal resistance.
- Make smaller movements.
- Exercise a shorter time.
- Keep arms and legs close to the body.
- Open your hands, slice the water, and keep wrists loose.

Two or three times each week, your workout should include a muscular development set. This promotes flexibility, range of motion, strength, and muscular endurance.

The cool-down in an aquatic workout should consist of slow, rhythmic activities. A good format for the cool-down is simply to reverse the warm-up activities.

Progressions for Water Fitness

You can easily progress in water fitness because you can manipulate three factors (resistance due to surface area, speed of movement, and type of movement) to reach the level of intensity you need. If you are less fit, start with low-level exercises such as walking in chest-deep water or slow jogging in waist-deep water. Use slow, rhythmic movements with small surface areas. If you are generally fit, exercise with larger surface areas, faster speeds, and angular motion to reach the right intensity. Once you learn how to adjust your intensity, you can exercise in the same class with others who are exercising at different intensities.

The key to progressively overloading the system and maintaining target heart rates is to control how surface area, speed, and type of movement interact. You can stay at the same intensity with a smaller surface area (for example, moving from chest-deep water to waist-deep water) if you increase the speed of movement (such as walking or jogging faster). You can also change from angular motion to curved motion without losing intensity as long as you increase the surface area and/or the speed.

Water Fitness for Muscular Development

The intensity of resistance training increases directly with the size of the surface area and the speed of movement. It will seem as though you are lifting more weight if your movements are faster and the surface area meeting resistance is larger.

Equipment

Several devices on the market today are designed to provide greater overload during resistance training. Some use the principle of buoyancy to increase exercise intensity. Wearing buoyant cuffs on wrists or ankles means that greater force must be used to move your limbs under water. Other devices increase the surface area of the limbs to provide resistance. Devices for aquatic resistance training are not recommended for the beginner. For most people, the water alone provides an adequate overload for improvements in strength and muscular endurance. However, the more advanced exerciser may need equipment to help maintain the proper intensity for his or her workout.

Buoyancy equipment includes Sea Hands and water wings. These devices ensure that the user must work against the buoyancy of the device, thereby intensifying the workout. Personal flotation devices designed for deep water workouts keep the body in a suitable position for water running, which allows the participant to use all limbs to increase resistance.

Resistance equipment such as Fitness Fins, Aquaflex, Dynabands, and Aquatoner increase the resistance to movement in the water to increase workout intensity (Figure 11-19).

Figure 11-19. Using resistance equipment increases the intensity of the workout.

Pressure and weight equipment such as wrist weights, ankle weights, weighted balls, and others increase the intensity of the workout by making limbs heavier but can also increase impact.

Safety Precautions

 Follow these guidelines in your muscular development sets to keep your water fitness safe:

- Use the right equipment. It is important to use equipment specifically designed for water fitness. Improvised equipment may cause injury. Always use equipment you can control. Once you begin to set a piece of equipment in motion, it can keep moving and strike your body. If you are not strong enough to stop and reverse the motion or to stabilize your body during the movement, you may be injured.

- Keep your body centred. Body alignment is especially important when you are using equipment for resistance training. Choose exercises in which your limbs move toward and away from the centre of your body.

Movements with limbs fully extended, such as leg or arm circles, may cause injury.

- Stabilize your trunk when you *lift*. The larger surface area of some devices requires more stability for safe lifting technique. When you perform lifting motions, keep your back flat, with the abdominal muscles tight, the knees slightly bent, and the feet flat on the pool bottom.

- Isolate and work one muscle group at a time. This focuses your attention and gives the best improvement for individual muscle groups. Be sure to exercise opposing muscle groups equally.

- Work major muscle groups first. If you work the smaller, assisting muscle groups first, they will fatigue early and limit the work you can do with major muscle groups.

- Plan your movements. First imagine where the piece of equipment will be at the end of the movement, then perform the action. Use exercises that involve a full range of motion and be sure to return fully to the starting position. Be sure the equipment stays in the water. Shock to joints and muscles when equipment passes into or out of the water can cause injury.

- Use correct breathing. Do not hold your breath. This increases your blood pressure and may increase your feelings of stress. Instead, adjust your breathing to the rhythm of the exercise. Exhale during the work phase and inhale during the recovery phase.

- Stop any exercise that causes sharp pain. Sharp pain can be a signal of a serious health problem. Seek immediate help for persistent pain in the chest or arm (pain that does not go away within 10 minutes and is not relieved by resting or changing position). Report any recurring pain to your health care provider.

Sample Water Fitness Workout

Set	Time/Distance	Intensity & Modes	Basic Moves
Goals	1 Length = 25 meters 1 Width = 8 meters		
BUOYANCY WARM-UP • Find Depth • Check Alignment • Adjust to Temperature & Bouyancy • Balance	3-5 minutes STATIONARY POSITION	• Light to Moderate • Flexuous Mode • Feel Warm • Increase Breathing Gradually	JOGGING • Arms Sculling KICKING • Arms Push & Pull • Rocking • Arms Pushing
CARDIO WARM UP • Adjust to Buoyancy & Increase Resistance • Balance & Stabilize	2-3 Minutes using 3-5 Lengths or 9-15 Widths	• Moderate Pace • Flexuous • Breathe Deeper • Light Sweat Should Begin on Forehead (Brow)	JOGGING • Arms Sculling • Arms Push & Pull
AEROBIC SETS			
1. STATIONARY RESISTANCE • Aerobic Conditioning • Muscular Strength • Endurance	4-6 Minutes STATIONARY POSITION 8-12 Repetitions	• Somewhat Hard to Strong • Flexuous • Deep Breathing • Sweat on Forehead	
2. JUMPING • Aerobic Conditioning • Muscular Strength • Endurance • High-Intensity Work	4-5 Minutes STATIONARY POSITION 8-12 Repetitions	• Somewhat Hard to Strong • Flexuous • Deep Breathing • Sweat on Forehead	JUMPING • Arms Push & Pull
3. WALKING • Aerobic Conditioning • Muscular Strength • Endurance • Trunk Stabilization	4-10 Minutes using 10-15 Lengths or 30-45 Widths	• Somewhat Hard to Strong • Flexuous & Rigid • Strong Muscular Contraction • Breathe Deeply Especially During High Intensity	WALKING • Arms Push & Pull
4. SCISSORS • Aerobic Conditioning • Muscular Strength • Endurance • Balance	4-6 Minutes STATIONARY POSITION 8-12 Repetitions and 4-6 Lengths or 12-18 Widths	• Somewhat Hard to Strong • Deep Breathing • Muscles May Begin to Fatigue • Sweat on Brow • Flexuous & Rigid	SCISSORS • Arms Push & Pull
5. ALL WAVE SET (TRAVEL) • Aerobic Conditioning • Muscular Strength • Endurance • Balance	4-15 Minutes using 16-29 Lengths or 48-60 Widths	• Somewhat Hard to Strong • Deep Breathing • Flexuous & Rigid • Body Very Warm • Sweating on Brow	WALKING JOGGING ROCKING KICKING JUMPING
FUNKY SET • Aerobic Conditioning • Have Fun!	4 Minutes Stationary & Travel	• Moderate to Somewhat Hard • Rigid	COMBINE A VARIETY OF MOVES
COOL DOWN • Balance Using Buoyancy • Release Tension	4-6 Minutes using 4-6 Lengths or 12-18 Widths	• Moderate • Flexuous • Lighter Breathing	WALKING, LEAPING KICKING, LIGHT REBOUND GO EASY
STRETCH • Flexibility • Balance • Relaxation	4-6 Minutes Stationary or Easy Travel for Active Stretching	• Light to Very Light • Feel Buoyant • Easy Breathing	COMBINE A VARIETY OF STRETCHING MOVES

WARM DOWN—REMOVE ALL EQUIPMENT. Perform fun moves, feel light, loose & bouyant. Kick—Leap—Skip—Rock—Release tension into the water...
GOOD JOB!
Warm up & get ready for gravity... LAND HO!

Adapted from: The Art & Science of Wave Aerobics Workout by Mary Sanders, Director, Wave Aerobics, Reno, Nevada.

SUMMARY

Regular aerobic exercise is beneficial in many ways. Water is an effective vehicle for reaching one's fitness goals with a low risk of injury. No matter what your level of ability, you can design a fitness program to meet your personal needs.

The success of your aquatic fitness program depends on its design. It should meet your fitness needs and your personal goals. Monitor your program and evaluate its success. If your current program is not meeting your needs, adjust it to reach your goals more effectively. If the program gives you the results you want, you are more likely to keep using it and enjoy the benefits of greater health. When you enroll in a water fitness exercise program, be sure that the instructors are trained in water exercise programs.

Boating Safety

Know how to operate a boat by taking a boating course. Have the required and recommended equipment on your boat. Plan your boating trip in known or mapped waters, file a float plan, and watch the weather.

Operate the boat safely, using common sense guidelines. Avoid drinking alcohol before and while boating. Know proper procedures for boarding and disembarking, weathering a storm, and other boating conditions.

Know how to perform reaching assists, self-rescue in different kinds of water conditions, and what to do if the boat is capsized or swamped. Know how to perform rescue breathing from a boat.

- One of the leading causes of drowning involves Canadians in small boats. Therefore it is important that you have certain basic knowledge and skills.

- You must appropriately be prepared for boating by wearing a PFD/lifejacket, securing the safety equipment, and knowing how the environment affects boating and how to write a float plan. When you are on the water you must know what rules to obey, how to monitor the weather, and how to use required equipment. In an emergency you must be able to self-rescue, perform a reaching assist from the boat, and assist another person or yourself back into the boat from deep water.

Canada abounds with beautiful lakes, rivers, and waterways that attract many boating enthusiasts each year. Some boaters are safety conscious, knowledgable, and experienced. But others think they need only put their boat in the water and aim it at their destination, with no knowledge of the risks involved or the precautions they should take. Every year serious injuries and deaths occur involving boaters who are not safety conscious.

Boats up to 5.5 metres long are called small craft. Although they can be very enjoyable for recreation, small craft are more likely to be involved in incidents than larger ones.

PREPARE FOR SAFE BOATING
Personal Preparedness

It is beneficial to know how to operate a boat safely. If you intend to be a passenger in a boat, ensure that operators are well versed in the operation of the particular craft. No matter how well they swim, all passengers on small craft should wear a Department of Transportation–approved lifejacket or PFD at all times.

To become acquainted with boat operation, take lessons to learn—

- Differences among types of craft.
- Effects of wind, water, and weather conditions.
- How to use boating equipment.
- Navigation rules.
- Safe boat handling and operation.
- Boat maintenance.
- Emergency procedures.

To find a boating course in your area, check with your local Red Cross office or the following organizations:

- Coast Guard Auxiliary
- Canadian Canoe Association
- Canadian Power and Sail Squadron
- Canadian Recreational Canoeing Association
- Canadian Yachting Association

Chapter 2 has additional information on many of these organizations. You may also learn about boating courses from local marinas and recreation facilities.

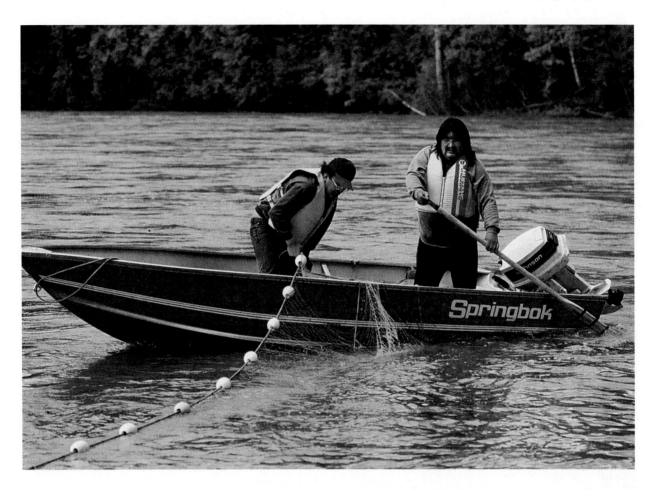

For information on navigation, contact your provincial ministry responsible for the management of waterways or government bookstores. For ocean charts, contact the Canadian Hydrographic Service for the Catalogue of Nautical Charts.

Float plan

Personal preparedness also includes being prepared for the possibility of an boating incident or mishap. Before your trip, file a float plan with a responsible person so that you can be found if you do not return or if you do not arrive at your destination at the time planned. If your trip is to last more than 1 day, you may be able to file a copy of your Float Plan with local police or law enforcement officers. Stick to your float plan route so that a search and rescue team can find you in the event of any mishap. Figure 12-1 is an example of a float plan form you can use.

Equipment

Being prepared for a safe boating experience includes having the right equipment and checking it in advance to be sure that it's functioning correctly. Some equipment is required by law, but other recommended equipment is also appropriate to ensure your safety.

Required equipment for power-boats and canoes

According to the Canadian Small Vessel Regulations and Collision Regulations (International with Canadian Modifications), all craft are required to carry certain equipment. Craft up to 5.5 metres in length must have the following on board:

- One approved PFD or lifejacket for each person on board (see Chapter 3, Water Safety)
- Two paddles or two oars and oar locks

Boat Name and Number: _____

Boat Size, Type, and Colour: _____

Sail _____   Power_____   Canoe _____   Other_____

Your Name _____

Address: _____

_____

_____

Number in Party: _____

Route Description:

Launch Point:_____   Date:_____

Routing:_____

_____

_____

Arrival Point:_____   Date: _____

                                        Time: _____

Call Search and Rescue at: _____

Date:_____   Time:_____

Person to contact in emergency

Name:_____

Address: _____

_____

_____

                                        Telephone: _____

Figure 12-1. Float plan.

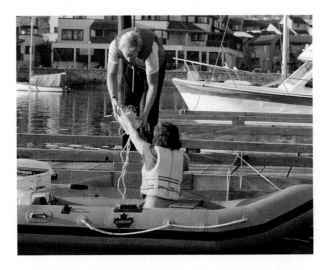

- One bailer or one manual pump
- One sound signaling device audible for half a nautical mile (0.93 kilometres)
- One class B1 fire extinguisher if your boat is equipped with an inboard motor, permanently fixed or built-in fuel tanks, or a cooking or heating appliance that burns liquid or gas fuel
- Lights that comply with collision regulations if traveling at night; a hand held flashlight for vessels without permanently fitted lights

Recommended equipment for powerboats and canoes

In addition to the equipment required by the Department of Transportation, it is recommended that the following equipment be carried on boating trips, depending on the length and type of trip you are taking. These items assist boaters and prevent or reduce the risk of an emergency situation:

- A first aid kit
- Additional PFD or lifejacket
- A change of clothes, in a watertight bag
- Extra paddles or oars
- Flares
- Rain gear (waterproof outer clothing)
- Matches (waterproofed)
- Knife

- Food supplies
- Tool kit and spare parts for the boat
- Throw bag or some form of throwable safety equipment to perform rescues
- Bow and stern ropes (painters)
- Radio for listening to weather reports
- Navigation charts or maps

Required and recommended equipment for personal watercraft

Under Canadian regulations, personal watercraft (PWC) and sailboards must be equipped with a Department of Transportation–approved PFD or lifejacket for each person on board. If you are the operator of a personal watercraft or sailboard, you should actually wear the PFD (Figure 12-2). When preparing for even a short day on the water, check your PFD for fit and serviceability.

The law also requires you to have a sound-signaling device on board and readily accessible. Other recommended items for PWC and sailboards include—

- Eyewear to protect against water spray and sun glare.
- Gloves for improved grip and comfort.
- Wet suit for comfort and added protection against sun, wind, abrasion, and hypothermia; wet suits also provide additional flotation.

Figure 12-2. Wear a PFD also on a personal watercraft or sailboard.

- Deck or tennis shoes with good traction or speciality aquatic shoes, to prevent loss of footing and to protect your feet from underwater hazards.
- Class B-1 fire extinguisher (PWC only).

Environment

The third aspect of being prepared involves paying attention to the environment *before* going boating. It involves choosing a safe place for boating and paying close attention to the weather.

Location

Follow these guidelines for staying in safe areas when boating:

- Keep your boat well away from swimming areas.
- Choose docking facilities with a separate area for small boats, for safer manoeuvring.

- Stay at least 30 metres away from diving flags, which signal that SCUBA divers are underwater nearby (Figure 12-3).
- Avoid boating above and below dams (see Chapter 4).
- Obey storm or gale warnings and small craft warnings in the area. These marine forecasts are broadcast to alert boaters to hazardous weather and water conditions.
- Be aware of tides and their effects on boats. Pay attention to depths in shallow areas at low tide.
- Avoid river currents and rapids unless you have adequate training.
- In a river watch for fallen trees along the banks with branches in the water ("sweepers"). Swimmers or small boats can get caught in the branches, especially when in a strong current.
- Before starting out, gather information about water conditions from charts and local boaters.
- In a waterway marked with buoys, know how to use the buoys as navigation aids.

Figure 12-3. Stay away from diving areas.

Weather

When boating, you must be able to predict weather conditions to lower the risk of being caught unexpectedly in a storm. Consider the weather both before you begin and while you are boating. Know the limitations of your craft and the effect of wind and water on it. How your boat handles in rough weather depends on many factors such as its size, shape, and load distribution.

There are many ways to forecast weather, including—

- Observing cloud patterns and the accompanying weather conditions.
- Listening to or reading weather forecasts from the Environment Canada Weather Service.
- Talking to local residents to gain information not readily available from official sources.
- Paying attention to meaningful observations such as: "Red sky at night, sailor's delight" (fair weather); "red sky at morning, sailor take warning" (poor weather).
- Noting signs of a storm coming, such as hearing static on the radio. This may be the first warning of a thunderstorm as far away as 150 km. Such a storm may arrive within 2 to 4 hours.

STAY SAFE WHILE BOATING

 In addition to preparing for safe boating, learn how to stay safe once you are on the water. This includes knowing how to navigate the boat safely, knowing how to use equipment, and staying aware of environmental factors.

Safety While Underway

Safety while the boat is underway involves both following boating laws and behaving appropriately while on the boat.

Boating laws

Under the Criminal Code of Canada, you are guilty of a criminal offence and liable to imprisonment or a fine if you operate a boat, air cushion vehicle, water skis, surfboard, or any towed object in a dangerous manner, including—

- Operating a vessel while impaired.
- Towing a person on skis after dark.
- Towing a person on skis without another person keeping watch.
- Failing to stop at the scene of an accident in which you are involved.

Under normal circumstances, power vessels must keep clear of sailboats, rowboats, and canoes.

The collision regulations require every vessel to maintain a constant lookout. You must also use every available means, such as radar and radio, to watch for any risk of collision.

Rules of the road

The rules of the road for boats are like traffic laws for cars: they help prevent collisions and other boating incidents that can cause serious injuries, damage to property, and death.

Determining right-of-way Boats with motors must give the right-of-way to boats under sail or those being rowed or paddled, except when a sailboat overtakes a motorboat. Even when you have the right-of-way, you should still operate your boat carefully and responsibly. Always signal your actions to other boats, according to the navigation rules.

Meeting When you approach another boat head-on or nearly so, keep to your right, just as you do when driving an automobile (Figure 12-4).

Crossing When two boats are crossing paths, the boat on the right has right-of-way. The boat on the left must slow down, change course, or pass behind the other boat. The boat on the left must prepare to stop or reverse course to avoid a collision (Figure 12-5).

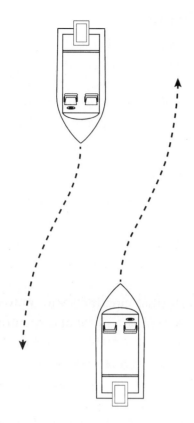

Figure 12-4. Stay to the right when meeting another boat head on.

Figure 12-5. The boat on the right has the right of way.

Exiting and entering the marina Follow the rules governing right-of-way. Always go slow and stay under the posted speed limit to avoid making a large wake when you're near docks, piers, or congested boat ramp areas. Watch out for swimmers, other boats, and other objects in the water.

Passing When one boat is overtaking another, the one being passed has the right-of-way. The boat that is passing may pass on either side after giving the proper signal such as one horn blast to signal passing on the right, two blasts to pass on the left; but the passing boat must keep clear of the boat being passed (Figure 12-6).

Warning: In a narrow channel, a small manoeuverable craft must not hamper the safe passage of a vessel that can navigate only inside the channel (e.g., less manoeuverable).

Safe behaviour in the boat

Follow these Do's and Don'ts:

Do's:

- Head for the nearest safe anchorage or landing when a storm threatens. Avoid the temptation to ride it out in open water.
- To avoid swamping small boats, slow down when passing, especially in narrow waters.
- Slow down in bad weather and when making sharp turns.

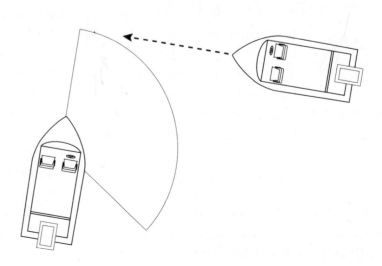

- Assist any boat in distress. Watch for distress signals. If you are not sure about a signal you see or hear, investigate.
- Slow down when passing an area where divers may be working.
- Stay clear of bathing beaches. Swimmers are hard to see in the water.
- Limit the number of people in the boat to the number indicated on the capacity plate.
- Remain seated when starting an outboard motor. The boat may suddenly move forward when it starts and cause you to fall.
- When approaching other boats while underway, establish your course early in accordance with the right-of-way rules.
- Stay alert for underwater obstacles such as rocks or fallen or submerged trees.

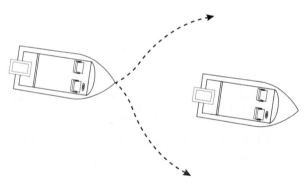

Figure 12-6. The boat being passed has the right of way.

Don'ts:

- Don't anchor too close to other boats.
- Don't cruise above the posted speed near an anchorage.
- Don't come near a river location where you see any sign of a lowhead dam.

Entering, exiting, and moving in a boat

Because a small boat or canoe can easily capsize when unbalanced or when hit by an unexpected wave, take special care when entering, exiting, or moving in a boat.

Boarding a boat and disembarking Make sure all passengers know how to board (get on) and disembark (get off) the boat safely.

- Wear nonskid deck shoes.
- Watch for waves or boat wakes that may throw you off balance.
- Alert those already on board that you are about to board or disembark.
- Have another person hold and help stabilize the boat while you board or disembark (Figure 12-7, **A** and **B**).

A   B

Figure 12-7, A and B. Stabilize the boat while boarding.

- Be careful not to step on equipment.
- Keep your weight low to the bottom of the boat to keep the boat stable.
- Use a paddle to stabilize a boat such as a canoe if it tips easily.

Boarding at a dock Make sure that the boat is tied at both the front (bow) and the back (stern). The lines should be snug but not so tight that they keep the boat from settling when weight is added.

Step aboard as close to the centre of the boat as you can. Reach down and grasp the side (gunwale) of the boat as you shift your weight to the foot in the boat. Then bring the trailing foot aboard. If the dock is much higher than the boat, sit on the dock and then move into the boat (Figure 12-8).

Boarding at a beach or shoreline Make sure the boat is floating and not partly resting on the bottom. Step over the bow or stern while you grasp the sides with both hands. Shift your weight to the foot in the boat. Keep your weight low to the bottom of the boat as you bring your trailing foot aboard (Figure 12-9).

Disembarking To disembark, reverse the steps used to board. Keeping your weight low, step ashore or onto the dock, carefully shift your weight to the leading foot, and then lift out your trailing foot.

Keeping the boat balanced For safety and best boating performance, the sides or gunwales of the boat should be parallel to the water with the weight or equipment and passengers evenly distributed.

- An overload forward causes the boat to plough (Figure 12-10, *A*).
- An overload aft causes the boat to "porpoise" (Figure 12-10, *B*).
- Balanced forward-aft load gives maximum performance (Figure 12-10, *C*).

Similarly, keep the load balanced side to side.

Changing Positions Normally, don't stand up or change seats in a small boat. If you must move, the easiest way to change positions is to return first to a dock or shore. But if you have to change positions in a small boat while out on the water, follow these guidelines:

- Only one person at a time should move.
- Keep body weight low and as near the centre of the boat as possible.
- Keep the boat trimmed by balancing the weight of one passenger against the weight of another (Figure 12-11).
- In heavy waves, change your position only when needed to correct the balance.

Figure 12-8. Board carefully from a dock.

Figure 12-9. Keep your weight low while boarding.

Figure 12-10. Keep the boat in trim with the load not too far forward (**A**), not too far aft (**B**), but well balanced (**C**).

A

B

C

Figure 12-11. Keep the boat in trim when changing positions.

Alcohol and boating

The criminal code of Canada treats drinking and driving a boat with the same severity as driving a car. First offenses can include prohibition from driving, fines, imprisonment, and prohibition from operating a vessel.

The operator and all passengers should stay sober. Passengers are equally at risk of falling in and not being able to reach safety. If the boat does hit something, both passengers and operators may be at risk.

For more information on the laws governing alcohol and vessels, contact your local Canadian Coast Guard or law enforcement office.

Boating and alcohol can be a deadly mix:
- The first drink of alcohol begins to affect balance, judgment, and reaction time—all of which are critical in the boating environment. Alcohol causes boaters to lose their balance and reduces the body's ability to protect against the effects of cold water. Alcohol contributes to faster loss of body heat and to the onset of hypothermia.

Boating and Drowning

- Boating fatalities cost Canada an annual average total cost of one hundred million dollars every year.

- Two thirds of all recreational boating drownings occur to people in powerboats up to 5.5 metres in length and canoes. In powerboats, the casualty typically falls overboard or the boat capsizes or swamps. Capsizing is the most common cause of canoeing drowning incidents. Most drownings occur on lakes, and the remainder on rivers and the ocean.

- In 90% of drownings from small powerboats and canoes, the casualty is male.

- 66% of powerboat drowning casualties and 50% of canoe drowning victims had been drinking alcohol (Figure 12-12).

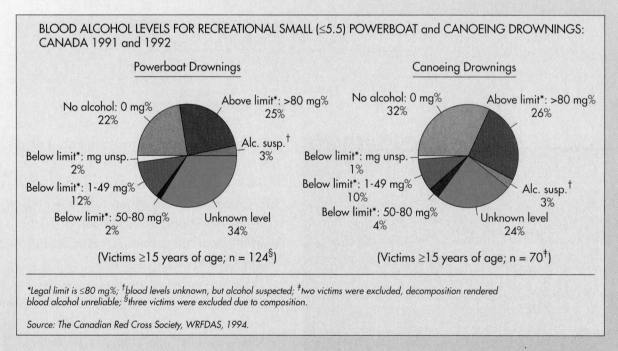

BLOOD ALCOHOL LEVELS FOR RECREATIONAL SMALL (≤5.5) POWERBOAT and CANOEING DROWNINGS: CANADA 1991 and 1992

Powerboat Drownings

- No alcohol: 0 mg% 22%
- Above limit*: >80 mg% 25%
- Alc. susp.[†] 3%
- Below limit*: mg unsp. 2%
- Below limit*: 1-49 mg% 12%
- Below limit*: 50-80 mg% 2%
- Unknown level 34%

(Victims ≥15 years of age; n = 124[§])

Canoeing Drownings

- No alcohol: 0 mg% 32%
- Above limit*: >80 mg% 26%
- Below limit*: mg unsp. 1%
- Below limit*: 1-49 mg% 10%
- Alc. susp.[†] 3%
- Below limit*: 50-80 mg% 4%
- Unknown level 24%

(Victims ≥15 years of age; n = 70[†])

*Legal limit is ≤80 mg%; [†]blood levels unknown, but alcohol suspected; [‡]two victims were excluded, decomposition rendered blood alcohol unreliable; [§]three victims were excluded due to composition.

Source: The Canadian Red Cross Society, WRFDAS, 1994.

Figure 12-12. Blood alcohol levels for recreational small powerboats (up to 5 metres) and canoeing drownings in Canada, 1991 and 1992.

- Only 8% of drowning casualties from small powerboats and canoes were properly wearing a personal flotation device (PFD) or lifejacket (Figure 12-13). Canoeists on lakes often do not use flotation devices because they underestimate the potential hazards of wind and waves—an attitude that can lead to death.

Information from The Canadian Red Cross Society, Highlights of Special Research Report on Drownings Among Recreational Boaters in Canada, 1994.

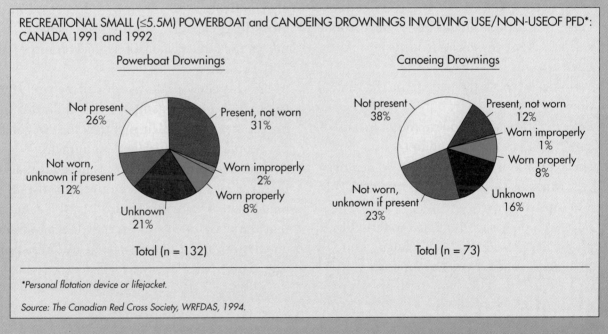

RECREATIONAL SMALL (≤5.5M) POWERBOAT and CANOEING DROWNINGS INVOLVING USE/NON-USEOF PFD*: CANADA 1991 and 1992

Powerboat Drownings

Not present 26%
Present, not worn 31%
Not worn, unknown if present 12%
Worn improperly 2%
Worn properly 8%
Unknown 21%

Total (n = 132)

Canoeing Drownings

Not present 38%
Present, not worn 12%
Worn improperly 1%
Worn properly 8%
Not worn, unknown if present 23%
Unknown 16%

Total (n = 73)

*Personal flotation device or lifejacket.

Source: The Canadian Red Cross Society, WRFDAS, 1994.

Figure 12-13. Recreational small powerboat (up to 5 metres) and canoeing drownings by use of PFD in Canada, 1991 and 1992.

- Alcohol intensifies the effect of disorientation caused by water entering the ear. An impaired person whose head is immersed can become so confused that he or she swims down to his or her death instead of up to the surface.
- Alcohol also severely diminishes a boater's ability to react to several stimuli at the same time, making it difficult to correctly judge speed and distance or track moving objects effectively.

Using Equipment Safely

- Wear a lifejacket or PFD approved by the Department of Transportation.
- Carry charts and publications in your boat that are up to date. Discard outdated ones.
- Sound your horn and use the spotlight only when necessary.
- Keep the bilges clean and free of oil, gasoline, and rags. Vent any enclosed areas into the open air.
- Periodically check the battery and its ventilation.
- Before starting an outboard motor, make sure it is set in neutral and in the straight-ahead position. A motor started while it is in gear can cause a small boat to turn suddenly and capsize.
- Keep some spare clothing in a watertight plastic bag. Also include a flashlight, knife, first aid kit, and emergency rations.

- Have the required and recommended safety equipment on board.
- Carry an anchor and a sufficient length of cable, rope, or chain (at least 7 times the anchorage depth at high tide). Be sure that the inboard end of the line is fastened securely.

Boat capacity

Overloading is dangerous. The number of people who can be carried safely depends on the type of boat, distribution of the occupants, and the equipment carried. Each operator must know the limitations of the vessel.

Every vessel up to 5.5 metres (up to 6 metres, since 1993) that can be powered by an engine of 7.5 k.w. (10 h.p.) or more must carry a capacity plate (Figure 12-14, *A*). This identifies that the boat complies with construction standards. It also indicates the recommended maximum gross load capacity, total engine power, and number of adults who can be safely transported in the vessel.

The capacity plate produced before 1993 (Figure 12-14, *B*) is still valid. It indicates the maximum load, which includes the weight of the people, engine, fuel, and equipment.

Virtually all motorized pleasure craft manufactured in Canada are required to display a metal plate or a decal (Figure 12-14, *C*) stating that the vessel meets or exceeds the minimum construction standards issued by Transport Canada.

Figure 12-14. A, Current capacity plate. **B,** Former capacity plate. **C,** Construction standards plate or decal.

Environmental Factors

Staying safe while boating also means monitoring the weather and knowing what to do in a storm or fog.

Monitoring the weather

You know the weather is changing when there is—

- Sudden, major wind direction change.
- Sudden temperature change.
- Cloud cover change.
- Barometric pressure change.
- Cloud elevation change.

Weathering a storm

If you are on the water and fog or a storm is approaching, follow these guidelines:

- Head for the nearest safe anchorage or landing.
- Slow down and keep the weight low in the craft.
- Take the waves on a slight angle.
- Move weight to the middle of the craft so that bow and stern ride higher. This helps to stabilize the boat and prevents taking on water.
- If fog moves in quickly and you are unable to make it to shore, sit quietly and listen for motors or horns that signal the approach of another boat.
- Use available navigational aids such as map or chart and compass to set a course for land.

KNOW HOW TO SURVIVE A BOATING EMERGENCY

 Even with thorough advance preparations and an understanding of how to stay safe while boating, an emergency can still occur. To survive such an emergency, be properly trained in rescue procedures for boating mishaps.

Reaching Assists

Reaching assists are used to extend your reach to rescue someone who has fallen out of a boat. Paddles, rope, PFDs, branches, and towels can be used. As a rescuer, you must be firmly secured in the boat and keep your weight low while offering an assist. Talk to the person in difficulty, encouraging him or her to calm down and hold on to the aid. Once the casualty has a firm grasp of the assist, you can pull him or her to safety (Figure 12-15). With a canoe, help the person into the craft at the midpoint. A rowboat or powerboat remains more stable if you bring the person in over the back of the boat (transom).

Assisting Someone Into a Craft

Assisting a person in distress into a small craft can be very difficult. If the individual is able to help, you can stabilize the craft and explain the best method to use. It may be best to paddle to shore with the person holding on to the craft (Figure 12-16), but if the person is exhausted or injured, consider the following factors:

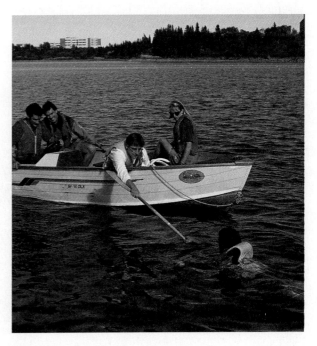

Figure 12-15. Reaching assist from boat.

- Distance to shore or other assistance
- Effect on craft of the additional weight
- Possible further injury to the person if he or she is pulled into the craft
- Water temperature

The rescuer has several options:

- Securing the person to the craft as the rescuer paddles or rows for help. However, if the water is cold, hypothermia can occur, and therefore it may be more important to remove the person from the water.

Figure 12-16. In warm water, if the casualty can hold on safely, paddle the craft to safety.

- Summoning help to transfer the casualty to a larger vessel.
- Pulling the person into the craft. Grab the casualty under the arms and, watching his or her head, pull up so that the armpits rest over the gunwales (or transom in motor or row boats). Pull the person in as far as the waist. At this point, swing the legs in to one side as you roll the casualty onto his or her back.

Climbing Back into a Canoe or Rowboat

If the canoe or rowboat is upright and not completely swamped, the person in distress can be directed to climb back into the craft. The person should place his or her hands at the bottom of the boat and kick vigorously to raise the hips to the gunwale or stern plate (Figure 12-17, *A*). The person then rotates the hips to sit on the bottom of the boat (Figure 12-17, *B*) and brings his or her legs into the boat (Figure 12-17, *C*). You can hand paddle an upright boat back to shore.

A

B

C
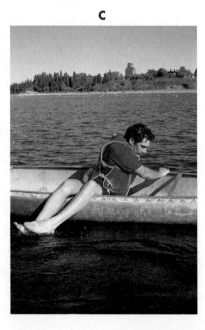

Figure 12-17, A to C. Climbing back into a canoe or rowboat.

Capsized or Swamped Boat

If your boat capsizes or becomes swamped, remain calm and assess the situation. Your first decision is whether to stay with the boat or leave it. If you stay with the boat, your actions depend on whether the water is warm or cold. Figure 12-18 shows this decision process.

Capsized canoe in a river

In this special situation, follow these guidelines:

- Hold onto the canoe, getting upstream of the boat. Hold onto your paddle if you can.

- If the water is too cold or the current is too dangerous, let the canoe go and head directly for shore. Don't try to swim upstream against the current.

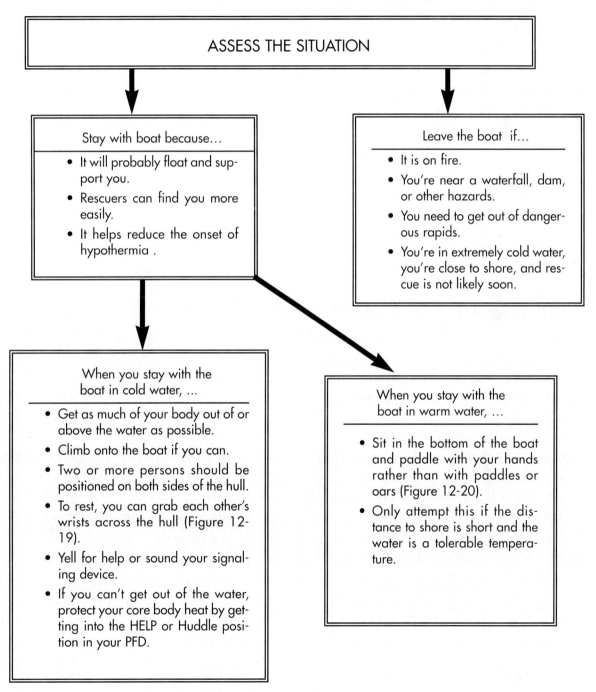

ASSESS THE SITUATION

Stay with boat because...

- It will probably float and support you.
- Rescuers can find you more easily.
- It helps reduce the onset of hypothermia .

Leave the boat if...

- It is on fire.
- You're near a waterfall, dam, or other hazards.
- You need to get out of dangerous rapids.
- You're in extremely cold water, you're close to shore, and rescue is not likely soon.

When you stay with the boat in cold water, ...

- Get as much of your body out of or above the water as possible.
- Climb onto the boat if you can.
- Two or more persons should be positioned on both sides of the hull.
- To rest, you can grab each other's wrists across the hull (Figure 12-19).
- Yell for help or sound your signaling device.
- If you can't get out of the water, protect your core body heat by getting into the HELP or Huddle position in your PFD.

When you stay with the boat in warm water, ...

- Sit in the bottom of the boat and paddle with your hands rather than with paddles or oars (Figure 12-20).
- Only attempt this if the distance to shore is short and the water is a tolerable temperature.

Figure 12-18. Assess the situation when the boat is swamped.

Figure 12-19. Grasp wrists across the hull of an over-turned boat in cold water.

Figure 12-20. In warm water, sit in the swamped craft and hand paddle to shore.

- Always float on your back, facing down-stream, with feet out before you to fend off obstacles.
- Head to the nearest bank or calm water by swimming on your back.
- Do not try to stand up in fast-moving water because your legs may become trapped in rocks as the current sweeps you over.

Craft-Over-Craft Rescue

Should a small craft overturn, the craft and its occupants can often be rescued by other small craft operators. The rescue craft provides buoyancy for the distressed craft to be pulled up and emptied of water.

Many combinations of craft-over-craft rescue are feasible, including canoe-over-canoe, canoe-over-kayak, and canoe-over-rowboat. The rescue depends on the weight of the craft and the strength of the rescuers.

The procedure is basically the same for all combinations, illustrated here with two canoes:

1. Coming onto the scene of an overturned craft, ensure that all boaters are safe and holding onto their craft or the rescue craft. Gather any floating gear and stow it in the rescue craft.

2. "T" the craft by bringing an end of the overturned craft amidship of the rescue craft. The rescuers may have to shift positions or turn around in their craft. If any boaters are in the water, have them take positions where they can be seen at all times. If the overturned craft is turned completely upside down, the air seal may have to be broken before lifting. Rock the craft slightly from side to side (Figure 12-21, *A*).

3. Lift the end of the overturned craft onto the rescue craft. Casualties may provide assistance by sinking the end of the overturned craft farthest away from the rescue craft. Lift one end to the gunwale *and* slide it over the gunwales of the rescue craft until it forms a cross (Figure 12-21, *B*).

4. In a cross position, the rescue craft is very stable. The rescuers can now flip the craft right side up (Figure 12-21, *C*) and return it to the water by sliding it over the gunwales (Figure 12-21, *D*).

5. The rescuers move the craft alongside their own and help the boaters back on board (Figure 12-21, *E*). This can be done by having them enter as they would from deep water, or by using the rescue craft for added stability. Equipment can then be put back in.

Figure 12-21, A to E. Craft-over-craft rescue.

Use common sense to modify this process as needed for other combinations of boats. For example, when rescuers are trying to put a canoe over a sailboard, only one person can stay on the board while the canoe is raised and cleared of water because the sailboard cannot bear as much weight as a larger craft.

Signaling and Reporting an Emergency

In an emergency you can signal others to call for help in several ways, depending on available equipment:

- Signal with four or more short blasts with an air horn or other sound source.

- Use a two-way radio.

- Use a flare.

- Wave your arms or paddle overhead in a horizon-to-horizon motion. This is a common way to signal that you need help.

When using a radio to call in your own emergency or one you see, quickly assess the situation first. Your assessment may determine the type of assistance provided. Be sure to note the weather and water conditions. Include in your radio report:

- Position of the boat

- Nature of the emergency

- Number of people on board

- Name and number of the boat, if applicable

- Description of the boat, including colour, type, length, and any distinguishing characteristics

- The assistance needed

Whom you contact in an emergency situation depends on the area. Rescue Coordination centres organize marine and air search and rescue operations throughout Canada, although in some areas the first contact might be the local RCMP or provincial or municipal police.

Rescue Breathing from a Craft

Rescue breathing for a casualty who has stopped breathing can be performed far more effectively if the casualty is removed from the water. However, you may have to give rescue breathing to a casualty in the water. The technique varies, depending on the craft, weather, and size of the casualty and rescuer.

1. Hold onto the casualty, keeping the casualty's mouth and nose clear of the water. If the casualty is wearing a flotation device, grasp it near the neck to provide head and neck support. If the casualty needs more support, hold the casualty under both arms or reach under one arm and hold onto the back of the casualty's head (Figure 12-22).

2. Position yourself so that you can lean over the casualty to begin rescue breathing.

The specific steps for providing rescue breathing are described in Chapter 14, Basic Life Support.

Figure 12-22. Rescue breathing done from small craft in deep water.

The Canadian Coast Guard

General

Under the jurisdiction of the Government of Canada, the Canadian Coast Guard contributes to the safe, efficient, and economical conduct of marine activities and to the protection of the quality of the marine environment in Canadian waters. Primarily, the Coast Guard coordinates marine search-and-rescue activities in cooperation with the Canadian Forces. Four Rescue Coordination Centres are staffed 24 hours a day in Victoria, British Columbia; Edmonton, Alberta; Trenton, Ontario; and Halifax, Nova Scotia. Rescue Coordination Sub-centres are also staffed to coordinate local marine search and rescue activities.

Rescue Coordination Centres organize all marine search and rescue operations throughout Canada. However, in certain areas local Royal Canadian Mounted Police or the provincial or municipal police are contacted when an emergency is suspected.

Prevention

Studies of search-and-rescue activities in recent years have acknowledged that the benefits of investing in programs focused on preventing loss of life far outweigh the costs of trying to rescue people once they are in trouble. As such, the Coast Guard puts a great deal of effort towards its Rescue and Environmental Response Loss of Life Prevention Program. This program consists of an overall strategy designed to decrease the frequency and/or severity of search-and-rescue incidents.

The primary client groups for the prevention program are pleasure craft operators and commercial fishermen who are involved in approximately 85% of search-and-rescue incidents annually. Various components that form the foundation of comprehensive, season-long campaigns include public service announcements, boating educational material, courtesy boat safety examinations, a Rescue and Environment Response 1-800 information hotline service, and other safety promotion activities.

SUMMARY

Boating is such a popular activity because of the great enjoyment it can bring. It is a wonderful way to experience Canada's many lakes, rivers, coasts, and waterways. Injury and death among boaters can be prevented if everyone prepares for safety on the water, follows the guidelines for safe boat operation, and knows what to do when an emergency does occur.

13

Rescue

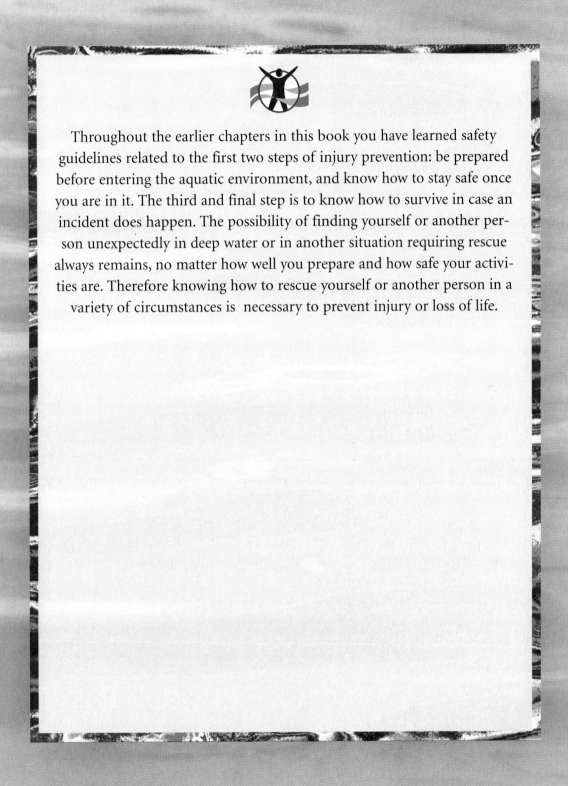

Throughout the earlier chapters in this book you have learned safety guidelines related to the first two steps of injury prevention: be prepared before entering the aquatic environment, and know how to stay safe once you are in it. The third and final step is to know how to survive in case an incident does happen. The possibility of finding yourself or another person unexpectedly in deep water or in another situation requiring rescue always remains, no matter how well you prepare and how safe your activities are. Therefore knowing how to rescue yourself or another person in a variety of circumstances is necessary to prevent injury or loss of life.

Should an emergency arise, you must know how to ensure your own safety and the safety of others by:

Performing self-rescue techniques:

- Heat escape–lessening position (HELP)

- Huddle position

- Staying with or entering an overturned craft

- Removal after falling through ice

Performing a reaching and throwing assist rescue to help someone in distress in the water

Most people who drown or become distressed in the water did not intend to get wet in the first place. They may have fallen from a boat, from shore, or from a snowmobile. Usually they were not wearing lifejackets or personal flotation devices (PFDs). Perhaps they thought, "It can't happen to me." But it can, and all too often it does.

Rescue is the term used for a variety of methods for helping a near-drowning casualty or distressed swimmer reach safety. These include skills for rescuing yourself or someone else. No matter how well you prepare in advance for water safety and how closely you follow the guidelines to stay safe while in, on, or around the water, you or someone in your group may become involved in a situation where rescue is needed. Knowing what to do can make the difference between life and death.

Partners in Prevention

This chapter was developed in collaboration with the Royal Life Saving Society Canada (RLSSC). RLSSC has been saving lives through drowning prevention since 1896. RLSSC lifesaving and lifeguarding programs are offered throughout Canada at pools, waterfronts, camps, and other settings. Most of the content in this chapter comes from or is based on *The Canadian Lifesaving Manual*, published by the RLSSC.

This chapter describes basic skills for rescuing yourself and others. It does not present detailed rescue procedures such as are used by lifeguards or skills needed to carry out rescues while in the water. Such skills are described in *The Canadian Lifesaving Manual*.

THE ROYAL LIFE SAVING SOCIETY CANADA
LA SOCIÉTÉ ROYALE DE SAUVETAGE CANADA

As you think about these rescue skills, be realistic. We are all familiar with movies that portray lifesavers as selfless heroes who put themselves in danger to save others. In real life, lifesavers must not be completely selfless. True, you must think of the well-being of the person needing rescue, but *you must always put your own safety first.* You are not a hero if you make a foolhardy rescue attempt that turns you into a second casualty. Therefore, as you will learn in this chapter, always choose rescue techniques that place you in the least possible danger.

SELF-RESCUE

Because of the risk of falling into the water, nonswimmers should wear a lifejacket or PFD whenever they are near water. This flotation device makes self-rescue or rescue by another more likely and easier.

Self-rescue can mean reaching safety by yourself or staying afloat long enough for someone to help you. In both cases, be prepared by knowing how to survive a sudden, unexpected entry or problem in the water.

The method you use for self-rescue depends on factors such as the water temperature and the presence of currents. The following sections describe self-rescue techniques for deep water, cold water, hot water, and water with strong currents.

Self-Rescue in Deep Water

In deep water, try to move to safety if you can. If you cannot, call out or signal for help. Stay on the surface by swimming, using surface support skills, or floating. (Chapter 8 describes these techniques.) Follow these guidelines to decide what to do:

- Consider swimming for safety if no one responds to your call for help within a few minutes. You can swim for safety if you are in known water and the distance you need to swim is appropriate for your swimming skills, your energy level, and the conditions at the time. Remember, distances over the water often appear shorter than they actually are.

- Treading water to stay at the surface requires less energy than swimming but more than floating. Treading water may result in less heat loss than motionless floating on the back.

- Motionless floating is useful for conserving energy while waiting for help or while resting. This is an effective survival skill in calm, warm water (20° to 24° C). Motionless floating is not recommended for self-rescue in cold water (10° C or lower) because much heat is lost through the head when it is fully or partially submerged. This results in a lowering of the body's core temperature.

Swimming self-rescue

Following are some tips for a swimming self-rescue:

- Check whether there is a current, wind, or tide you can use to your advantage in planning your swimming route. An onshore current or wind may aid your progress toward shore.

- Use any buoyant object to help you stay afloat while you swim.

- Although a PFD or lifejacket may make swimming a little more difficult, do not remove it.

- Unless you are in warm water, swim with your head up because of the heat loss that will occur when the head is submerged in cold water.

- Do not swim too fast. Pace yourself and keep your breathing relaxed and controlled.

Treading water self-rescue

Chapter 8 describes different types of surface support. Treading water is one alternative. You can also alternate among different leg movements to reduce fatigue.

Floating self-rescue

Chapter 8 also describes the different kinds of floats you can use while waiting to be rescued. Your goal is to choose the position that allows you to be motionless with nose and mouth above the water. Remember that keeping your lungs full of air helps you float. Hold your breath when floating motionless; blowing out fully may make you sink. Try to stay calm and control your breathing; panic makes it more difficult to float motionless.

Self-rescue after a boat incident

If you are in a boat that swamps or capsizes, think carefully before you choose to swim to safety. In general, it is safer to stay with the boat and wait to be rescued. See Chapter 12, Boating Safety, for more information.

Clothing

Remove clothing in cold water only if wearing it threatens your life. Clothes can trap water and add insulation. In warm water you can remove any clothing that is weighing you down unless you are wearing a PFD. Use these methods:

- *Shoes or boots:* Get in a tuck position and remove one shoe at a time.
- *Jacket:* In a back float position, use both hands to unfasten and remove the jacket.
- *Pants:* If necessary, unfasten the pants while treading water in a vertical position or while floating. Then get in a tuck position and slide the pants off.
- *Shirt:* Unfasten and remove the shirt in either a back float or backward-leaning position.
- *Pullover shirt or sweater:* Grasp the base of the shirt or sweater with crossed arms and pull it over your head and arms in a single

movement. Note that taking off this type of clothing may be quite difficult and use a great deal of energy.

- *Other clothes:* There is no need to remove clothing that does not interfere with swimming movements.

Self-Rescue in Cold Water

Cold water is more dangerous than warm, but you can use different survival skills to reach safety or stay at the surface until rescued. First, you need to know the effects on the body of sudden immersion in cold water. Several reflex "shock" responses occur because of the immediate drop in skin temperature:

- The gasp reflex causes a sudden breathing in followed by involuntary hyperventilation. This may cause water to be breathed into the airway.
- The ability to hold the breath is greatly reduced.
- Heart rate and blood pressure both increase.

Continued exposure to the cold causes a rapid decline in strength and in the ability to use the fingers, hands, and limbs. This makes it more difficult to hold onto rescue aids.

Because of the immediate effects of cold water, the priority is to get out of the water as fast as possible. If you can, use a quick burst of energy to get out, remove wet clothing immediately, and dry off and keep warm. (See Chapter 4 for information on preventing and treating hypothermia.)

If you cannot get out immediately, take action to extend your survival time while waiting to be rescued. Follow these guidelines:

- If you expect to be in the water a long time, move slowly and deliberately to conserve heat. Because your strength and ability to move will diminish, any manoeuvre that requires strength should be done right away.

- Keep on any clothing that will help you conserve heat.

- If you are not wearing a PFD or life-jacket, tread water.

If you are wearing a PFD or lifejacket, use the HELP or Huddle position to reduce heat loss while waiting for rescue (see Chapter 4).

Cramps

Cramps are a threat in cold water self-rescues. Cramps occur when your muscles become cold or tired from swimming. The muscle contracts suddenly, usually in the arm, foot, or calf. Try to relax it by not moving, by changing position of the limb, or by massaging the area. To massage a cramp of the calf muscles, take a deep breath, roll face-down, extend your leg and flex your ankle, and massage the cramp (Figure 13-1).

Self-Rescue in Hot Water

Hot water (over 37° to 40° C) such as in a spa or hot tub can cause dizziness and weakness. Often you do not feel these effects until you stand up to get out of the water.

Follow these guidelines if you stand up in hot water and feel dizzy:

1. Move to a horizontal position and crawl out of the water.

2. Once out, lie on your side until you feel better.

Figure 13-1. Massage the muscle to relieve a leg cramp.

3. Call for help if the dizziness does not pass soon.

Rest before starting regular activities after experiencing dizziness. Drink water or other fluids before getting in hot water. This replaces fluids lost and prevents negative effects such as dizziness and muscle weakness.

Self-Rescue in Currents

In the ocean you may experience strong under-tows or rip currents. In a river you may experience powerful currents or hydraulics. Use the guidelines in the following sections for self-rescue from these kinds of currents.

Undertows

Undertows are backwash currents that occur when the water from a wave flows back into the ocean from a beach. The greater the slope of the beach or the size of the wave, the greater the strength of the undertow. Undertows can also occur in wave pools.

An undertow can knock you down and carry you outward, often into deeper water, and then send you back to shore. Follow these self-rescue guidelines:

1. Stay calm and prepare to be carried back to shore.

2. When the next wave carries you back to shore, regain your footing, stand up, and walk out of the waves.

Rip currents

Rip currents can occur when water from waves that accumulates near shore rushes seaward through a break in the surfline, such as between sandbars or in an underwater gulley. A rip current is the most dangerous hazard at ocean beaches because it can quickly carry you out into deeper water. Unlike the situation with an undertow, however, you are not returned to the beach by the next wave. A rip current can carry you a distance from shore.

You may notice a rip current if you see a break in the surfline, an area of darker water near the beach, or an area that looks muddy (because of the sand carried in the current).

Follow these steps for self-rescue:

1. Don't try to fight the current. The current will weaken and dissipate as it moves seaward.

2. Swim across the current and back to safety.

Lateral (side) currents often feed into rip currents. Lateral currents can be dangerous because you can be carried out of your depth or into a rip current. Too often people don't even recognize they are moving in a lateral current. Periodically check your location in relation to a landmark on shore. You can usually swim out of the lateral current to reach shore (Figure 13-2).

River currents

Never underestimate the power of a river current, even if it seems slow. You may find yourself swept into a river current from an overturned boat, from a section of river bank that suddenly collapses, or from a shallower area where you were wading. Rescue yourself following these guidelines:

1. Don't fight the current.

2. Turn onto your back and try to stay on the surface.

3. Move feet-first with the current (Figure 13-3).

4. Watch for obstacles and debris ahead and try to avoid them.

5. Manoeuvre diagonally out of the current to safety.

Hydraulic currents

Hydraulic currents are recirculating currents that occur just below low-head dams. These are dams in which the top of the dam is below the water's surface. These dams look innocent because the hydraulic usually can't be seen, but they are very dangerous because the current is strong enough to hold you once it catches you. It can suck you underwater and smash you against the bottom or other objects.

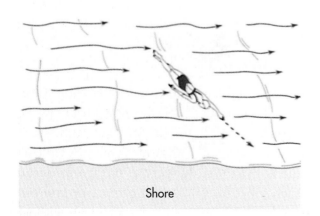

Figure 13-2. Angle toward shore when in a lateral current.

Figure 13-3. Travel downstream feet-first in a river current.

If caught in a hydraulic current, follow these guidelines for self-rescue:

1. Stay calm and don't try to fight the current.

2. If you can, grab a large object such as a rock or boat and wait for help.

3. Watch out for debris caught in the current, such as tree branches.

4. If you can't grab a secure object to hold onto, you can swim underwater away from the bottom of the hydraulic current. Let the current pull you under and then swim with the downstream current away from the dam. You may have to repeat this effort.

RECOGNISING A PERSON IN TROUBLE IN THE WATER

Before you can rescue someone who is in trouble in the water, you have to recognize that the person is in danger. In a crowded or noisy aquatic setting, you may not automatically notice the problem. Watch for these signs of someone in danger:

• Fear on the face of someone in the water

• Lack of progress of a person trying to swim

• A distressed call for help

• An overturned boat

• An inflatable toy apparently abandoned in the water

• A crowd gathering

People in danger of drowning may be either distressed swimmers or drowning casualties, as described in the following paragraphs.

Distressed Swimmer

A distressed swimmer can be a novice swimmer with limited swimming ability, a tired or weak swimmer or someone who is ill or injured. A swimmer who is disoriented after playing in or falling into the water may also become a distressed swimmer. Unless rescued, a distressed swimmer usually becomes a drowning casualty. Signs of a distressed swimmer vary but may include (Figure 13-4):

• The person's body position approaches vertical.

• The person is making little forward progress.

• Distress is obvious on the person's face.

• The person may be able to call or wave for help.

• If injured or ill, the person may be holding the affected area of the body.

• The person may be facing an apparent point of safety such as the shore, a raft, or a boat.

Drowning Casualties

Drowning casualties are not able to support themselves at the surface. Even a good swimmer

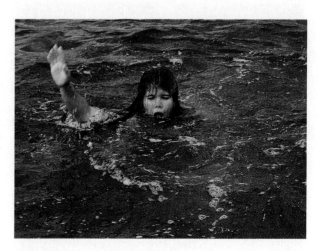

Figure 13-4. A distressed swimmer can stay afloat and usually calls out for help.

can become a drowning casualty as a result of an illness or injury. The casualty may not struggle if affected by illness, an injury such as a blow to the head, alcohol or other drugs, hyperventilation, fatigue, or unconsciousness.

All struggling drowning casualties demonstrate an identifiable pattern of behaviour called the instinctive drowning response. Because the person is unable to breathe, he or she cannot call out for help. All energy is used in trying to get or keep the face out of the water to breathe. The signs of a drowning casualty are (Figure 13-5):

- The person is vertical in the water, with legs not being used for propulsion or treading water.
- Fear may show on the face.
- The person's arms may be flailing up and down, as he or she tries to rise in the water to breathe, rather than trying to swim forward.
- The struggle is uncontrolled and lasts only a short time.

It is important to understand that the drowning person's response is instinctive—not rational or within the person's control once the body starts its struggle for air. This is one reason why

Figure 13-5. An active drowning casualty struggles to stay afloat and is unable to call out for help.

you should never just swim up to a drowning person to try to rescue him or her. Even if that person is a child or loved one, he or she is acting instinctively and may grab you ferociously about the head or other body area and refuse to let go long enough for you to get into position for a rescue. In such cases you too are likely to become a drowning casualty. Even professional lifeguards are trained to use caution when approaching a drowning casualty without equipment for the person to grab onto— because the body's instinctive response is so powerful.

RESCUE OF OTHERS: DECISION MAKING

When you recognize a distressed swimmer or drowning casualty, you must first check for hazards in the area.

Hazards

In any rescue situation there may be hazards in the environment that could endanger you or cause further danger to the casualty. Remove such hazards from the area when you can, or remove the casualty from the hazards:

- Water
- Poisonous gas, such as engine exhaust or chlorine gas
- Other poisons
- Live electrical wires
- Debris, broken glass
- Extreme cold or heat
- Animals

The Ladder Approach to Rescue

After considering hazards and before starting the rescue, you need to *decide* which rescue method to use. No one technique works in all instances, as you will see in the following sec-

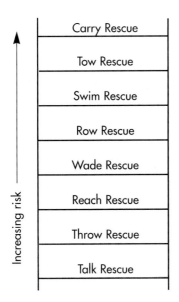

Figure 13-6. The ladder approach to water rescue.

tions. The general principle for decision making is to use the least risky method that will work and for which you are equipped.

This principle can be easily understood in terms of the ladder approach illustrated above (Figure 13-6). Start at the bottom rung of the ladder: use that method if it will work, or take a step up to the next rung and try that one. Consider every rung before moving to a higher, more risky rescue method, and always use the lowest rung possible.

These types of rescue are described in the following sections.

Talk Rescue

From a dry, safe location, give the person clear, simple instructions about what to do, along with verbal encouragement.

- From a crouched position, tell the casualty, "Watch me, keep your head up, kick your feet, and grab the side...."
- Eye contact and positive encouragement can have immediate results on a casualty at close range, without putting you in any danger.

Throw Rescue

If the casualty is a short distance away and a suitable buoyant object is available, throw the object so the casualty can grasp it for support (Figure 13-7).

- Be careful not to hit the casualty on the head when throwing the object.
- Encourage the casualty verbally, and direct him or her toward safety.
- Remember that wind and waves make it harder to throw accurately.

Reach rescue

If you can find a suitable rescue aid, extend it and pull the casualty to safety. If the casualty is close enough, even a towel can work. A pole or branch can work with a casualty who is farther away.

- A buoyant object works best, because it can help support the casualty in the water so that you don't have to both lift and pull. A rope attached to the buoyant object can extend your reach even farther.
- Keep your centre of gravity as low as possible.
- Anchor yourself by holding onto a solid object such as a tree root, ladder, or dock with your free hand to prevent being pulled into the water.

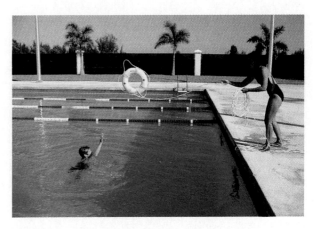

Figure 13-7. Performing a throw rescue.

Wade rescue

When the casualty cannot be rescued from shore and if the water is shallow, wade into the water with a rescue aid and extend it to the casualty (Figure 13-8).

- Minimize the risk by keeping your feet on the solid bottom at all times or by grasping a solid object such as dock or ladder with your free hand.

- With others to help you, form a human chain by taking hold of each other's wrists. The rescuer nearest the casualty extends the rescue aid and encourages the casualty. Another rescuer guides the chain back to shore (Figure 13-9).

Row rescue

The row rescue is riskier because you do it in open water from a small boat.

- Try to manoeuvre the boat so that you approach the casualty from downwind to lower the chances of pushing the boat into the casualty and causing injury.

- Follow the ladder approach to first talk to the casualty, then throw him or her a life-jacket, PFD, or boat cushion, and if necessary reach a paddle or throwing line to the casualty.

- When the casualty has grasped the rescue aid firmly, decide whether to row to shore towing the casualty in the water or to help the casualty onto the boat. The choice you make takes into account the casualty's condition and size, the boat's stability, your distance from shore, the water temperature, your skill, and the number of rescuers.

How a small boat is used in a rescue depends on the size and type of boat:

- *Canoes* can be very unstable and should be used only by experienced canoeists in a rescue. It is very difficult to get a casualty into the canoe.

- *Inflatable boats* have varying stability. Those with outboard motors are more easily manoeuvred and are easily used in a rescue.

- *Kayaks, rowing sculls, and paddleboards* have limited stability, but the casualty can hold on to them to be towed to safety. You can also use them as a buoyant rescue aid to support the casualty in the water.

- *Powerboats* that are not too large or difficult to manoeuvre work well for rescues. When near the casualty, cut the power to avoid injuring the person.

Figure 13-8. Performing a reach rescue after wading in close to casualty.

Figure 13-9. Creating a human chain to rescue a casualty.

- *Rowboats* are easy to manoeuvre and are stable. The casualty can be helped into the boat over a square stern. Rescue breathing can be given over the stern to a casualty still in the water.

- *Sailboards* should be sailed to a casualty only by skilled board sailors. However, the sail can be taken off, and the board used as a paddleboard for a rescue.

- *Sailboats* require experience and skill to be used for a rescue. To approach the casualty, manoeuvre the boat from downwind and stop alongside the casualty. Depending on the size and shape of the sailboat, the casualty may be brought aboard or towed to shore in the water.

- *Personal watercraft* can be used in an emergency to transport a casualty to safety if the person can be brought aboard. Otherwise, the casualty can hold onto the watercraft until further help arrives.

Swim rescue

You may have to enter the water during a rescue if the casualty's condition gets worse, if the casualty cannot be reached with a throwing assist, or if no craft is available for rescue.

- Enter the water with a buoyant rescue aid (such as a rescue tube or flutter board) and swim to the casualty.

- Minimize your personal risk by stoping before you reach the casualty and pushing the buoyant aid to the casualty from a safe distance away. Avoid even indirect contact with the casualty.

- Move back as the casualty grasps the aid, maintain eye contact, and encourage the casualty to kick or paddle to safety while holding onto the aid.

Tow rescue

When you try the swim rescue, the casualty may not be able to propel himself or herself to safety while holding the buoyant rescue aid.

- Pull from the other end of the rescue aid to tow the casualty to safety (Figure 13-10).

- As this indirect contact brings you close to the casualty, ensure your own safety by being ready to move away quickly at any time.

Carry rescue

If all else fails, you may have to use the carry rescue. This may occur if the casualty cannot support his or her head above the water while holding onto the rescue aid, if no rescue aid is available and the casualty is not responding to verbal encouragement, or if the casualty is unconscious.

- Calm the person before making contact. Throughout the rescue keep reassuring the casualty.

- Never make contact with a violently struggling person. Try to calm the person, or wait until he or she is subdued and just starting to submerge.

Figure 13-10. Towing a casuality to safety.

- Always maintain control of your own body and that of the casualty. If you think you're losing control, break away and start over.

- There are many types of water rescue carries. Some offer only minimal assistance, whereas others directly control the casualty. An assistive carry, such as an armpit carry, should be used when the casualty is conscious and can provide some help to the rescuer (Figure 13-11). A more controlling carry, such as a cross-chest carry, should be used with an unconscious casualty.

RESCUE OF OTHERS: RESCUE SKILLS

The ladder approach helps you to decide what kind of rescue to make. The rescue skills themselves—*how* to do the rescue—are described in this section. This process begins with using an assisted aid and entering the water and includes removing the casualty and follow-up care and activities.

Figure 13-11. An assistive carry can be used when the casualty is conscious and calm.

Assistive Rescue Aids

An assistive rescue aid is an object you use in the rescue, whether it is to extend or throw to the casualty. It allows the casualty to grasp onto something and be pulled to safety, and it may provide buoyant support as well.

Your choice of what assistive rescue aid to use depends on the situation and the available aids. Different techniques are used with the different assistive rescue aids.

Choosing an assistive rescue aid

Consider the following factors when choosing an assistive rescue aid:

- *Availability:* The object must be readily available at the moment needed.

- *Buoyancy:* Floating objects support the casualty higher in the water and let you rest if needed during the rescue.

- *Manageability:* The assistive rescue aid must be easy to handle on land and in the water, and easy to transport to the casualty.

- *Strength:* The assistive rescue aid must be strong enough to accomplish the rescue.

- *Your own fitness and strength:* Be sure you can carry and use the assistive rescue aid effectively.

- *The immediate surroundings:* Make sure the aid can be manoeuvred in the available space.

Types of assistive rescue aids

Assistive rescue aids include the following (Figure 13-12):

- *Lifejackets and PFDs:* Because of their buoyancy, these are effective aids that can be thrown or extended to the casualty.

- *Throw bags:* Throw bags are a white-water rescue aid. They consist of a bag with a length of rope that streams out of the bag while in flight. With practice, you can throw these bags a good distance accurately.

Figure 13-12. Assistive rescue aids include rescue tubes, throw bags, and ring buoys.

- *Kickboards:* Kickboards and flutter boards are available in many facilities and can be used as assistive aids.

- *Improvised buoyant aids:* Buoyant objects such as large plastic bottles, plastic coolers, gasoline cans, paddles, boards, and branches can all be used in rescues. Poles, oars, paddles, and sticks make good extensions because they are usually light and strong and can be extended easily to the casualty.

- *Reaching poles:* Reaching poles are used when the casualty is within reaching distance. Poles vary in length and material. Some are lightweight, and some are electrically insulated. Reaching poles with a hook on one end are called "shepherd's hooks."

- *Ring buoys:* Ring buoys are required at pools and beaches in many provinces and territories. They are also found at many docks and marinas. A length of rope (appropriate for the environment) allows them to be thrown to someone at a distance.

- *Rescue cans and rescue tubes:* Rescue cans (buoys) and tubes come with a length of rope and strap that slips over the shoulder. These can be used as reaching assists or as aids to tow or carry distressed swimmers or drowning casualties.

- *Clothing as Towing Aids:* Shirts and pants can be used as towing assistive rescue aids if you must enter the water to reach the casualty. Swim with the pants or shirt over your shoulders, with the legs or sleeves stretched forward over your shoulders and back under your arms. If the casualty is calm, pass the legs or sleeves under his or her arms and back over the shoulders, and hold both sleeves or pant legs in one hand as you swim back to safety.

Using assistive rescue aids

Assistive rescue aids are extended or thrown to the casualty. Follow the guidelines described in the following paragraphs.

To extend an assistive rescue aid to the casualty—

- Keep your centre of gravity low to avoid being pulled into the water.

- If the casualty is just out of reach, lie down at a 45-degree angle on the side of the dock or pool with legs spread for stability. With one shoulder over the edge of the dock or pool deck, you have the longest reach.

- If a rigid reaching pole or other aid is not available, use any material at hand such as clothing, a towel, or a blanket to reach to the casualty. You may have to "flip" the flexible aid to the casualty.

- After extending the aid, crouch or drop to one knee, staying as far from the water's edge as you can.

- Be careful not to jab a struggling casualty with the aid.

- Pull the aid back in hand over hand, moving gradually to the edge to secure the casualty.

- Only if no assistive rescue aid at all is available, reach with an arm from the position lying down with legs spread. Keep a firm grip on the pool edge, dock, or boat.

To extend a reaching pole to the casualty (Figure 13-13)—

- Make sure the casualty can grab the pole without being injured.

- Control the pole to avoid injuring anyone around you.

- Stay low when reaching to ensure your own stability.

- When the casualty has grasped the end of the pole, bring it back in hand over hand.

- Let the casualty contact the edge of the pool or dock before using your hand to secure him or her. Reach out to a casualty only if he or she has trouble grasping the edge of the pool or dock.

To use a throwing assist—

- Secure the trailing end of the rope by a method such as tying it to a dock or making a knot at one end and holding it under one foot.

- For greater accuracy in the throw, tie a lightly weighted buoyant object such as a semi-filled plastic container on the end of the line (Figure 13-14). This throwing assistive aid should be prepared and in place. Do not spend time locating equipment when there is an emergency.

- Consider currents and other factors that can affect your throw. Throw upstream so that the current will carry the assisted aid to the casualty.

- Throw past the casualty with a pendulum swing. For greatest distance, throw at an upward angle of 45 degrees.

- After throwing, drop to one knee or lie flat on your stomach for greater stability.

- When the casualty has grasped the aid, pull it back slowly hand over hand.

- Let the casualty contact the edge of the pool or dock before using your hand to secure him or her. Reach out to casualties only if they have trouble grabbing the edge of the pool or dock on their own.

Figure 13-13. Using a reaching pole in a rescue.

Figure 13-14. Use a lightly weighted buoyant object on a line for a throwing assist.

Keep a throwing rope on your dock, boat, or other setting. Keep the rope permanently knotted at the end and uniformly coiled to save time in an emergency.

Entries

In an emergency you may need to enter the water rapidly and safely if you can't use a reaching or throwing rescue. In this case you must use a method appropriate for the situation. Possible entries include:

- Wading or jumping
- Slip-in entry
- Stride jump
- Shallow dive
- Compact jump

These entries are described fully in Chapter 7, Entering the Water.

Removals

Once you have brought the casualty to the edge of the water using any rescue technique, you need to remove him or her from the water *unless you suspect that the person has a spinal injury*(described in a later section). There are different ways to remove a casualty, depending on these factors:

- The casualty's condition
- The availability of others to help
- Your strength and abilities
- Characteristics of the site, including water depth, water conditions, and the height of the deck, dock, or shoreline.

When you've brought a casualty to safety, you should get him or her out of the water as quickly as possible without risking injury to either of you. To lift or carry a casualty, remember to let your legs do the work, not your back. Keep your back as straight as possible. Usually someone else is nearby to help you.

Removal methods include the shallow water assist, the beach drag, and the lift from water.

Shallow-water assist

If the casualty is a tired or beginning swimmer who has been helped to a depth where he or she can stand, you may use the shallow-water assist. This person may be able to walk with some support. The following directions apply to a casualty on your right side; use the reverse for the left.

1. Stand with the casualty at your right side.

2. Place your right hand around the casualty's waist and duck your head under the casualty's left arm.

3. With your left hand firmly grasp the casualty's left arm, which is now over your shoulder, slowly assist the casualty up the pool steps or onto the shore (Figure 13-15).

Beach drag

You may use the drag assist for an unconscious or ill casualty on a sloping shore or beach. Because the water helps support the casualty's weight for part of the distance, this method works well with a heavy casualty.

Figure 13-15. Shallow-water assist.

Once you are in water at a depth where you can stand, move behind the casualty. Secure a hold at the armpits and support his or her head if needed. Walk backward slowly toward the beach, pulling the casualty. The water supports the casualty's body. Keep your back as straight as you can and let your legs do the work (Figure 13-16).

When you can rest the casualty on the beach with head and shoulders out of the water, you may stop and call for help. Or you may drag the casualty completely from the water by moving your arms forward under the casualty's armpits and interlacing your fingers in front of his or her chest. Moving backwards, pull the casualty onto the beach. You may use a two-person drag if another person is present to help you (Figure 13-17).

Lift from water

This removal is used for unconscious casualties or those who are unable to assist in removing themselves from the water. The procedure described here assumes that you are in the water with the casualty; if you are already on land, you can start the lift from Step 3.

If you have to lift a casualty from the water onto a dock, pier, or pool deck, be very careful to avoid injuring both yourself and the casualty. If you do not think that you can perform the lift safely, remain in the water with the casualty until further assistance arrives—either another adult who can help or an emergency care professional. If you suspect that the casualty has a spinal injury, do not use this lift.

1. When you have towed the casualty to the pier or edge of the pool, get a good grasp on the edge and rotate him or her to face the pier or pool side. Support the casualty with your knees while you reach under the casualty's armpits and grasp the edge. Ensure that the casualty's nose and mouth remain out of the water.

2. Place the casualty's hands, one on top of the other, on the deck. Then place one of your hands on top of the casualty's hands, move to one side of the casualty, and climb or crawl out of the water (Figure 13-18, *A*).

3. Keeping hold of the casualty's hands, pivot to face him or her. Transfer your hold to the casualty's shoulder and armpit region and rotate the casualty so that his or her back is against the deck.

Figure 13-16. Beach drag.

Figure 13-17. Two-rescuer beach drag.

4. Stand as close to the edge as possible, bend your knees, place your elbows under the casualty's armpits, and with your hands grasp his or her wrists. Remember to let your legs rather than your back do the work when pulling the casualty from the water. Keep the casualty's mouth above water at all times (Figure 13-18, *B*).

5. When the casualty's hips clear the edge of the deck, step back with one leg and rest him or her in a sitting position on the edge of the deck as you drop to one knee (Figure 13-18, *C*).

6. Gently lower the casualty onto his or her back in a position where you can care for the airway and check for breathing and pulse.

A   **B**   **C**

Figure 13-18, A to C. Steps for lifting a casualty to the pool deck.

Follow-up

After the casualty is out of the water, evaluate his or her condition and provide first aid as needed (see Chapter 14). If possible, get help to move the casualty to a more comfortable environment for recovery.

Call Emergency Medical Services (EMS) if necessary. Always call if the casualty is unconscious or became a distressed swimmer or drowning casualty because of sudden illness or injury. Other situations in which you should call EMS are listed in Chapter 14, which also describes how to make the call.

Write down any information you have about the incident while it is still fresh in your mind. Note things such as the conditions, what you observed, and who else witnessed the incident.

RESCUE OF SPINAL INJURY CASUALTIES

Serious injuries can occur to the skull or bones of the spine (vertebrae) or to the brain or spinal cord when one's head strikes the bottom or some object underwater. As you learned in earlier chapters in this book, most spinal injuries can be prevented, but they do occur. People do dive into shallow water and fracture their necks. People do strike their heads against underwater rocks and injure their spinal cords. Therefore you need to know how to rescue a casualty with a spinal injury in a way that prevents additional injury. Skillful care can be the difference between an injury that heals and permanent paralysis.

Chapter 14 describes how to give first aid for casualties of life-threatening injuries—how to call emergency medical services and care for the airway, breathing, and circulation. For a casualty with a possible spinal injury, follow the same principles. The primary difference is that, during the rescue and giving of first aid, you take additional steps to immobilize the spine to ensure no additional injury occurs.

NOTE: The following material describes the basic principles for rescuing and giving first aid to a casualty with an aquatic spinal injury. The RLSSC provides more detailed information in its lifesaving training courses.

Recognising a Spinal Injury

When you see that a person in the water needs help, you cannot know immediately whether the person may have a spinal injury. The most important reason to suspect a possible spinal injury is the nature or cause of the incident. Suspect a spinal injury if the casualty—

- Dove into shallow water.
- Dove into another swimmer, or was dived on by another swimmer.
- Hit the head against the pool wall while diving or swimming.
- Dove from a height or from a diving board or water slide.
- Fell from a height.
- Has an obvious head injury.
- Is unconscious for no known reason.

Note that a person does not have to hit the bottom, wall, or another object very hard to cause a spinal injury. In most cases of spinal injuries, the impact is not even forceful enough to cause a bruise on the skin—yet it may break the person's neck!

Also suspect a spinal injury if the casualty displays any of these signs and symptoms:

- Pain, swelling, bruising, or deformity at the site of the injury
- Numbness, tingling, lack of sensation, or difficulty moving arms or legs
- Signs of a head injury
- Unconsciousness
- Blood or fluid in the ears
- Unequal pupils

If you suspect a spinal injury, call EMS to ensure that trained professionals will be on the scene.

Approaching a Casualty with Spinal Injury

Even the movement of water against the person's body can be enough to cause additional injury in a casualty with a spinal injury. Therefore avoid an approach that causes a lot of splashing. Slip into the water and approach carefully to minimize waves.

Immobilising a Spinal Injury Casualty

A casualty with a spinal injury is often found floating face-down in the water. In this case you need to roll the casualty over so that he or she can breathe but in a way that keeps the spine immobile to prevent further injury. Use the technique called the Canadian rollover in which the casualty's head and neck are splinted between the person's own arms, as described in the following paragraphs.

This technique can be used in a variety of circumstances with casualties of different sizes. It is especially useful when the casualty is in shallow water or when the casualty is much smaller or larger than the rescuer. Follow these steps:

1. Stand at one side of the casualty just below the shoulders.

2. Grasp the casualty's arms midway between the elbow and the shoulder, with your right hand on the casualty's right arm and your left hand on the casualty's left arm.

3. Gently float the casualty's arms up alongside his or her head, parallel to the water's surface.

4. Position the casualty's arms extending against his or her head (Figure 13-19, A).

5. With your fingers squeeze the arms against the head to splint the head and neck. Extend your thumbs and place them on the back of the casualty's head.

6. Lower your body to chest depth, and move the casualty slowly forward and to a horizontal position, gliding the casualty's body to the surface.

7. As the casualty becomes horizontal in the water, keep moving forward slowly and rotating the casualty toward you until he or she is face up with head resting in the crook of your arm (Figure 13-19, B and C).

8. Now you can check the airway and assess the casualty's breathing and pulse (Figure 13-19, D).

For a casualty found floating face up on the back, immobilize the head and neck in the same manner, splinting the casualty's head with his or her own arms extended.

If the casualty is in deep water, immobilize the head and turn the casualty over to facilitate breathing. Note that this technique in deep water is very difficult and should be practiced. Move the casualty to shallow water, when possible.

Care for the ABCs of a Spinal Injury Casualty

Chapter 14 describes in detail the process for checking an aquatic casualty for a life-threatening condition. To do this, remember the ABCs:

A—Airway

B—Breathing

C—Circulation (pulse)

The technique of securing the casualty to a backboard should be left to trained lifeguards or other emergency personnel. If you have immobilized the head and neck and checked the ABCs, you have performed a good spinal rescue.

Figure 13-19. A, Use arms to splint head and neck. **B** and **C,** Rotate the body while slowly gliding forward. **D,** Keep head in line with rest of the body until help arrives and assess casualty's breathing and pulse.

SUMMARY

In any water-related activity, few people anticipate they may suddenly be in a situation requiring rescue. But it can happen almost any time. A violent wave or gale can overturn a boat, a section of riverbank can give way where you are walking, or an unnoticed rip tide may sweep you seaward without warning. *Any time* you are around water, your safety depends on knowing what to do in case the unexpected happens—and it does happen, all too often. Know the techniques of self-rescue for different water conditions, and know how to recognize and rescue someone else, using the rescue aid and method safest for both the casualty and yourself. Finally, since spinal injuries are common aquatic incidents, know how to recognize and care for a casualty with such an injury.

Basic Life Support

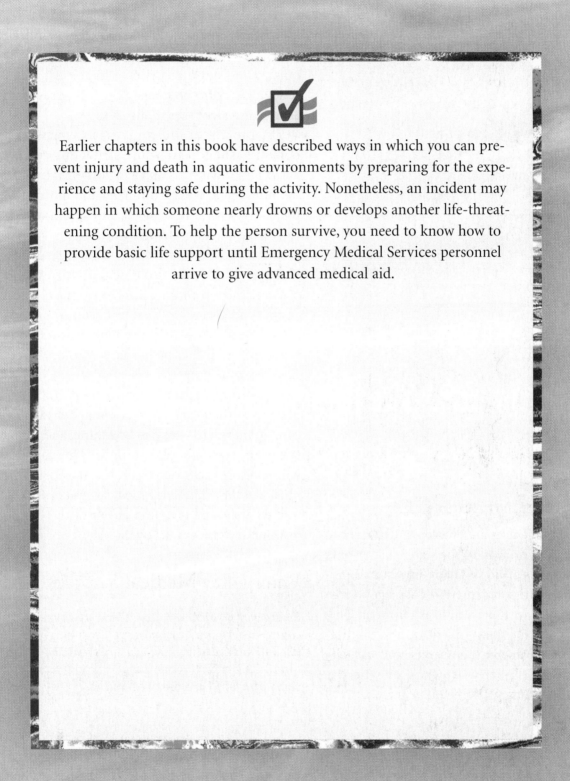

Earlier chapters in this book have described ways in which you can prevent injury and death in aquatic environments by preparing for the experience and staying safe during the activity. Nonetheless, an incident may happen in which someone nearly drowns or develops another life-threatening condition. To help the person survive, you need to know how to provide basic life support until Emergency Medical Services personnel arrive to give advanced medical aid.

The Canadian Red Cross recommends that all Canadians take a first aid course; but, if you choose not to take such a course, you should at least become proficient in the following skills:

- **Contacting the Emergency Medical System**

- **Performing rescue breathing for an adult, child, or infant**

- **Assisting a conscious and unconscious casualty with a blocked airway**

AQUATIC EMERGENCIES

Aquatic emergencies are problems that occur to people in, on, or around the water that require rescue or medical aid. In many situations a person may need first aid; therefore it's a good idea for everyone to take a first aid course. This chapter describes first aid for a critical, life-threatening problem: the unconscious casualty who may have nearly drowned or who has stopped breathing for some other reason.

Drowning

You've seen it a hundred times in movies, television programs, and cartoons. People who are drowning wave their arms and shout, "Help, I'm drowning!" They slip under the surface and rise up again, and the third time down is their last. But, in reality, most people who are near-drowning cannot or do not call for help. They spend their energy just trying to keep their head above water. They might slip under water quickly and never resurface. Chapter 13, Water Rescue, describes in detail a drowning casualty, as well as a swimmer in distress.

The process of drowning starts whenever a person gasps for air while struggling to stay afloat and inhales a small amount of water into the lungs. The water stimulates the muscles of the larynx (voice box) to go into spasm, which closes the airway. This natural body response prevents more water from entering the lungs. However, this spasm also blocks the airway and prevents air from entering. Without air, the casualty suffocates and soon becomes unconscious. Sometime after the person loses consciousness, the muscles relax, and more water may enter the lungs.

In a drowning, the person's breathing stops first. Soon the heart stops. A rescued drowning casualty may have stopped breathing, and his or her heart may have also stopped. This casualty will soon die without basic life support. You must call the emergency medical system (EMS) immediately and give first aid until these professionals arrive to take over.

Emergency Medical Services

Emergency medical services (EMS) are trained and equipped personnel, including police, fire-fighters, and ambulance personnel, who are dispatched through a local emergency number to give emergency care for ill or injured casualties.

The EMS is a coordinated system that exists throughout the country to provide emergency assistance to casualties with injury or sudden illness and to transport them to a hospital.

Within the EMS, different parts are linked together like a chain (Figure 14-1). When you call the local emergency number, you are the first link. The dispatcher who answers is the second link. The EMS professionals who come to the scene, such as police, fire-fighters, and emergency medical attendants (EMAs), are the third link. The hospital emergency department professionals form the fourth link. All this begins with your telephone call.

> *An emergency medical attendant (EMA) is someone trained in a provincially approved Emergency Medical Attendant program. There are several different levels of EMAs, including ambulance attendants and paramedics.*

The EMS system varies from community to community. Many areas have a 911 telephone system, whereas others have a specific local number. The level of training of the ambulance attendants and EMAs may also vary. But the overall system and the principles of calling EMS are the same in all provinces.

When to call EMS

The guidelines described in this chapter apply in any emergency, regardless of whether the casualty has almost drowned or has another injury or sudden illness. However, if the individual is drowning, follow the steps outlined in Chapter 13, Water Rescue, to first secure the casualty at a safe location.

Remember, do not put yourself at risk to save another, especially if you do not have the physical skills and knowledge of the environment. In these cases always call EMS immediately.

In any emergency situation on land, quickly check the injured or ill person to see if he or she

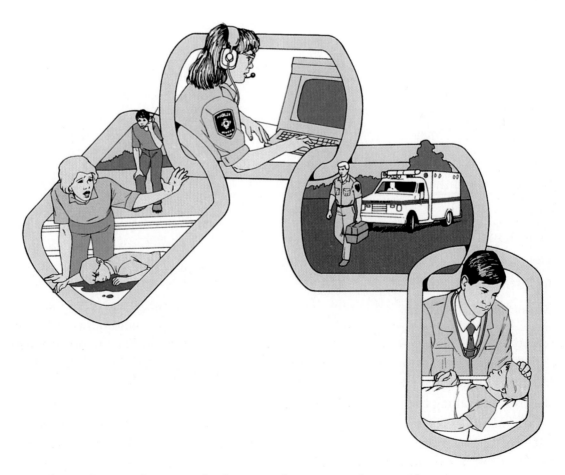

Figure 14-1. The EMS system is a network of community resources that provides emergency care.

is unresponsive. With an unconscious casualty, call EMS immediately.

If the casualty is conscious, sometimes you may not be sure if you should call EMS. An injured or ill person may tell you not to call an ambulance because he or she is embarrassed about creating a scene. Or you may be unsure if the casualty's condition is serious enough to require going to a hospital. As a general rule, call EMS personnel for any of the following conditions:

- Unconsciousness or altered level of consciousness
- Breathing problems (difficulty breathing or no breathing)
- Persistent chest pain or pressure
- No pulse
- Severe bleeding
- Vomiting blood or passing blood
- Poisoning
- Convulsions, severe headache, or slurred speech
- Injuries to head, neck, or back
- Possible broken bones

Also always call EMS if the casualty is involved with any of the following:

- Fire or explosion
- Poisonous gas
- Downed electrical wires
- Swift-moving water
- Motor vehicle collision
- A casualty who cannot be moved easily

In other cases, trust your instincts. If you think there is an emergency, there probably is. Do not lose time calling friends or family members. Call EMS for professional help immediately. It is better for professionals to come and find out they are not needed than not to come in an emergency when they were needed.

How to call EMS

If you can, send someone else to call the emergency number so that you can stay with the casualty to keep giving first aid. The dispatcher who answers the local emergency telephone number will send the appropriate help to the scene.

*A **dispatcher** is the emergency medical services person, usually in a communications centre, who answers the emergency telephone number and decides which EMS professionals to send to the scene and who may give advice regarding first aid to be given until EMS professionals arrive.*

When you tell someone to call for help, do the following:

✔ 1. Send a bystander, or possibly two, to make the call.

✔ 2. Give the caller(s) the EMS telephone number to call. This number is 911 in many places. Tell the caller(s) to dial O for the Operator only if you do not know the local emergency number. Sometimes the emergency number is on the inside front cover of the telephone book or on the pay phone.

✔ 3. Tell the caller(s) what to tell the dispatcher. Most dispatchers will ask for these important facts:

    a. *Where the emergency is located.* Give the exact address or location and the name of the city or town. Give the names of nearby intersecting streets (cross streets or roads), landmarks, the name of the building, the floor, and the room number. If the casualty is being moved, give that location. (If there is any risk that arriving EMS personnel may not locate you immediately, give additional information about how to reach you and, if needed, have someone meet them when they arrive.)

b. *Telephone number from which the call is being made.* Give any other available phone number for a call back.

c. *Caller's name.* NOTE: Give these first three pieces of information first so that the dispatcher can still act even if the call is cut off.

d. *What happened*—for example, a motor vehicle collision, fall, fire.

e. *How many people are involved.*

f. *Condition of the casualty*—for example, pulled from the water, nonresponsive, not breathing. The dispatcher may ask for additional information.

g. *The first aid being given.*

✔ 4. Tell the caller(s) not to hang up until the dispatcher hangs up. Be sure the dispatcher has all the information needed to send the right help to the scene.

✔ 5. Tell the caller(s) to report to you after making the call and tell you what the dispatcher said.

If you are alone with the casualty, call out loudly for help. Shouting may attract someone who can help you by making this call. If no one comes, get to a phone as fast as you can to call EMS. Then return to the casualty to keep giving help. With an infant or child under age 8, give emergency care for 1 minute first, and then go to the telephone to call EMS.

Your role in the EMS system

Once you recognize the emergency, calling EMS is the most important thing you and other bystanders can do. Early arrival of EMS personnel increases the casualty's chances of surviving a life-threatening emergency. Once help is on the way, your next priority is to give basic life support for the casualty's ABCs: airway, breathing, and circulation.

Basic Life Support: the ABCs

Basic life support is the term for first aid to keep the casualty alive until EMS professionals arrive and give more advanced care. Whenever you encounter an unconscious casualty, regardless of whether the person is found on dry land or was rescued from the water, you must first check the casualty's airway, breathing, and circulation and give basic life support care if needed. It is easy to remember these steps because they are called the ABCs:

A: *Airway*

B: *Breathing*

C: *Circulation*

These are described in detail in the following sections.

Try to check the ABCs without moving the casualty. If you must move the him or her, roll the casualty gently onto the back, keeping the head and spine in as straight a line as possible (Figure 14-2).

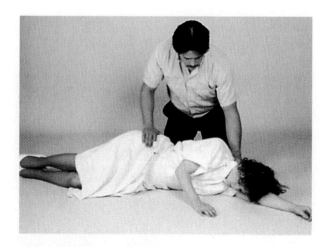

Figure 14-2. If the casualty's position keeps you from checking the ABCs, roll the casualty gently onto the back while supporting the head and neck.

A—Check the Airway

Be sure the casualty has an open airway. The airway is the pathway from the mouth and nose to the lungs. Any person who can speak or cry is conscious and has an open airway.

If the person is unconscious, you must ensure that the airway is open. To do this, tilt the head back and lift the chin (Figure 14-3, *A*). This moves the tongue away from the back of the throat and lets air reach the lungs. However, do not use the head-tilt method for a casualty you suspect of having a spinal injury (see Rescue of Spinal Injury Casualties in Chapter 13). Instead, to avoid injuring the spine further, use the technique called the modified jaw thrust. The steps for the modified jaw thrust are:

1. Grasp the casualty's lower jaw on both sides of the face where it forms an angle close to the ears.

2. Using both hands, move the lower jaw forward (upward) without tilting the head backward (Figure 14-3, *B*).

3. If rescue breathing is required, DO NOT move one hand to pinch the nostrils closed; instead, seal the nose with your cheek.

When the airway is open, check for breathing in the same manner as you do for a casualty not suspected of having a spinal injury. You can give rescue breathing while the casualty floats in the water with head and neck immobilized. However, if the casualty does not have a pulse, you must remove him or her promptly to the pool deck or beach and begin cardiopulmonary resuscitation (CPR).

When the person's airway is blocked by food or some object, you must remove the blockage first, as described in the later section on choking.

B—Check Breathing

Next check for breathing. Someone who can speak or cry is breathing. Watch an unconscious person carefully for signs of breathing. The chest should rise and fall, but you must also listen and feel for breathing. Put your face close so you can hear and feel air coming out the nose and mouth while you watch the rise and fall of the chest. Take the time to look, listen, and feel for breathing for a full 3 to 5 seconds (Figure 14-4).

Rescue breathing is the technique of breathing for a nonbreathing casualty.

If the casualty is not breathing, you must help the person to breathe by breathing air into the casualty's mouth. Follow these steps:

A
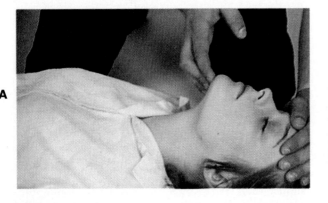

B

Figure 14-3. **A,** If you do not suspect a head or spine injury, tilt the head and lift the chin to open the airway. **B,** Use the jaw thrust technique for a casualty suspected of having a head or spine injury.

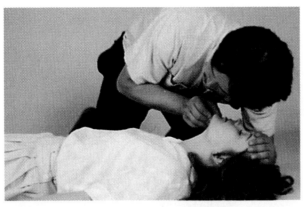

Figure 14-4. To check for breathing, look, listen, and feel for breathing for a full 3 to 5 seconds.

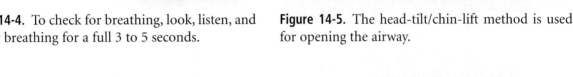

Figure 14-5. The head-tilt/chin-lift method is used for opening the airway.

1. Gently tilt the casualty's head back with one hand and lift the chin with the other (Figure 14-5).

2. Gently pinch the casualty's nose shut with the thumb and index finger of your hand that is on the casualty's forehead.

3. Take a deep breath and make a tight seal around the casualty's mouth with your mouth (Figure 14-6).

4. Breathe slowly into the casualty until you see the casualty's chest rise. Each breath should last about 1 to 1 ¹/₂ seconds. Pause between breaths to allow you to take a breath and to let the air flow back out of the casualty's lungs. Watch the casualty's chest rise each time you breathe in to ensure that your breaths are actually going in.

5. If you do not see the casualty's chest rise and fall as you give breaths, you may not have the head tilted far enough back to open the airway. Retilt the casualty's head and try again to give breaths. If your breaths still do not go in, the casualty's airway is obstructed, and you must clear it first (see following section on choking).

Rescue breathing can be given to a casualty while still in shallow water but is easier to do effectively if the casualty is out of the water.

Figure 14-6. To breathe for a non-breathing casualty, pinch the nose shut, seal your mouth around the casualty's mouth, and breathe slowly into the casualty.

Note: Rescue breathing is used for a casualty who is not breathing but who has a pulse. You must check to see if the casualty has a pulse. If the casualty does not have a pulse, give CPR instead of rescue breathing alone (see later section).

Rescue breathing for children and infants

Rescue breathing for children and infants follows the same general procedure as that for adults. The differences are based on the child's or infant's different physique and faster heartbeat and breathing rate (Figure 14-7). The following is a summary of the differences:

- Use the head-tilt/chin-lift position to open the airway as for an adult, but move the head very gently. For an infant, use the neutral or "sniffing" position, and seal your mouth over both the infant's nose and mouth.

- For an adult, give full breaths in rescue breathing. For a child use smaller breaths, and for an infant use puffs of air. Breathe in only enough air to make the chest rise.

- Give rescue breathing to adults at the rate of 1 breath every 5 seconds (12 per minute); give rescue breathing to children at the rate of 1 breath every 3 seconds and to infants at the rate of 1 puff every 3 seconds (15 per minute).

- See p. 286, First Aid for an Unconscious Adult, for the detailed steps for rescue breathing.

- For both adults and children, check the pulse at the carotid artery in the neck. For infants, check the brachial pulse. (See pp. 281 and 285 for descriptions of finding pulse locations.)

Choking

An airway obstruction is blockage of the airway that prevents air from reaching a person's lungs. Choking is the result of a partial or complete blockage of the airway by a foreign object.

If your breaths do not go into the casualty when you attempt to give rescue breathing, the casualty has an airway obstruction. You must try to clear this before continuing with rescue breathing or CPR.

If an unconscious adult has an obstructed airway, keep the person on his or her back and follow these steps:

1. With the heel of one hand just above the navel and the other hand on top of it, thrust into the abdomen in an upward direction. Do this 5 times. This is called an abdominal thrust.

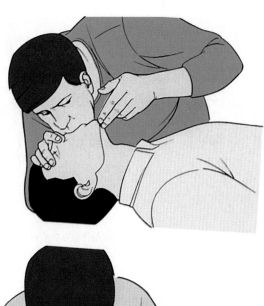

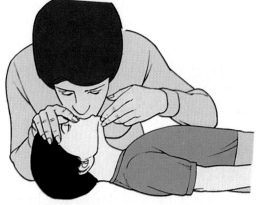

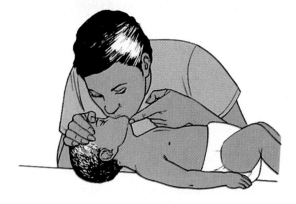

Figure 14-7. Rescue breathing for adults, children, and infants has only minor variations.

2. Use a finger sweep to check inside the casualty's mouth for the object that caused the obstruction.

3. Try to give 2 full breaths again. If the breaths do not go in, repeat the abdominal thrusts and finger sweep.

See p. 286, First Aid for an Unconscious Adult, for the detailed steps for a casualty with an obstructed airway.

With a noticeably pregnant unconscious casualty or any larger adult to whom you cannot deliver abdominal thrusts effectively, give chest thrusts. Kneel facing the casualty. Place the heel of one hand on the centre of the casualty's breastbone and your other hand on top of it (Figure 14-8). Give 5 quick thrusts. Each thrust should compress the chest 3.5 to 5 cm. After giving 5 chest thrusts, do a finger sweep, open the airway, and give 2 full breaths as you normally would for an unconscious choking adult. Repeat the sequence until the obstruction is dislodged, you can breathe into the casualty, or EMS arrives and takes over.

Children with airway obstruction First aid for an unconscious child over age 1 who is choking is similar to that for an adult. Consider the child's size when you provide care. Obviously you cannot use the same force when giving abdominal thrusts to expel the object. Otherwise, use the same method you use for an adult.

Infant with airway obstruction With the infant on its back, first look for an object in the throat and try to remove it. Open the airway by lifting the chin, and check for breathing. If the infant is not breathing, put your mouth over both the infant's nose and mouth and give two slow breaths, allowing 1 to 1^1/$_2$ seconds per breath. If the breaths go in but the infant is not breathing, continue with rescue breathing. If the breaths do not go in, use backblows and chest thrusts to clear the obstructed airway.

C—Check Circulation

The last step of the ABCs is to check the circulation. This step involves checking for a pulse.

The carotid arteries are major blood vessels bringing blood to the head and neck.

If a person is breathing, the heart is beating and you do not need to check the pulse. If the person is not breathing, you must check the pulse. To check circulation, feel for the pulse in the carotid artery in the neck on the side closest to you (Figure 14-9). To find the pulse, find the Adam's apple and slide your fingers into the groove at the side of the neck. The pulse may be hard to find if it is slow or weak. If at first you do not find a pulse, start again at the Adam's apple and slide your fingers into place. When you think you are in the right spot, keep feeling for at least 5 to 10 seconds.

Cardiopulmonary resuscitation (CPR) is first aid combining rescue breathing and chest compressions for a casualty whose breathing and heart have stopped.

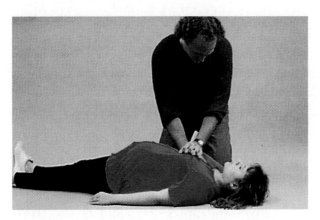

Figure 14-8. Position an unconscious casualty on the back for chest thrusts.

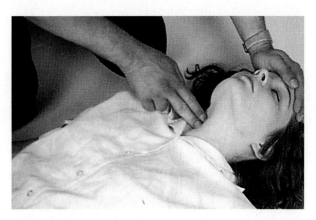

Figure 14-9. Determine if the heart is beating by feeling for a carotid pulse on the side of the neck closest to you.

If the casualty does not have a pulse, you *must* give CPR.

1. Position an adult casualty flat on the back on a firm surface, with the head on the same level as the heart. Kneel beside the casualty midway between the chest and the head so you can give compressions and breaths (Figure 14-10).

2. Lean over the chest and place your hands in the correct position over the lower half of the sternum. To find the correct hand position for chest compressions for an adult or child:

   • Find the lower edge of the casualty's rib cage. Slide your middle and index fingers up the edge of the rib cage to the notch where the ribs meet the sternum (Figure 14-11, A). Place your middle finger on this notch. Place your index finger next to your middle finger.

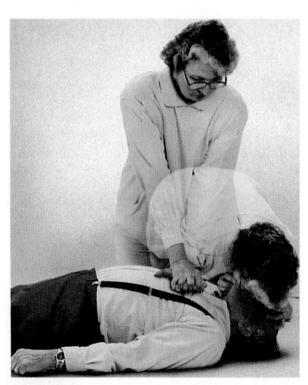

Figure 14-10. Position yourself so that you can give rescue breaths and chest compressions without having to move.

• Place the heel of your other hand on the sternum next to your index finger (Figure 14-11, B). The heel of your hand should rest along the length of the sternum.

• Once the heel of your hand is in position on the sternum, place your other hand directly on top of it (Figure 14-11, C).

• Use the heel of your hand to apply pressure on the sternum. Try to keep your fingers off the chest by interlacing them or holding them upward. Pushing with your fingers can cause inefficient chest compressions or damage to the chest.

• Depending on your own strength and abilities, you may use an alternate hand position, grasping the wrist of the hand on the chest with the other hand (Figure 14-12). Practicing chest compressions on a manikin is recommended; you can also discover what position works best for you.

3. Compress the chest by alternately pressing straight down and releasing in a smooth, uniform pattern. Straighten your arms and lock your elbows with your shoulders directly over your hands (Figure 14-13). When you press down in this position, you will be pushing straight down onto the sternum. Push with the weight of your upper body, not with the muscles of your arms. Push straight down. Do not rock back and forth. After each compression, release the pressure on the chest without losing contact with it, and let the chest return to its normal position before starting the next compression (Figure 14-14). Each compression should push the sternum down 3.8 to 5 cm. Maintain a steady down-and-up rhythm, and do not pause between compressions.

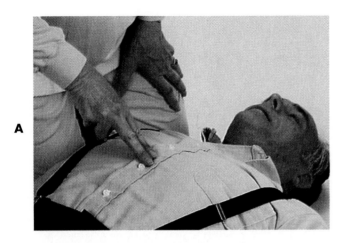

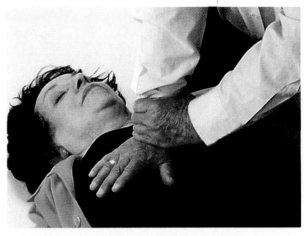

Figure 14-12. Grasping the wrist of the hand positioned on the chest is an alternate hand position for giving chest compressions.

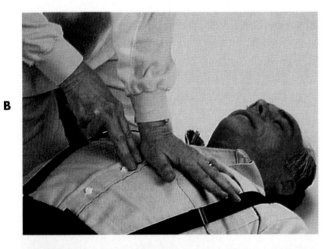

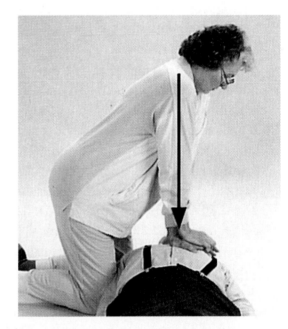

Figure 14-13. With your hands in place, position yourself so that your shoulders are directly over your hands, arms straight and elbows locked.

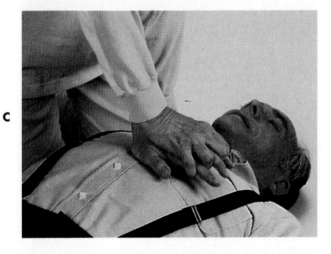

Figure 14-11 A, Find the notch where the lower ribs meet the sternum. **B,** Place the heel of your hand on the sternum, next to your index finger. **C,** Place your other hand over the heel of the first. Use the heel of your bottom hand to compress the sternum.

4. Give compressions at the rate of 80 to 100 per minute. As you do compressions, count aloud, "One and two and three and four and five and six and. . ." up to 15. Counting aloud helps you pace yourself. Push down as you say the number and come up as you say "and." You should do the 15 compressions in about 9 to 11 sec-

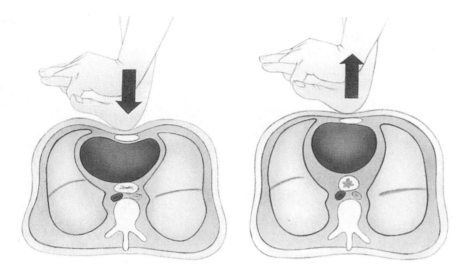

Figure 14-14. Push straight down with the weight of your body; then release, allowing the chest to return to the normal position.

onds. Even though you are compressing the chest at a rate of 80 to 100 times per minute, you will only actually do 60 compressions in a minute because you must also do rescue breathing.

5. Do 4 cycles of 15 compressions and 2 breaths. For each cycle, give 15 chest compressions, and then open the airway and give 2 full breaths (Figure 14-15). This cycle should take about 15 seconds. For each new cycle of compressions and breaths, find the correct hand position first.

After 4 cycles of CPR in about a minute, check to see if the casualty has a pulse. Then continue CPR. Check the pulse again every few minutes. See page 286, First Aid for an Unconscious Adult, for detailed CPR steps.

CPR for children and infants

CPR for infants and children is similar to the technique for adults. Because of their smaller bodies, infants and children have faster heart and breathing rates. A different hand position is used to give compressions, as well as different cycles of compressions and breaths. Figure 14-16 compares these techniques for adults, children, and infants.

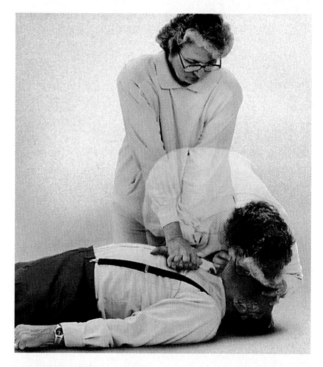

Figure 14-15. For adults, give 15 compressions, and then 2 breaths.

The hand position on the sternum is the same for children as for adults. The main differences are that for a child you compress with just one hand (with elbow locked) and compress only 2.5 to 3.8 cm. The number of compressions and breaths in the cycle is also different. Remember to be gentle in using the head-tilt/chin-lift technique for opening the airway.

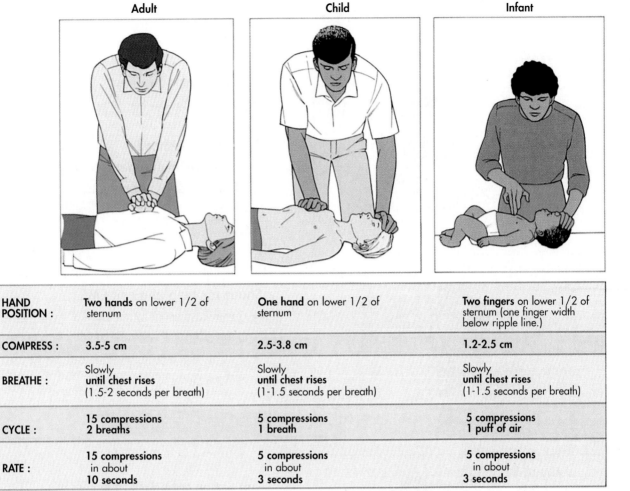

	Adult	Child	Infant
HAND POSITION :	**Two hands** on lower 1/2 of sternum	**One hand** on lower 1/2 of sternum	**Two fingers** on lower 1/2 of sternum (one finger width below ripple line.)
COMPRESS :	3.5-5 cm	2.5-3.8 cm	1.2-2.5 cm
BREATHE :	Slowly **until chest rises** (1.5-2 seconds per breath)	Slowly **until chest rises** (1-1.5 seconds per breath)	Slowly **until chest rises** (1-1.5 seconds per breath)
CYCLE :	15 compressions 2 breaths	5 compressions 1 breath	5 compressions 1 puff of air
RATE :	15 compressions in about 10 seconds	5 compressions in about 3 seconds	5 compressions in about 3 seconds

Figure 14-16. The technique for chest compressions differs for adults, children, and infants.

For infants under 1 year, use your middle and ring fingers only for chest compressions. Find the correct position by first imagining a line drawn between the nipples. Place your middle three fingers of the hand closest to the feet on the breastbone below this line, with the index finger at the line. Then lift the index finger so that the middle two fingers are spaced slightly below the nipple line. Compress only 1.2 to 2.5 cm. Remember also to tilt the head back only to the neutral or sniffing position and to give small puffs of air rather than forceful rescue breathing.

Pulse check in infants

Before starting CPR for adults and children, check the pulse to see if the heart is beating. It is very difficult to find a pulse in infants under 1 year old. Therefore, unless you have special training, you should not spend more than a few seconds searching for a pulse in an infant who has stopped breathing. Except in cases in which the infant is choking, an infant who has stopped breathing usually does not have a pulse, and you should start CPR immediately.

For infants, check the brachial pulse inside the upper arm instead of the carotid pulse in the neck. Place two fingers close to the bone on the underside of the arm, nearer the armpit than the elbow. Press gently and feel for the pulse for 5 to 10 seconds.

FIRST AID FOR UNCONSCIOUS ADULT

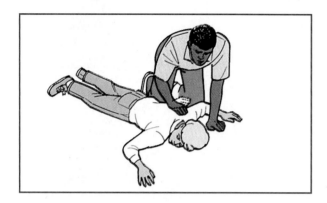

☐ **Check for responsiveness.**
- Tap or gently shake person.
- Shout, "Are you OK?"

  If person responds. . .

  Determine if other first aid is needed.

  If person does not respond. . .

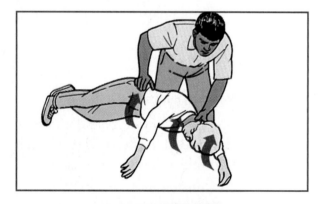

☐ **Shout for help and call EMS.**
- Summon someone who can help and call EMS, or place the call yourself if no one is available.
- If alone with a child, continue care for 1 minute, then call EMS yourself.

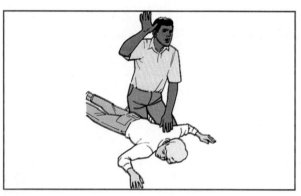

☐ **Roll person onto back (if necessary).**
- Kneel facing person.
- Place one hand to cradle the head and neck, and place the other hand on person's hip.
- Roll person toward you, moving the body and head as a single unit. Remember to support the back of head and neck.

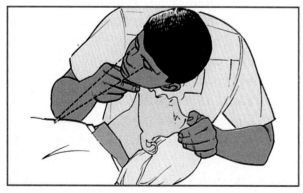

☐ **Open airway and check for breathing.**
- Tilt head back and lift chin.
- Look, listen, and feel for breathing for 3 to 5 seconds.

  If person is breathing. . .

  Keep airway open.

  Monitor breathing.

  Position the casualty on the side with airway open, so that any fluids can drain from the mouth.

If person is not breathing. . .

☐ **Give 2 full breaths.**

- Pinch nose shut and seal lips tightly around person's mouth.
- Give 2 full breaths, allowing 11/2 to 2 seconds per breath.
- Watch chest to see that your breaths go in.

  If breaths go in. . .

  Check pulse.

  If person has a pulse but is not breathing, continue rescue breathing:

- Maintain open airway with head-tilt/chin-lift.
- Pinch nose shut.
- Give 1 full breath every 5 seconds.
- Watch chest to see that your breaths are going in.
- Recheck pulse and breathing every few minutes.

  If person has no pulse and is not breathing, do CPR.

  If breaths do not go in. . .

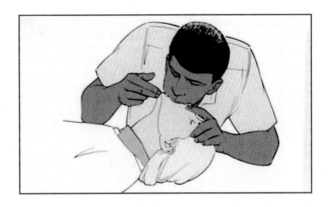

☐ **Retilt person's head and repeat breaths.**

- Pinch nose shut and seal your lips tightly around person's mouth.
- Give 2 full breaths.

  If breaths still do not go in. . .

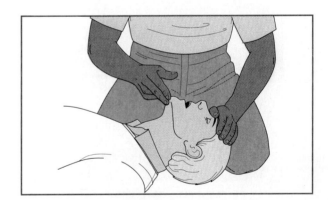

☐ **Give 5 abdominal thrusts.**

- Place heel of one hand just above the navel.
- Place other hand directly on top of first hand.
- Press into person's abdomen with upward thrusts.
- 5 chest thrusts on obese or pregnant

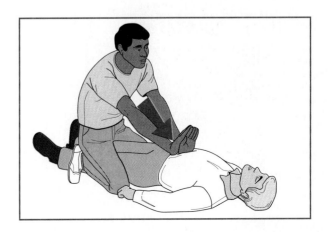

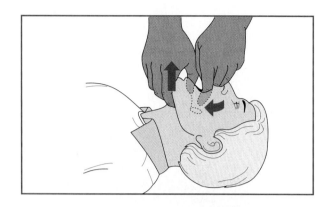

☐ **Do finger sweep.**

- Grasp both tongue and lower jaw between your thumb and fingers and lift jaw.
- Slide finger down inside of cheek to base of tongue.
- Attempt to sweep object out.
- Don't Finger sweep child.

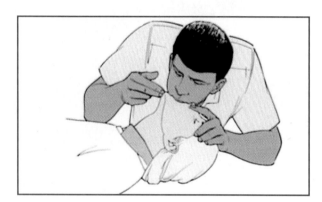

☐ **Open airway and give 2 full breaths.**

- Tilt head back.
- Pinch nose shut.
- Seal your lips tightly around person's mouth.
- Give 2 full breaths.
- Watch chest to see if your breaths go in.

   If breaths do not go in. . .
   repeat thrusts, finger sweep, and breathing steps until. . .
   Obstruction is removed.
   Person starts to breathe or cough.
   EMS personnel take over.
   If breaths go in. . .

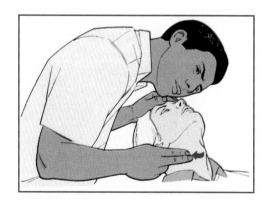

☐ **Check for pulse.**

- Feel for pulse for 5 to 10 seconds.
   If person has a pulse and is not breathing. . .
   Continue rescue breathing.
   If person does not have a pulse. . .
   Begin CPR.

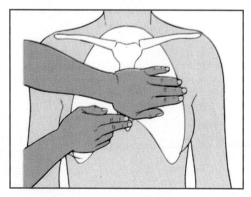

☐ **Find hand position.**

- Locate notch at lower end of sternum, using hand closest to the feet.
- Place heel of other hand on sternum next to fingers.
- Remove hand from notch and put it on top of other hand.
- Keep fingers off chest.

Give 15 compressions.
- Position shoulders over hands.
- Compress sternum 3.8 to 5 cm.
- Do 15 compressions in approximately 10 seconds (80 to 100 compressions per minute).
- Compress down and up smoothly, keeping hand contact with the chest at all times.

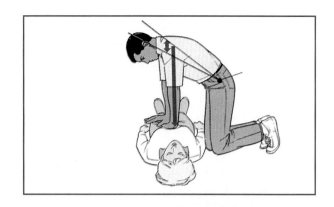

Give 2 full breaths.
- Open airway with head-tilt/chin-lift.
- Pinch nose shut and seal your lips tightly around person's mouth.
- Give 2 full breaths, each lasting 1$\frac{1}{2}$ to 2 seconds.
- Watch chest to see that your breaths are going in.

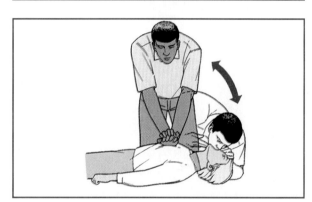

Repeat compression/breathing cycles.
- Do 3 more cycles of 15 compressions and 2 breaths.

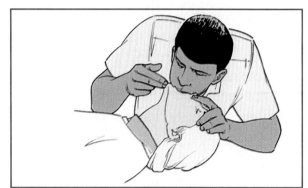

Recheck pulse.
- Feel for pulse for about 5 seconds.

  If person has a pulse and is breathing. . .

     Put the person on the side.
     Keep airway open.
     Monitor breathing.
     Await arrival of EMS.

  If person has a pulse but is still not breathing. . .

     Do rescue breathing until EMS arrives.

  If person does not have a pulse and is not breathing. . .

Continue CPR until EMS arrives.

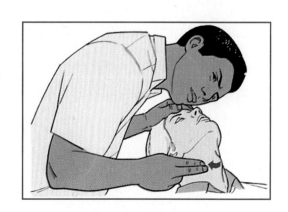

When to stop CPR

Once you begin CPR, do not stop. Stop CPR only if—

- Your personal safety is threatened.
- The casualty's heart starts to beat on its own.
- Another trained rescuer arrives on the scene and takes over.
- You are too exhausted to continue.

If the casualty's heart starts but he or she is still not breathing, keep giving rescue breathing. If the casualty is breathing and has a heartbeat, turn the person onto the side, keep the airway open, and carefully monitor the ABCs until EMS arrives.

SUMMARY

Hopefully, neither you nor anyone in your group will ever need to use the basic life support techniques described in this chapter. But drownings and other incidents do occur, and these techniques can and do save lives. Remember that you do not need to know the cause of a casualty's condition to treat it: CPR for someone who has had a heart attack is the same as for a drowning casualty. Knowing how to perform basic life support is an important first aid skill, and it is recommended that you take a course in CPR and first aid to learn these skills, along with other measures that can help save lives. Always have with you a first aid kit (see Appendix A).

Appendix

FIRST AID KIT

Keep a first aid kit readily available in your home, automobile, workplace, and recreation area (Figure A-1). Store it in a dry place and replace used and outdated contents regularly. A first aid kit should contain the following:

1. Emergency telephone numbers for EMS, your regional poison contre, and personal physicians. Include the home and office phone numbers of family members, friends, or neighbors who can help.

2. Sterile gauze pads (dressings), in small and large squares to place over wounds.

3. Adhesive tape.

4. Roller and triangular bandages to hold dressings in place or to make an arm sling.

5. Adhesive bandages in assorted sizes.

6. Scissors.

7. Tweezers.

8. Safety pins.

9. Ice bag or chemical ice pack.

10. Disposable gloves such as surgical or examination gloves.

11. Flashlight, with extra batteries in a separate bag.

Figure A-1. Be prepared for emergencies with a well-stocked first aid kit.

12. Antiseptic wipes or soap.

13. Pencil and pad.

14. Emergency blanket.

15. Syrup of ipecac.

16. Eye patches.

17. Thermometer.

18. Coins for pay phone.

19. Red Cross first aid manual.

Illustration Credits

CHAPTER 1

p. 12, Figure 1-7, Mike Ridewood/Canadian Sport Images; **p. 14, lower right,** Canapress; **p. 15, lower left,** Canapress; **p. 15, lower right,** Canadian Sport Images; **p. 16, lower left and right,** Ted Grant/Canadian Sport Images; **p. 17, lower left and right,** Ted Grant/-Canadian Sport Images; **p. 19, Figure 1-8,** Benjamin Rondel/First Light

CHAPTER 2

p. 20, top right, Daniel Reinders; **p. 20, middle right,** Ted Grant /Canadian Sport Images; **p. 20, bottom left,** F. Scott Grant/Canadian Sport Images; **p. 20, bottom center,** F. Scott Grant /Canadian Sport Images; **p. 22, F.** Scott Grant /Canadian Sport Images; **p. 24,** Patrick Morrow/First Light; **p. 27, top right,** Steve Chenn Photography/First Light; **p. 28, bottom left,** Steve Short/ First Light

CHAPTER 3

p. 32, middle left, Myron Kozak

CHAPTER 4

p. 59, Figure 4-15, Wendy Shattil/Rozinski/Tom Stack & Associates

CHAPTER 5

p. 66, top left, Chris Harris/First Light; **p. 66, top right,** Jerry Kobalenko/First Light; **p. 66, middle left,** Alan Marsh/First Light; **p. 66, bottom center,** Ron Watts/First Light; **p. 69, Figure 5-1,** Paul von Balch/First Light; **p. 72, Figure 5-4,** Donald Standfield/First Light

CHAPTER 6

p. 87, Figure 6-11, Michelle Mayes

CHAPTER 10

p. 184, bottom right, Bill Ross/First Light

CHAPTER 12

p. 231, top, Myron Kozak

COVER

top, Stephen Simpson, F. P. G. International

BACK COVER

bottom, Paul von Balch/First Light

Index

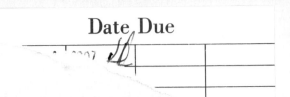
Red Cross Divisional Addresses and Telephone Numbers

British Columbia/Yukon Division
4710 Kingsway, Suite 400
Burnaby, British Columbia
V5H 4M2
Telephone: (604) 431-4200
Fax: (604) 431-4275

Saskatchewan Division
2571 Broad Street
Regina, Saskatchewan
S4P 3B4
Telephone: (306) 352-4601
Fax: (306) 757-2407

Ontario Division
5700 Cancross Court
Mississauga, Ontario
L5R 3E9
Telephone: (416) 890-1000
Fax: (416) 890-1008

New Brunswick Division
405 University Avenue
P.O. Box 39
Saint John, New Brunswick
E2L 3X3
Telephone: (506) 648-5000
Fax: (506) 648-5095

P.E.I. Division
62 Prince Street
Charlottetown, P.E.I.
C1A 4R2
Telephone: (902) 628-6262
Fax: (902) 566-6385

Alberta/NWT Division
737-13th Avenue, S.W.
Calgary, Alberta
T2R 1J1
Telephone: (403) 541-4400
Fax: (403) 541-4444

Manitoba Division
200-360 Broadway Avenue
Winnipeg, Manitoba
R3C OT6
Telephone: (204) 982-7300
Fax: (204) 942-8367

Quebec Division
6-Place du Commerce
Ile-des-Soeurs
Verdun, Quebec H3E 1P4
Telephone: (514) 362-2929
Fax: (514) 362-9991

Nova Scotia Division
1940 Gottingen Street
P.O. Box 366
Halifax, Nova Scotia
B3J 2H2 (for street address)
B3J 2P8 (for post box address)
Telephone: (902) 423-9181
Fax: (902) 422-6247

Newfoundland/Labrador Division
7 Wicklow Street
P.O. Box 13156, Station "A"
St. John's, Newfoundland
A1B 4A4
Telephone: (709) 754-0461
Fax: (709) 754-0728